ISPF: The Strategic Dialog Manager

ISPF: The Strategic Dialog Manager

Joseph A. Azevedo

Intertext Publications
McGraw-Hill Book Company
New York, NY

Library of Congress Catalog Card Number 88-82419

10 9 8 7 6 5 4 3 2 1

ISBN 0-07-002673-4

IBM is a trademark of International Business Machines, Inc.
System One is a trademark of System One Corporation.

Intertext Publications/Multiscience Press, Inc.
One Lincoln Plaza
New York, NY 10023

McGraw-Hill Book Company
1221 Avenue of the Americas
New York, NY 10020

Dedication

This book is dedicated to

Bruce L. DeSautel

and

Robert B. McArdle

I am deeply grateful to Bruce DeSautel, Chairman of the EDP Division at Miami-Dade Community College (Retired), for having such confidence in me while I was a student there that he created a special position so that I could assist any student with *any* kind of problem in the field of data processing.

Being exposed to thousands upon thousands of different types of errors and difficulties that each student faced and presented to me for assistance, provided me with more experience, knowledge and insight into this field than I could ever have achieved on my own in about ten years of work. For this great headstart, I thank you, Professor!

I am equally grateful to Robert McArdle, Senior Director at System One Corporation (one of the largest computer reservations systems facilities in the world), for providing me with the environment where I was able to research and develop new processes, tools, facilities, etc. When ISPF was announced by IBM a few years ago and I suggested to Bob that we should investigate the applicability of ISPF at System One, without hesitation he immediately encouraged me to pursue it to whatever extent possible.

This being a new product, it meant that I had to learn it first and then teach it to the others in the company. This opportunity enabled me to develop a course whose contents led SHARE representatives to request that I present it at their conferences (four consecutive times).

Again, Bob allowed me to take time away from work to attend the various conferences and to make these lengthy presentations. At the same time, it made me aware of the tremendous need for a good book on this subject. Thus, if it had not been for Bob McArdle's support, this book might never have been possible.

Contents

Acknowledgements

I am indebted to William J. Smith, Systems Software Specialist at Syntex (U.S.A.) Inc., and to Jay Ranade, Series Editor-in-Chief at McGraw-Hill Book Company for having taken the time to review the book for technical content as well as style. Their encouraging and complimentary comments were a great morale boost for my finishing this project.

I also want to thank my wife Barbara and my son Joey for their support, understanding and cooperation throughout this lengthy but interesting process.

Preface

This book is designed to show anyone who has any interest in IBM's ISPF (Interactive System Productivity Facility) how the product works and how anyone can use it to develop new full-screen interactive applications.

Every effort has been made to make this a clear, concise, and yet comprehensive presentation of what might otherwise appear to be a very complex subject. In addition, the material is presented in such a manner that the reader will be able to develop new applications by simply following the exact guidelines presented in this book. Everything needed to develop and implement a new application will be presented here and in its proper order.

This book is designed in a structured fashion using a top-down approach. This means that information is presented in layers of succeedingly greater levels of detail. As such, one only needs to read down to the level of desired knowledge without losing the overall concept of how the product operates.

An executive, for example, who might be curious as to what ISPF provides, might read only the overview section and get a very good idea of what the product offers. A manager, wanting a little more detail, would continue reading into the various services available. A group leader or a systems designer, needing still more detail, would continue reading into the various component definitions. Finally, a developer, needing all the detailed knowledge of the product, would read the complete book.

Some coverage of PDF (Program Development Facility) will also be provided to the extent that it complements ISPF by providing the basic tools with which to create the various dialog components as well as to test them. Coverage of TSO CLISTs and CMS EXECs as well as COBOL and PL/I will be done only to the extent necessary to understand how they can interact with ISPF.

The Presentation Overeiw on the following page provides a graphic representation of this book's organization. A similar figure will be used at the beginning of each new section so that the reader will always be sure of the context of that section in relation to the others.

It is worthwhile to note that throughout this book *data* has been used to represent both the singular and the plural form. Although technically the singular form should be *datum*, its usage has been avoided since it appears forced.

Finally, in order to maintain continuity of thought, the various components of one complete *and useful* application will be used throughout this book. This particular application has been specifically developed for illustrative purposes as well as for its usefulness in developing other applications. Each component of this dialog application was specifically designed with simplicity and clarity in mind while at the same time providing a variety of cases to demonstrate the various services provided by ISPF.

Readers are free to copy and install, for their own use, the various components of the Data Dictionary System illustrated in this book. However, those readers who wish to save the time to key the nearly 100,000 keystrokes for these components may receive a diskette copy (5-1/4-inch floppy) of these items by sending $15.00 to cover the cost of materials, postage, and handling to:

> Joseph A. Azevedo
> 6135 SW 146 Ct.
> Miami, FL 33183

ISPF — THE DIALOG MANAGER

OVERVIEW

DIALOG SERVICES

COMPONENT SYNTAX AND CODING

- PANEL   DEFINITIONS
- MESSAGE   DEFINITIONS
- FUNCTION   DEFINITIONS
- SKELETON   DEFINITIONS
- TUTORIAL   DEFINITIONS

DEVELOPING A COMPLETE APPLICATION

- THE   DESIGN   PHASE
- THE   DEVELOPMENT   PHASE
- THE   TEST   PHASE
- THE   IMPLEMENTATION PHASE

APPENDICES

- ISPF/TSO INTERFACES
- ISPF/CMS INTERFACES
- ISPF/PLI INTERFACES
- ISPF/COBOL INTERFACES
- ISPF FULL SYNTAX SUMMARY
- ISPF VARIABLES & COMMANDS

Presentation overview.

ISPF — The Dialog Manager

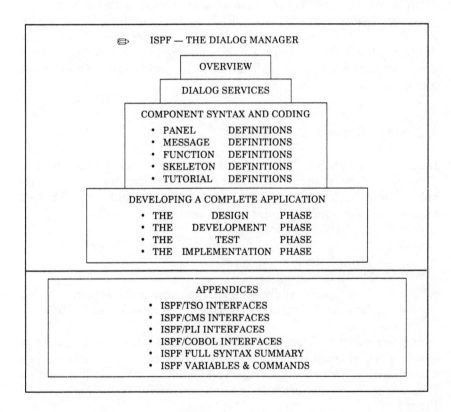

The ISPF Concept

ISPF — the Interactive System Productivity Facility — is an IBM product designed to improve productivity by simplifying and standardizing the process of communicating with an end-user in a variety of operating environments. This process, the dialog, is effected through full-screen displays, which simply prompt the user either to select a desired logical path or to provide the data necessary to carry out a given task.

Through these dialogs, any user with a minimum amount of knowledge can become productive in almost any environment. The end-user is able to concentrate on the desired results and not be concerned with the detailed knowledge of a particular operating system or its command language requirements.

ISPF, while fairly simple to learn, enables one to develop some very sophisticated applications. PDF — the Program Development Facility — is an example of one such application. It was also developed by IBM to simplify the majority of tasks required by a programming staff. Any installation can develop other applications along the same lines as PDF.

A Strategic Cross-System Product

IBM has announced ISPF to be a strategic cross-system product. This commitment guarantees users that this facility will be supported by a variety of operating systems in a highly standardized manner and for a long time into the future.

At present, ISPF is supported under:

• VM   — Virtual Machine
• MVS — Multiple Virtual Storage
• VSE — Disk Operating System/Virtual Storage Extension
• PCs — Personal Computer/Disk Operating System (as EZVU)

The advantages of having a standardized product across so many systems are so beneficial that at least one installation has developed a compatible version that operates under TPF — Transaction Processing Facility (formerly known as ACP — Airline Control Program).[1]

---

[1]   This ISPF/TPF version was developed by the programming staff of System One Corporation at the Doral Computer Center in Miami, Florida, a subsidiary of Texas Air Corporation.

Flexible Programming Language Support

ISPF functions can be programmed in a variety of languages to suit the preferences of most users. One may use programming languages such as:

- FORTRAN   — FORmula TRANslation
- COBOL   — COmmon Business-Oriented Language
- PL/I   — Programming Language I
- PASCAL   — (Named after Blaise Pascal)
- Assembler — The most basic programming language

Interpretive command languages are also supported depending on the operating environment:

- CLIST   — TSO Command LIST
- EXEC2   — CMS EXEC2 Language
- REXX   — CMS REXX Language
- APL2   — A Programming Language 2

The Environment for This Book

In order to keep the presentation of ISPF at the simplest level, an operating system, its environment, and a specific language had to be chosen so that the various topics throughout this book could be illustrated. Consequently, the following primary selections have been made:

- Operating system: MVS
- Sub-environment: TSO
- Language: CLIST

These selections were based on their popularity and simplicity. Nevertheless, variations of any of the choices made will be discussed wherever appropriate or in a separate appendix at the end of the book.

The ISPF Version Used

The material presented here is based on Version 2 of ISPF. Different installations may have slightly different versions, but the concepts presented will still apply.

The Syntax Notation in This Book

In order to be consistent with the syntax notation familiar to most users of IBM products, the following rules will apply:

- Upper-case entries are generally coded as shown
- Lower-case entries generally indicate a variable
- Braces surrounding multiple items indicate that a choice must be made: {item | item}
- Brackets surrounding a single item indicate that the item is optional: [item]
- Brackets surrounding multiple items indicate that a choice is to be made, but the entry is entirely optional: [item | item]
- Ellipses indicate that multiple occurrences of the preceding entry may be used: item...

1

ISPF Overview

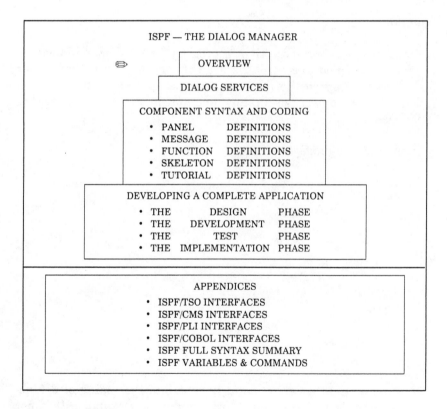

ISPF — THE DIALOG MANAGER

OVERVIEW

DIALOG SERVICES

COMPONENT SYNTAX AND CODING
- PANEL   DEFINITIONS
- MESSAGE   DEFINITIONS
- FUNCTION   DEFINITIONS
- SKELETON   DEFINITIONS
- TUTORIAL   DEFINITIONS

DEVELOPING A COMPLETE APPLICATION
- THE   DESIGN   PHASE
- THE   DEVELOPMENT   PHASE
- THE   TEST   PHASE
- THE   IMPLEMENTATION   PHASE

APPENDICES
- ISPF/TSO INTERFACES
- ISPF/CMS INTERFACES
- ISPF/PLI INTERFACES
- ISPF/COBOL INTERFACES
- ISPF FULL SYNTAX SUMMARY
- ISPF VARIABLES & COMMANDS

An ISPF dialog is composed of any number of elements arranged in various combinations from the following set of components:

- FUNCTIONS
- PANELS
- MESSAGES
- TABLES
- FILE SKELETONS

Each of these components will be discussed quite extensively in Chapters 3 through 7; for now, though, we are only concerned with the general purpose and description of each of these items.

Functions

A function is nothing more than a program or a command-language procedure designed to control the logic of a given task within a user dialog. Depending on the preference of the application developer, a function may be written in any one (or more) of the following languages:

- Command Languages:

  - CLIST
  - EXEC2
  - REXX
  - APL2[1]

- Programming Languages:

  - FORTRAN
  - COBOL
  - PL/I
  - PASCAL
  - Assembler

In order to gain a very general insight into the coding of a function, let us look at Figure 1-1, a brief and simple example. It is not important, at this time, that we understand exactly what each state-

---

[1]   Although technically APL is a programming language, in an ISPF environment it is treated as if it were a command language.

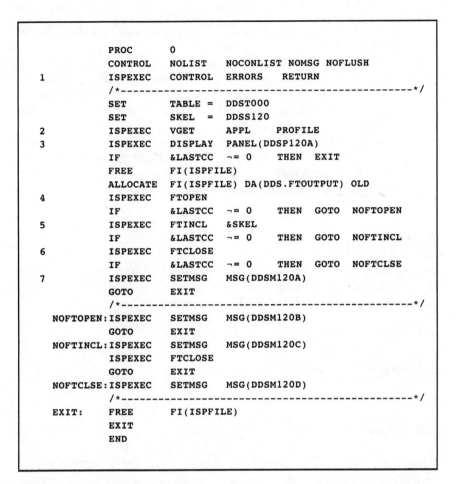

```
              PROC       0
              CONTROL    NOLIST    NOCONLIST NOMSG NOFLUSH
   1          ISPEXEC    CONTROL   ERRORS    RETURN
              /*------------------------------------------------*/
              SET        TABLE =  DDST000
              SET        SKEL  =  DDSS120
   2          ISPEXEC    VGET      APPL     PROFILE
   3          ISPEXEC    DISPLAY   PANEL(DDSP120A)
              IF         &LASTCC  ¬= 0      THEN   EXIT
              FREE       FI(ISPFILE)
              ALLOCATE   FI(ISPFILE) DA(DDS.FTOUTPUT) OLD
   4          ISPEXEC    FTOPEN
              IF         &LASTCC  ¬= 0      THEN   GOTO   NOFTOPEN
   5          ISPEXEC    FTINCL    &SKEL
              IF         &LASTCC  ¬= 0      THEN   GOTO   NOFTINCL
   6          ISPEXEC    FTCLOSE
              IF         &LASTCC  ¬= 0      THEN   GOTO   NOFTCLSE
   7          ISPEXEC    SETMSG    MSG(DDSM120A)
              GOTO       EXIT
              /*------------------------------------------------*/
   NOFTOPEN: ISPEXEC    SETMSG    MSG(DDSM120B)
              GOTO       EXIT
   NOFTINCL: ISPEXEC    SETMSG    MSG(DDSM120C)
              ISPEXEC    FTCLOSE
              GOTO       EXIT
   NOFTCLSE: ISPEXEC    SETMSG    MSG(DDSM120D)
              /*------------------------------------------------*/
   EXIT:     FREE       FI(ISPFILE)
              EXIT
              END
```

Figure 1-1   Sample ISPF Function.

ment is accomplishing. The intent is simply to acquire a concept for the manner in which various services may be requested.

Very generally, the purpose of this function (as it relates to ISPF) is basically to:

1. Inform ISPF of how to CONTROL ERROR conditions.
2. Request ISPF to retrieve (VGET) the contents of the variable *appl* from a pool of variables possibly stored in a previous pass.

3. Request ISPF to DISPLAY a data entry panel called DDSP120A.
4. Instruct ISPF to OPEN a file (ISPFILE) in preparation to write some output as a result of a file tailoring (FT) process.
5. Have ISPF perform the file tailoring (FT) by including (INCL) a predetermined "skeleton" (DDSS120) which will control the output format and content.
6. Request ISPF to CLOSE the file tailoring process.
7. Inform ISPF of a MeSsaGe number (DDSM120A) to be inserted into whatever panel will be redisplayed next as this function terminates and returns to the point of invocation.

Panels

Panels are the full-screen displays that the end-user sees. They can be structured in a variety of ways depending on their purposes. Generally, there are four major types of panels:

• Selection panels (menus)
• Data entry panels
• Table display panels
• Tutorial panels

Selection panels

Selection panels (often called "menus") show the list of options representing the different paths available to the user. After the user indicates the desired selection, and depending on the complexity of the application, the next display may be another lower-level selection panel, or it may lead directly into a data or table display panel.

As an example of a selection panel, Figure 1-2 shows one of the most popular menus, which most developers will recognize immediately — the PDF primary option menu.

Data Entry Panels

These are the panels through which data is entered or retrieved from the system. Depending on the request, the user may see a panel re-

```
-------------- ISPF/PDF PRIMARY OPTION MENU --------------
OPTION  ===>

   0  ISPF PARMS   - Specify terminal and user parameters
   1  BROWSE       - Display source data or output listings
   2  EDIT         - Create or change source data
   3  UTILITIES    - Perform utility functions
   4  FOREGROUND   - Invoke language processors in foreground
   5  BATCH        - Submit job for language processing
   6  COMMAND      - Enter TSO command or CLIST
   7  DIALOG TEST  - Perform dialog testing
   T  TUTORIAL     - Display information about ISPF/PDF
   X  EXIT         - Terminate ISPF using log and list defaults

Enter END command to terminate ISPF.
```

Figure 1-2   Sample Selection Panel.

questing the entry of some data fields, a panel to display the contents of some other data fields, or a mixture of the two.

Figure 1-3 illustrates one such panel that performs both functions.

Table Display Panels

Tables are the equivalent of data files (a more detailed explanation will be given later in this section).

Since displaying a table involves a repetitive process for each of its entries (rows), a table display panel is a specialized version of a data display panel. We simply define how we want each row to be processed, and ISPF automatically repeats that definition for as many rows as it needs to display.

Figure 1-4 illustrates a table display panel.

Tutorial Panels

Tutorial panels are designed to provide assistance to the end-user at any level of an application. Generally, the dialog is designed so that a particular process points to a particular tutorial panel. Then, if the

```
-------------------- DDS DATA ENTRY PANEL  ---------------------
COMMAND ===>


PLEASE ENTER OR VERIFY THE FOLLOWING ITEMS:
ACTION TO PERFORM:    ADD


APPLICATION ID . . . DDS.          Maximum 4 alphanumeric chars
VARIABLE NAME. . . . ........       Maximum 8 alphanumeric chars
POOL TYPE. . . . . .               P=Prof, S=Shr, F=Funct, N=N/A

DATA TYPE. . . . . . . .....        CHAR,NUMER,PANEL,MSG,TABLE,etc
FIELD LENGTH . . . . . .....        Maximum field length (32767)
DESCRIPTION. . . . .  ............................... Max 30 chars
```

Figure 1-3   Sample Data Entry Panel.

user should request HELP at that point, that particular tutorial panel would be presented to the user.

These panels normally contain nothing more than text in a manner similar to a page in a book. Mechanisms are available whereby

```
------------------- DDS TABLE DISPLAY PANEL  -------- ROW 1 OF 6
COMMAND ===>                                    SCROLL ===> CSR

ENTER:   A (ADD), C (CHANGE), OR D (DELETE)   ON THE DESIRED LINE(S)

CMD APPL VARIABLE POOL DATA  FIELD  FIELD DESCRIPTION AND COMMENTS
CDE  ID    NAME   TYPE TYPE LENGTH


    DDS  APPL      P   CHAR     4   APPLICATION IDENTIFICATION
    DDS  CLASS     P   CHAR     1   PREFERRED OUTPUT CLASS ON JOBS
    DDS  DESCRIPT  F   CHAR    30   FIELD DESCRIPTION
    DDS  DTYPE     F   CHAR     5   DATA TYPE (NUMER OR CHAR)
    DDS  LENTH     F   NUMER    5   MAXIMUM FIELD LENGTH
    DDS  PTYPE     F   CHAR     1   VARIABLE POOL CLASSIFICATION
```

Figure 1-4   Sample Table Display Panel.

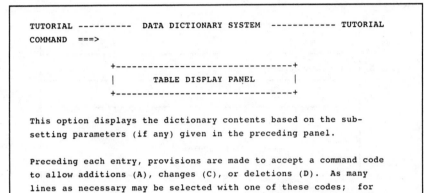

```
TUTORIAL ----------  DATA DICTIONARY SYSTEM  ------------ TUTORIAL
COMMAND  ===>


              +---------------------------------+
              |      TABLE DISPLAY PANEL         |
              +---------------------------------+


   This option displays the dictionary contents based on the sub-
   setting parameters (if any) given in the preceding panel.


   Preceding each entry, provisions are made to accept a command code
   to allow additions (A), changes (C), or deletions (D).  As many
   lines as necessary may be selected with one of these codes;  for
   each line selected, an expanded panel display will be provided to
   allow the user to add/change/delete the selected entries.
```

Figure 1-5   Sample Tutorial Panel.

the user can continue to the next "page" or the previous one, skip to an index for a keyword search, to the table of contents for a topic location, and more. In short, one can use it in much the same manner that one uses any book (see Figure 1-5).

So flexible is this facility that one could exploit it to allow online access to very large documents, standards, courses, etc. And the best part is that its usage is so simple that one does not even have to be a programmer to develop such on-line documents. A complete application could be developed consisting of nothing but tutorial panels.

Messages

As a user proceeds through a dialog, it is important to keep that user informed of any errors detected or of certain actions taken. This information is normally relayed through messages that overlay certain predetermined sections of the screen.

Although it is possible to vary the location of these messages, usually it is best to adhere to the convention of always displaying any short messages on the top right corner of the screen, while longer ones are displayed on the third line of the screen (see Figure 1-6).

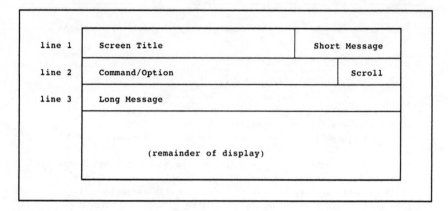

Figure 1-6   Standard ISPF Screen Design.

Short Messages

In the majority of cases, a thought can be conveyed to the user with a message that does not exceed 24 characters in length. When this is the case, the developer can take advantage of the ISPF built-in short message mechanism, which will display that short amount of text by overlaying it on the rightmost positions of the current screen title.

To illustrate, suppose that we were faced with the table display screen previously shown in Figure 1-4. If we were to press the Enter key without making any selections, we would receive a message as shown in Figure 1-7.

An interesting variation of this concept is the ability to display the identification of the current panel on the leftmost positions of the current screen title. This can be very useful when tracing activity through the system.

This process is activated through the commands PANELID ON and PANELID OFF. With PANELID ON, the previous display would look like Figure 1-8.

Long Messages

In most cases, the short message would be sufficient to remind the user of the needed selection. There may be times, however, when a

```
----------------- DDS TABLE DISPLAY PANEL  - SELECT A LINE OR END
COMMAND ===>                                    SCROLL ===> CSR

ENTER:  A (ADD), C (CHANGE), OR D (DELETE)  ON THE DESIRED LINE(S)

CMD APPL VARIABLE POOL DATA  FIELD  FIELD DESCRIPTION AND COMMENTS
CDE  ID    NAME   TYPE TYPE LENGTH

     DDS  APPL      P   CHAR    4   APPLICATION IDENTIFICATION
     DDS  CLASS     P   CHAR    1   PREFERRED OUTPUT CLASS ON JOBS
     DDS  DESCRIPT  F   CHAR   30   FIELD DESCRIPTION
     DDS  DTYPE     F   CHAR    5   DATA TYPE (NUMER OR CHAR)
     DDS  LENTH     F   NUMER   5   MAXIMUM FIELD LENGTH
     DDS  PTYPE     F   CHAR    1   VARIABLE POOL CLASSIFICATION
```

Figure 1-7   Sample Short Message Display.

longer explanation is necessary. In this case, requesting HELP
(usually PF1) would automatically display the long message.

To use the same example, pressing PF1 (HELP) would cause the
message to appear on the screen (see Figure 1-9).

```
DDSP110B -------- DDS TABLE DISPLAY PANEL  - SELECT A LINE OR END
COMMAND ===>                                    SCROLL ===> CSR

ENTER:  A (ADD), C (CHANGE), OR D (DELETE)  ON THE DESIRED LINE(S)

CMD APPL VARIABLE POOL DATA  FIELD  FIELD DESCRIPTION AND COMMENTS
CDE  ID    NAME   TYPE TYPE LENGTH

     DDS  APPL      P   CHAR    4   APPLICATION IDENTIFICATION
     DDS  CLASS     P   CHAR    1   PREFERRED OUTPUT CLASS ON JOBS
     DDS  DESCRIPT  F   CHAR   30   FIELD DESCRIPTION
     DDS  DTYPE     F   CHAR    5   DATA TYPE (NUMER OR CHAR)
     DDS  LENTH     F   NUMER   5   MAXIMUM FIELD LENGTH
     DDS  PTYPE     F   CHAR    1   VARIABLE POOL CLASSIFICATION
```

Figure 1-8   Using the PANELID Option.

```
------------------ DDS TABLE DISPLAY PANEL  - SELECT A LINE OR END
COMMAND ===>                               SCROLL ===> CSR
YOU MUST ENTER "A", "C", OR "D" UNDER "CMD CDE", OR "END" (PF3)
ENTER: A (ADD), C (CHANGE), OR D (DELETE)  ON THE DESIRED LINE(S)


CMD APPL VARIABLE POOL DATA  FIELD  FIELD DESCRIPTION AND COMMENTS
CDE ID    NAME    TYPE TYPE LENGTH

    DDS  APPL     P    CHAR     4   APPLICATION IDENTIFICATION
    DDS  CLASS    P    CHAR     1   PREFERRED OUTPUT CLASS ON JOBS
    DDS  DESCRIPT F    CHAR    30   FIELD DESCRIPTION
    DDS  DTYPE    F    CHAR     5   DATA TYPE (NUMER OR CHAR)
    DDS  LENTH    F    NUMER    5   MAXIMUM FIELD LENGTH
    DDS  PTYPE    F    CHAR     1   VARIABLE POOL CLASSIFICATION
```

Figure 1-9   Sample Long Message Display.

Tutorials

Under some circumstances, the user may still be unsure as to what action to take next. Should this be the case, requesting HELP one more time would place the user into a TUTORIAL mode by displaying a panel appropriate to the screen in question.

Continuing with the same example, pressing PF1 (HELP) again would display the tutorial panel already shown as Figure 1-5.

Tables

As previously mentioned, tables are the equivalent of data files. These tables represent a two-dimensional matrix of data where the *rows* are similar to logical records on a file, and the *columns* are similar to data fields within a record (see Figure 1-10).

Although tables may reside on disk, to process them they must be in core (the computer memory). This allows for faster processing of the table, but it also imposes some limitations on the size of the table that one can control.

Tables may be used in an exclusive mode (private) or they may be shared with other users. If a table is shared, however, only one user at a time may have write access to it.

appl id	variable name	pool type	data type	field len	field description and comments
DDS	ACCT	P	CHAR	15	USER ACCOUNT DATA FOR JOB STMT
DDS	APPL	P	CHAR	4	APPLICATION IDENTIFICATION
DDS	CLASS	P	CHAR	1	PREFERRED OUTPUT CLASS ON JOBS
DDS	CPY	F	NUMER	3	NUMBER OF COPIES TO PRINT
DDS	DDSC000	N	CMD	0	APPLICATION START-UP COMMAND
DDS	DDSM110B	N	MSG	0	SELECT LINE OR END

Figure 1-10   Sample ISPF Table: 6 Rows x 6 Columns.

One may access the various rows of a table in a variety of ways:

- *By key field(s).* If each row is associated with a special identifier such as an employee number, a unique name, etc., then this field (or a combination of multiple fields) can become the *key* for this row. In Figure 1-10, the key for each row is the unique combination of the "appl id" and "variable name" fields.
- *By data field(s).* Regardless of whether key fields are or are not present, it is possible to retrieve one or more records by matching on any other data fields. Our application will be retrieving rows based on "pool type" and/or "data type" as well as on keys.
- *By row number.* One can also retrieve rows by specific row numbers. It is possible to control the "row pointer" to any position within the file and read the contents of that row. Thus, whether one wishes to "step" through the file in a predetermined sequence, or access rows in a random fashion, services are available to satisfy these needs.

File Skeletons

File skeletons are preformatted files where the basic structure of the desired output is established, but the variable data has to be inserted on demand. This process is called *file tailoring*. File tailoring can be used to construct job streams, create output reports, or produce any file that may be used for some other process.

```
//&ZUSER.A JOB (&acct.,&room.,TLIST),&uname.,MSGCLASS=&class.,
//              USER=&ZUSER.,NOTIFY=&ZUSER.,PASSWORD=&pass.
/*JOBPARM       COPIES=&cpy.
//S1      EXEC PGM=IEBGENER
//SYSUT1    DD DSN=&ZUSER..DDS.FTOUTPUT,DISP=SHR
//SYSUT2    DD SYSOUT=*,DCB=(&ZUSER..DDS.FTOUTPUT,RECFM=FBA)
//SYSPRINT  DD SYSOUT=*
//SYSIN     DD DUMMY
//
```

Figure 1-11   Sample ISPF Skeleton to Construct a Job Stream.

Job Streams

Figure 1-11 illustrates a skeleton used to construct a job stream.

In this simple (but representative) case, the file tailoring process of this skeleton will consist of nothing more than substituting all the variables (*&name.*) with the corresponding values that have been collected by an ISPF application in a dialog with a user.

Output Reports

Another example of file tailoring, this time a little more elaborate, demonstrates the ability to produce an output report (see Figure 1-12). This particular skeleton will produce a report with up to 50 lines per page containing headings on each page followed by various lines showing the contents of table rows that meet certain selection parameters.

Very briefly, for now, any line that begins with a ")" indicates an ISPF file tailoring control statement; any other line simply contains data to be copied to the output (if applicable) after variable substitution.

For a very quick overview of the logic in this file skeleton, please refer to the reference numbers shown:

1. The)DEFAULT statement simply indicates a series of characters that will have special meaning to the file tailoring services.

```
)DEFAULT  )&?!<|>                                                   1
)TB   2 8 19 25 32 41                                               2
)SET  LINES = 255                                                  3
)CM -------------------------- start loop for all table rows
)DOT &table                                                        4
)CM    --------------------------- start row selection process
)SEL    &sappl = *      |      &sappl = &appl                      5
)SEL    &spool = *      |      &spool = &ptype
)SEL     &sdata = *    |    &sdata = &dtype
)CM       - row selected if all 3 true -
)SEL         &LINES > 50
)CM          ------------------------- start heading routine
1DDS TABLE ENTRIES FOR: APPL=&sappl.,PTYPE=&spool.,DTYPE=&sdata.
0APPL  VARIABLE  POOL    DATA    FIELD    FIELD DESC AND COMMENTS
  ID     NAME    TYPE    TYPE   LENGTH
)BLANK                                                             6
)SET LINES = 5
)CM          ----------- end heading routine/resume row processing
)ENDSEL                                                            7
   &appl !&varname !&ptype !&dtype !&lenth !&descript
)SET LINES = &LINES + 1
)ENDSEL
)ENDSEL
)ENDSEL
)CM    --------------------------------- end selection process
)ENDDOT                                                            8
)CM --------------------------------- end loop for table rows
```

Figure 1-12   Sample ISPF Skeleton to Produce a Report.

2. The)TB statement will indicate the logical tab positions for spacing of data entries whenever the tab character is found (! in this example).

3. The)SET statement will allow manipulation of variables within the file tailoring process.

4. The)DOT statement will allow iterative processing for each row of a given table until the corresponding)ENDDOT is found.

5. The)SEL statement in conjunction with its corresponding)ENDSEL statement bracket any number of lines whose process is predicated on the results of condition(s) given in the)SEL statement.

     In this particular example, several)SEL statements are nested within the "higher" ones providing the equivalent of "AND" logic.

6. The)BLANK statement simply indicates that a blank line is to be generated on the output file.

7. The)ENDSEL statements close out the)SEL statements in reverse order.

8. Finally, the)ENDDOT statement closes out the loop initiated by the)DOT statement.

Dialog Organization

It should also be useful to see how each of these components relates to the others. Figure 1-13 provides an example of how an application could be structured.

In the illustration, the application begins with a menu. It could, just as well, begin with a function, which might prepare the environment. As a matter of fact, the latter is often the case. The point is that you can establish any number of levels defining the structure of your application where menus are given until the exact task is identified.

At that point, you need some logic to carry out the task — that is where the function normally comes in. Using data or table display panels, the function communicates with the end-user either showing or requesting the appropriate data and then acting on it.

Summary

At this point, we should have a good understanding of the five dialog component types which, again, are:

- FUNCTIONS   — The programs or command procedures
- PANELS   — The full-screen displays
- MESSAGES   — The text inserted over a panel
- TABLES   — The "data files"
- FILE SKELETONS — The preformatted output

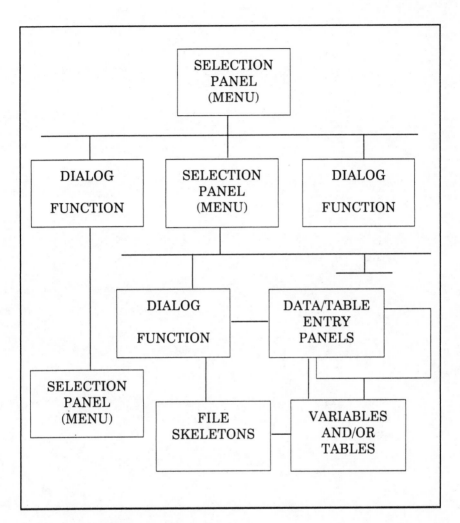

Figure 1-13 ISPF Component Interaction.

2

ISPF Services

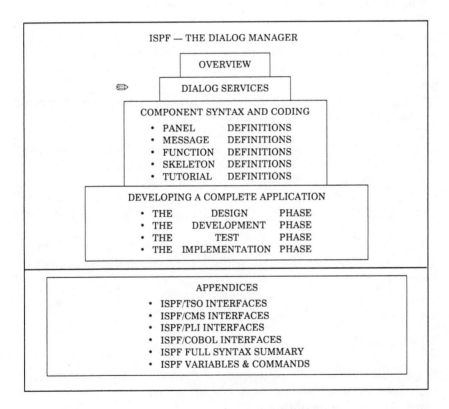

ISPF — THE DIALOG MANAGER

OVERVIEW

DIALOG SERVICES

COMPONENT SYNTAX AND CODING

- PANEL   DEFINITIONS
- MESSAGE   DEFINITIONS
- FUNCTION DEFINITIONS
- SKELETON DEFINITIONS
- TUTORIAL DEFINITIONS

DEVELOPING A COMPLETE APPLICATION

- THE   DESIGN   PHASE
- THE   DEVELOPMENT   PHASE
- THE   TEST   PHASE
- THE   IMPLEMENTATION PHASE

APPENDICES

- ISPF/TSO INTERFACES
- ISPF/CMS INTERFACES
- ISPF/PLI INTERFACES
- ISPF/COBOL INTERFACES
- ISPF FULL SYNTAX SUMMARY
- ISPF VARIABLES & COMMANDS

Now that we know what the various dialog components are and how they interact with each other, the next step is to determine what services are available that will allow us to manipulate and control these various components.

Generally, ISPF provides services to perform many complex tasks such as:

• Displaying screen images and messages
• Building and maintaining tables
• Generating output files
• Defining and controlling symbolic variables
• Interfacing with programs such as EDIT and BROWSE
• Controlling operational modes

The ability to perform all these tasks with simple ISPF service calls enables an application developer to concentrate on the overall purpose of the application without excessive concern for how each elementary detail is actually carried out. This is one of the reasons why ISPF is such a good programming tool as well as a great productivity aid.

For convenience of presentation and understanding, we can group all the ISPF services into five major classes:

• DISPLAY SERVICES   — To display panels and messages
• TABLE SERVICES   — To process data tables
• FILE TAILORING SERVICES   — To process file skeletons
• VARIABLE SERVICES   — To process variables in any pool
• OTHER SERVICES   — To interface with other products

Each of these services will be covered in greater detail in Chapters 3 through 7. For now, though, we will want to get a general idea of what they provide.

DISPLAY Services

Display services enable us to display selection panels, data panels, table panels, and overlay messages on panels. The actual service names and their functions are:

• DISPLAY — Display data panel
• TBDISPL — Display table panel
• SETMSG — Display message on panel

TABLE Services

Table services provide us with general services such as creating, opening, closing, or erasing tables, as well as more detailed operations such as adding, deleting, retrieving, etc., specific rows of a table.
The actual service names and their general descriptions follow.

Table-Wide Operations

* TBCREATE — Create a table
* TBOPEN — Open a table for processing
* TBSORT — Sort a table
* TBQUERY — Query information about the table
* TBSTATS — Obtain statistical data on the table
* TBSAVE — File a copy of the table and continue
* TBCLOSE — Close a table and disconnect it from use
* TBEND — End processing of a table without saving
* TBERASE — Remove a table from the system (DELETE)

Single Row Operations

* TBADD — Add a row to a table
* TBDELETE — Delete a row from a table
* TBEXIST — Check existence of a particular key
* TBGET — Retrieve a row from a table
* TBMOD — Modify a row in a table
* TBPUT — Store a row in a table
* TBSARG — Set search arguments for a table scan
* TBSCAN — Search for next row that matches search argument
* TBVCLEAR — Clear table variables to null

Row Pointer Operations

* TBTOP — Point to top of table (row 0)
* TBSKIP — Skip to the row following the current
* TBBOTTOM — Point to bottom of table (last row)

FILE TAILORING Services

As previously indicated, file tailoring consists of creating an output file, reading an input skeleton with data and control statements which dictate the contents of the output file, then closing the created file and, if necessary, erasing it when no longer needed.

The services available for this type of process are:

- FTOPEN — Create an output file for file tailoring
- FTINCL — Include a skeleton to control output
- FTCLOSE — Close out the file tailoring process
- FTERASE — Erase the created output file

VARIABLE Services

Variable data that flows in and out of the various panels displayed is held in areas referred to as variable pools. ISPF provides three classes of pools.

Application Profile Pool

This pool contains data that is held across any number of sessions. It can be used by any component of a given application for items that need to be "remembered" from one session to another. Because retrieval of data is by variable name, the dialog developer must be careful when assigning names to this pool, since carelessness could result in destruction of similarly named entries. (This happens to be one of the reasons why the application presented in this book was developed and offered to the readers.)

Shared Pool

This pool contains data that is to be known for as long as an application is in control, but will be discarded when the application is exited. It is used to enable data to flow from one application component to the other.

Again, care needs to be exerted in the naming of variables to avoid unintentional duplication and subsequent destruction of similarly named variables within this application.

Function Pool

This pool contains data that is to be known only to this particular function. As such, duplication of names from one function to another has no consequences (unless, of course, the variables are copied into one of the other pools).

Variable Access

Locating needed variables from the various pools for panel displays is performed by scanning the function pool first, then the shared pool, and finally the profile pool. If not found, a null value is returned.

Writing, however, is normally limited to the function pool unless explicitly stated otherwise. In the case of selection panels, variables are written to the shared pool; if such a variable should exist in the profile pool but not in the shared one, then it is written to the profile pool.

Figure 2-1 shows the scope and relationship of the variable pools to various dialog components. Please note that, although command procedure (CLIST, EXEC, REXX, etc.) variables are automatically known in the function pool, program variables are not (even if they should have the same name). It is possible to correlate the program and function pool variables, but this requires specific service calls to ISPF.

Variable Operations

The following is a complete list of variable services and their descriptions.

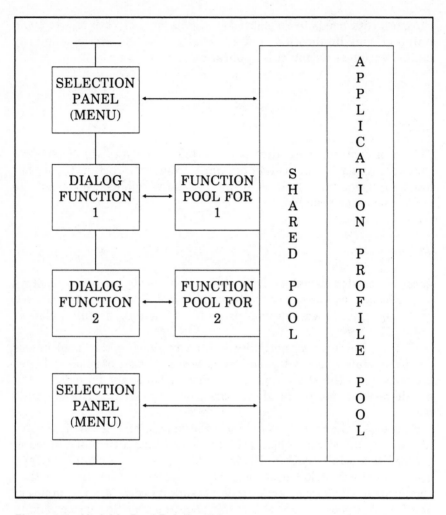

Figure 2-1   Variable Pool Relationships.

General-Purpose Services

• VGET   — Retrieve a variable from the shared or profile pool
• VPUT   — Store a variable in the shared or profile pool

Program-Related Services

- VCOPY — Copy a pool variable into a program variable
- VREPLACE — Copy a program variable into a pool variable
- VDEFINE — Correlate a program variable to a pool variable
- VDELETE — Cancel a variable correlation between program and pool
- VRESET — Cancel correlation of all variables

Other Services

Finally, there are a few other miscellaneous services designed to further simplify and enhance the functionality of any dialog application. These services are:

- CONTROL — Specify screen-handling and error-handling options
- SELECT — Display selection panel
- PQUERY — Obtain information on a particular panel
- GETMSG — Obtain information on a particular message
- LOG — Write dialog messages to a log file
- BROWSE — Invoke the BROWSE program from a dialog
- EDIT — Invoke the EDIT program from a dialog
- ISREDIT — Invoke EDIT macros from a dialog
- EDREC — Edit recovery table processing
- LIBDEF — Define ISPF libraries for a dialog
- LM*xxxxxx* — Use PDF library access services
- GR*xxxxxx* — Establish GDDM interface processes

Summary

At this point, we should understand not only the five types of components that make up a dialog, but the various services available from ISPF that allow us to manipulate these components. For a very quick review, then, the various classes of services available are:

- DISPLAY SERVICES — To display panels and messages
- TABLE SERVICES — To process data tables

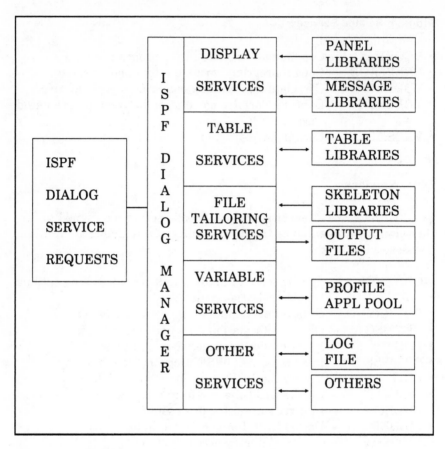

Figure 2-2   Service Relationships.

- FILE TAILORING SERVICES — To process file skeletons
- VARIABLE SERVICES   — To process variables in any pool
- OTHER SERVICES   — To interface with other products

All of these services are requested through one common point which is the Dialog Manager. Figure 2-2 shows the relationships of the various services to the Dialog Manager and the files involved in the process.

Finally, although the syntax of each service call will be discussed in detail in later sections, it should be helpful at this time to note the simplicity of requesting any of the services discussed.

The general format of each call is:

```
☞ ISPEXEC service parameter [parameter ...]
```

Thus, to display a data panel called DDSP110A, we would code:

```
☞ ISPEXEC DISPLAY PANEL(DDSP110A)
```

3

Panel Definitions

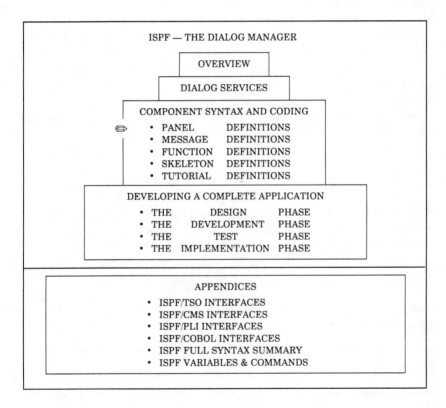

ISPF — THE DIALOG MANAGER

OVERVIEW

DIALOG SERVICES

COMPONENT SYNTAX AND CODING
- PANEL   DEFINITIONS
- MESSAGE   DEFINITIONS
- FUNCTION   DEFINITIONS
- SKELETON   DEFINITIONS
- TUTORIAL   DEFINITIONS

DEVELOPING A COMPLETE APPLICATION
- THE   DESIGN   PHASE
- THE   DEVELOPMENT   PHASE
- THE   TEST   PHASE
- THE IMPLEMENTATION PHASE

APPENDICES
- ISPF/TSO INTERFACES
- ISPF/CMS INTERFACES
- ISPF/PLI INTERFACES
- ISPF/COBOL INTERFACES
- ISPF FULL SYNTAX SUMMARY
- ISPF VARIABLES & COMMANDS

Now that we have a general understanding of what the dialog components are and how they interact with ISPF, it is time to begin the actual coding of each one. It is not the intent of this book to simply repeat the information that is already available in the IBM manuals.

Although all parameters for a given item will be shown, the emphasis will be on clarity, organization, and meaningful applications for these items with as many illustrations as possible.

Previously, we saw FUNCTIONS listed as the first type of component, but now we will begin with PANEL and MESSAGE definitions since the design of most applications normally starts with input and output processes. Once we know these components in detail, we can use that knowledge to prototype any application. (Prototyping an application is a process whereby a systems designer provides a modeling of the various inputs and outputs involved in a given application. This modeling should simulate the end product as closely as possible, the purpose being to enable the end-user to evaluate the system flow before final approval.) Furthermore, since the prototype process mechanism will be the same as that of the end product, we will be prototyping *and coding* the real application simultaneously. A great time-saver!

An ISPF panel contains both the text that is to be displayed on the screen and the logic immediately associated with the processing of any variables for that panel. The various sections that can be coded in a panel are:

-)ATTR   — Optional : Define field attributes for 3270 panel
-)BODY   — Required : Define panel design and contents
-)MODEL   — Optional : Define model for table display process
-)INIT   — Optional : Define logic to perform before displays
-)REINIT   — Optional : Define logic to perform before redisplays
-)PROC   — Optional : Define logic to perform after displays
-)END   — Required : Define end of panel definition

Each of these sections is identified by a header statement in the form of:

```
⇨ )section-id [parameter [parameter ...]]
```

possibly followed by one or more lines defining the contents of that section.

)ATTR Section

The)ATTR section enables us to select specific characters to represent special attributes to control the manner in which portions of the panel will appear to the end-user. We will be able to indicate whether or not some words will be highlighted and with which color, whether or not they can be modified by the user, etc.

This section is entirely optional, and in many cases one will not have to be concerned with it. If we wish to code it, the format is as follows.

ATTR Header

```
☞ )ATTR   [DEFAULT(abc  |  %+_)]
```

This header statement indicates that we are about to define the attribute characters that we will use in our panel definition. It also allows us a short form of defining three characters to represent the most commonly used combinations of attributes. If this section is omitted, the three default characters and their attributes will be:

```
☞ % TYPE(TEXT )   INTENS(HIGH)
☞ + TYPE(TEXT )   INTENS(LOW )
☞ _ TYPE(INPUT)   INTENS(HIGH)   CAPS(ON)   JUST(LEFT)
```

Of course, if we were to need any of these characters as part of the text to be displayed, we would have to select some other ones to control the display.

For example, if we actually needed to use the "+" symbol in our text, we could select another character, the "$" for example, to represent those attributes. In this case, the)ATTR header statement would be coded as follows:

```
☞ )ATTR  DEFAULT(%$_)
```

ATTR Section

If we need more than three characters, or if we wish to modify their attributes, we can use the attribute section to enter as many attributes for as many characters as we wish. The syntax of each entry in this section is as follows:

```
☞ char [TYPE    (TEXT  | INPUT   | OUTPUT  | DATAIN  | DATAOUT)]
       [COLOR (WHITE  | RED     | BLUE    | GREEN
                      | PINK    | YELLOW  | TURQ)]
       [INTENS (HIGH  | LOW     | NONE)]
       [HILITE(BLINK  | USCORE  | REVERSE)]
       [CAPS    (ON   | OFF     | IN      | OUT)]
       [JUST   (LEFT  | RIGHT   | ASIS)]
       [PAD    (NULLS | USER    | char)]
       [PADC   (NULLS | USER    | char)]
       [SKIP      (ON | OFF)]
       [ATTN      (ON | OFF)]
       [AREA(DYNAMIC | GRAPHIC)]
       [EXTEND    (ON | OFF)]
       [SCROLL    (ON | OFF)]
       [USERMOD(code)]
       [DATAMOD(code)]
```

Very briefly, *char* can be either any character available on your keyboard, or a 2-digit hexadecimal code. TYPE indicates whether a field in the panel is to be used for plain TEXT (constants), for INPUT data (unprotected), for OUTPUT data (protected), for input fields in a DYNAMIC area (DATAIN), or output (DATAOUT).

The COLOR, INTENSity, and HILITE attributes are self-explanatory except, perhaps, for INTENS(NONE). This option indicates a field whose contents will not be visible. An application of this would be, for example, to accept a password while keeping it invisible to any observers.

The CAPS option indicates whether or not data is to be translated to upper case into and out of the panel (ON I OFF), only when coming from the panel (IN), or only when going to the panel (OUT).

The JUSTification option instructs ISPF how to place variable data onto a field on a panel. Although JUST(LEFT) is most common, there will be times when it will be desirable to align entries on the right — JUST(RIGHT); a column of numbers would be a good example (which we will use later). JUST(ASIS) will enable you to maintain any leading blanks just as typed by the user.

Once the data is justified onto the panel field, the next concern is the PADding option. Specifying PAD('_') or PAD(_), for example, would cause any data shorter than the panel field to be extended with "_" either on the left or the right, depending on how JUSTification had been specified. It is possible to leave the choice of this character to the user by specifying PAD(USER), in which case the choice given through the PDF option 0.1 would be selected.

The PADConditional option applies only to fields that are entirely blank or null. In this case, one can specify some other padding character.

The SKIP option allows you to control whether you want the keyboard to lock up when a user types beyond the end of an input field — SKIP(OFF) — or whether to automatically advance to the next input field — SKIP(ON). Thus, if you want to override the default — SKIP(OFF) — you would have to specify SKIP(ON) on the TEXT field that is to be skipped immediately following the INPUT field in question.

The remaining parameters are for more unusual conditions. The ATTN indicates whether a text field is or is not light-pen selectable. The AREA allows you to define a section of the panel as a DYNAMIC area or a GRAPHIC one. All the other parameters (EXTEND, SCROLL, USERMOD, DATAMOD) relate to DYNAMIC areas which we will discuss later under "DYNAMIC Area Considerations."

ATTR Example

To simplify the understanding of this section (and others to come) let us look at an example. In this case, we will be using the default attribute characters (%, +, _) plus some others.

```
)ATTR DEFAULT(%+_)
/*  % TYPE(TEXT )  INTENS(HIGH)                                      */
/*  + TYPE(TEXT )  INTENS(LOW )                                      */
/*  _ TYPE(INPUT)  INTENS(HIGH)  CAPS(ON)  JUST(LEFT)                */
    $ TYPE(INPUT)  INTENS(HIGH)  CAPS(ON)  JUST(LEFT)   PAD(_)
    ! TYPE(INPUT)  INTENS(HIGH)  CAPS(ON)  JUST(RIGHT)  PAD(_)
    ¬ TYPE(INPUT)  INTENS(NON )  CAPS(ON)  JUST(LEFT)

)BODY
...
)MODEL
...
)INIT
...
)REINIT
...
)PROC
...
)END
```

Figure 3-1   Sample)ATTR Section Definition.

Suppose that we want three additional variations of input field definitions. Two of these will provide display padding of "_" so that the user can readily see the full length of the field. However, one is to be padded on the right, while the other is to be padded on the left. Finally, since we are about to ask for a password, we want it hidden from any possible observers.

The coding of our)ATTR section, then, would be as shown in Figure 3-1.[1]

)BODY Section

With the)ATTR section completed, we proceed to the)BODY of the panel — a required section (for obvious reasons). This is the section

----

[1]   Please note that the sequence /* . . . */ simply indicates a comment within the panel definition. Comments will be ignored completely unless, of course, they are found *within* the actual body of the panel.

that actually contains the screen format that we wish to "paint" on
the CRT. As before, we have the section header followed by the body
proper.

BODY Header

```
☞ )BODY  [DEFAULT(abc)]  [WIDTH(width)]  [EXPAND(xy)]      [KANA]
         [CMD(fldname)]  [SMSG(fldname)]  [LMSG(fldname)]  [ASIS]
```

Simply coding)BODY with no other parameters will be sufficient for
most applications. When necessary, the DEFAULT parameter serves
the exact same purpose as the one described in the)ATTR header. If
the only need is to change any of the three default characters, that
option could be specified here without even coding the)ATTR section
at all.

WIDTH allows you to override the default screen format of 80
columns. Since this value may come from a variable, it is possible to
have panels whose width may expand to the capabilities of a given
terminal. This option works with the EXPAND option which indicates a pair of characters that will designate the section(s) of the
panel that can expand to meet the desired WIDTH.

Consider the example in Figure 3-2.

When ISPF interprets line 1, it substitutes *&width* with the actual
value it contains (suppose 132). It now knows that this panel will be
formatted for 132 characters — WIDTH(132) — and it will scan each
line for the given delimiters ("/") in order to EXPAND it to the
specified width.

```
)BODY  WIDTH(&width) EXPAND(//)                               1
%------/-/------ DDS TABLE DISPLAY PANEL -----/-/----------   2
%COMMAND ===>_ZCMD         / /            +SCROLL ===> CSR +   3
%                                                             4
...
```

Figure 3-2 Handling Variable Screen Widths.

When it processes line 2, it finds two sets of "/-/" on that line. It will repeat the "-" an equal number of times on each set until the line fits the 132-character width.

Line 3 contains one set of "/ /" causing blanks to be inserted on that line (and at that position) until it has a length of 132 characters. Finally, line 4 has no expand characters. It will simply be padded with blanks on the right until it also has a length of 132 characters.

The end result of all this is that the panel would still have the same general layout, but it would appear "stretched" to fill the screen width as simulated in Figure 3-3.

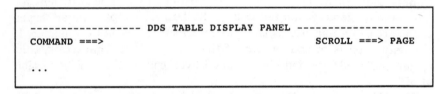

Figure 3-3   Display of Panel with EXPAND Option.

The other parameters of the)BODY header, SMSG, LMSG, and CMD, enable you to override the positioning of the short and long messages as well as the field that is to be treated as the input command. Although these three parameters may have their uses in some very unusual applications, generally one should not deviate from what has been established as a standard. To do so will only confuse the end-user.

The ASIS parameter indicates that even if the end-user attempts to change the normal locations of the command line or long message (possibly through the PDF option 0.4), the panel is to be processed as designed.

Finally, the KANA parameter alerts ISPF that KATAKANA characters are to be found in the panel body.

BODY Section

This section is the one where the actual screen layout and contents are established. It is made up of any text and variables that we wish to have displayed. The text is nothing more than a string of characters; the variables are names assigned to represent fields whose contents may change.

The rules for naming variables are quite simple: 1 through 8 (6 in FORTRAN) alphanumeric characters (A–Z, $, @, #, 0–9), the first of which must not be numeric. Thus, ALPHA, X123, $VAL, @#$, are all valid names (except for APL where variables cannot contain $, @, #), but 1ABC is not because it begins with a numeric character.

When we wish to reference the value that a name represents, we precede the name with an "&"; if we wish to reference the name proper (not its value), we use the name without the "&". (The exception to this is in the body of a panel for a field identified as INPUT. In this case, the "&" is omitted since it implies a variable.)

If we reference a variable immediately followed by some other variable or string, we delimit the name with a period. For example, &VAR1.&VAR2 would generate a string consisting of the contents of VAR1 immediately followed by those of VAR2.

In a panel body, various fields or parts of output text can have different attributes by simply using different attribute characters that have been defined (or implied) in the)ATTR section. Furthermore, the lengths of the various fields are determined by the size of the areas between attribute characters.

BODY Example

For this illustration, let us continue with the panel already started under the)ATTR section and now shown in Figure 3-4.

To begin, the title line (immediately following the)BODY header) is preceded with a "%" symbol, the character which, by default, represents TYPE(TEXT) INTENS(HIGH). This will give us a highlighted title.

The string "COMMAND ===>" on the following line is similarly highlighted. Immediately following it, we have our first input field, "ZCMD". We know that it is an input field because it is preceded by the "_" symbol which, also by default, represents TYPE(INPUT) INTENS(HIGH). The length of this ZCMD field continues until the next attribute character is found, which is the "%" marking the beginning of the next line.

The line "PLEASE . . ." is nothing more than TEXT displayed in low intensity. Eventually, we arrive at a series of six lines that con-

```
)ATTR DEFAULT(%+_)
/*  % TYPE(TEXT )  INTENS(HIGH)                                      */
/*  + TYPE(TEXT )  INTENS(LOW )                                      */
/*  _ TYPE(INPUT)  INTENS(HIGH)  CAPS(ON)  JUST(LEFT)                */
    $ TYPE(INPUT)  INTENS(HIGH)  CAPS(ON)  JUST(LEFT)   PAD(_)
    ! TYPE(INPUT)  INTENS(HIGH)  CAPS(ON)  JUST(RIGHT)  PAD(_)
    ¬ TYPE(INPUT)  INTENS(NON )  CAPS(ON)  JUST(LEFT)

)BODY
%-------------- DDS JOB SUBMISSION PARAMETERS --------------
%COMMAND ===>_ZCMD
%
+   PLEASE ENTER/VERIFY THE FOLLOWING ITEMS:
+
+   YOUR NAME. . . . . .$uname    +        JOB stmt pgmr's name
+   ACCOUNTING INFO. . .$acct              +Job acct parameters
+   ROOM NUMBER. . . . .$room     +        Room nbr for delivery
+   OUTPUT CLASS . . . .$z+                Output print classes
+   NUMBER OF COPIES . .$cpy+              Nbr of copies to print
+   ACCESS PASSWORD. . .¬pass     +        Dataset access (if req)

)MODEL
...
)INIT
.ZVARS = class
)REINIT
...
)PROC
...
)END
```

Figure 3-4   Sample)BODY Section Definition.

tain input fields, the lengths of which are controlled by the location of the attribute character that follows them. Thus, *uname* has a length of 8 characters, *acct* has a length of 17, etc.

One variable that has special significance is the *z*. In this case, we thought about calling this field *class*, but since we wanted it to represent a one-character entry, the name would have exceeded the size of the panel field. As such, we use this special *z* variable called a "place holder."

The use of place holders allows us to name fields in any manner desired without concern for the lengths of the data that they represent. Eventually, of course, we must somehow correlate the various place holders to the actual variable names that they represent. This is accomplished through an assignment statement ("=" statement) in the)INIT section. In the example, we see that *class* is being assigned to the special variable called ".ZVARS" (more on this later). With this knowledge, ISPF now knows that the z variable really represents the variable *class*, which will receive a one-character field.

DYNAMIC Area Considerations

DYNAMIC areas are special segments whose contents are to be determined entirely by some other process (a function most likely). These areas may be defined with any type of panel: menu, data entry or table display panels.

To define a DYNAMIC area, first we choose an attribute character (and code it in the)ATTR section) that will be used to identify the desired area. Then, in the)BODY section, we bracket the area on the left and on the right with the chosen character. Lastly, we construct the string that is to be distributed through the designated area. The interesting part about the string is that it is made up of data and other attribute characters that will control how the data within the area is to be displayed.

To illustrate the total process, please refer to Figure 3-5. In this example, a small panel area is defined as a DYNAMIC area and it is referenced by the name *window*. This variable represents a string where the needed attribute characters controlling DATAIN (input), DATAOUT (text), etc., would already be intermixed with the data.

When displaying this panel, ISPF would distribute the contents of the string into the area proceeding from left to right and from top to bottom until the entire area is filled.

You will note that in this case only two lines were defined for *window*, but since we indicated EXTEND(ON), the area will be extended into as many lines as the screen can accommodate after the "fixed" lines up to this point have been taken into account. The dialog component developing the contents of *window* can inquire about the number of lines through a built-in function called LVLINE (this will be discussed a little later in the panel logic sections).

Let us assume that the contents of *window* reflected some input as well as some text fields. If the user were to change any of the input fields, the attribute byte for that field would be changed (to a "!" in

```
)ATTR
 | AREA(DYNAMIC) EXTEND(ON) SCROLL(ON) DATAMOD(!)


)BODY
%--------------- SAMPLE DYNAMIC AREA PROCESSING --------------
%COMMAND ===>_ZCMD
%
+    FIELDX . . . . . _fieldx +
+    FIELDY . . . . . _fieldy    +      +|window                |+
+                                       +|                       |+
+
+ You may scroll UP or DOWN through the window.


)PROC
 &lines = LVLINE(window)   /* nbr lines visible this screen */
)END
```

Figure 3-5   Sample DYNAMIC Area Definition.

this case), since we had requested that through the DATAMOD(!) option in the)ATTR section.

Essentially, what this means is that we want to be told if the user modified the data displayed. If we had chosen USERMOD, we would be requesting that we wanted to be told if the user modified any of the fields even if it consisted of nothing more than overtyping with the same characters.

GRAPHIC Area Considerations

GRAPHIC areas are panel sections whose contents are to be controlled by GDDM to develop graphs, pictures, etc. The process to define this area is very similar to that of the DYNAMIC one except that we use the GRAPHIC attribute (see Figure 3-6).

Once the panel is defined, a call to GDDM with the panel name would allow GDDM to extract the dimension of the GRAPHIC area and to plot the necessary picture based on subsequent calls to GDDM.

```
)ATTR
  | AREA(GRAPHIC) EXTEND(ON)


)BODY
%-------------- SAMPLE DYNAMIC AREA PROCESSING --------------
%COMMAND ===>_ZCMD
%
+    FIELDX . . . . . _fieldx +
+    FIELDY . . . . . _fieldy  +       |window                      |
+                                      |                            |
+


)PROC
  &lines = LVLINE(window)   /* nbr lines visible this screen */
)END
```

Figure 3-6   Sample GRAPHIC Area Definition.

)MODEL Section

The)MODEL section is only found on panels for table displays. This means that the panel display must be invoked through the service TBDISPL.

The unique feature of this section is that we will be defining how we want one row of a table to be displayed, and the TBDISPL service will automatically reuse that model definition for each row to be displayed.

MODEL Header

The syntax for this header is:

```
⇨ )MODEL  [ROWS (ALL | SCAN)]   [CLEAR(vname1 [vname2 ...])]
```

Generally, no parameters are necessary. In a few cases, however, you may wish to limit the number of rows to process based on some search arguments. If this is the case, specifying ROWS(SCAN) would cause the TBDISPL service to examine each row to see if it matches the arguments set by the TBSARG in the function driving this display. Only successful matches would be shown.

The CLEAR parameter is used even less frequently. Although we often think of ISPF tables as "even" two-dimensional matrices, it is possible for any number of rows to have some extra column(s) not present on the others (for example, some extra remarks). These additional fields in particular rows are referred to as "EXTENSION VARIABLES."

When a table is being processed, each row retrieved causes the contents of each variable to reflect the new values of that row, except for extension variables that do not exist in a particular row. The result is that if these variables are not cleared before reading the next row, they may contain the data that applied to a preceding row. This problem can be eliminated by coding CLEAR(ext-var-name1, ...).

MODEL Section

This is where we define the actual appearance for each row of the table that is to be displayed. Whether the model for each row is to occupy just one line on the display or more (up to 8 lines) is entirely up to us. One interesting point, however, is that ISPF will display as many sets of the model as will fit on a screen without splitting up a multiline set.

Another interesting feature of a table display panel is that it allows scrolling of the data — not generally available in any other panel type (except for those with DYNAMIC areas). What is more, when scrolling a table display, the headings will remain stationary so that each column will always be properly identified.

The actual syntax for this section, then, is exactly the same as that for the)BODY section already discussed. The only difference is that we only define how one row is to appear.

MODEL Example

For this illustration, we will have to switch to a different panel from the one we have been using. Please refer to Figure 3-7 for the following explanation.

```
)ATTR DEFAULT(%+_)
  /* % TYPE(TEXT   )  INTENS(HIGH)                             */
  /* + TYPE(TEXT   )  INTENS(LOW )                             */
  /* _ TYPE( INPUT)  INTENS(HIGH)  CAPS(ON )  JUST(LEFT )   */
     ¬ TYPE(OUTPUT)  INTENS(LOW )  CAPS(ON )  JUST(LEFT )
     ! TYPE(OUTPUT)  INTENS(LOW )  CAPS(ON )  JUST(RIGHT)
```

```
)BODY
%------------------ DDS TABLE DISPLAY PANEL  ---------------
%COMMAND ===>_ZCMD                        %SCROLL ===>_AMT +
%
+ENTER:  %A+(ADD), %C+(CHANGE), OR %D+(DELETE) COMMAND(s)
+
%CMD APPL VARIABLE POOL  DATA   FIELD  FIELD DESC AND COMMENTS
%CDE  ID   NAME    TYPE  TYPE   LENGTH
+
```

```
)MODEL  ROWS(SCAN)
  _z+¬appl¬varname + ¬z+ ¬dtype+!lenth+¬descript            +
```

```
)INIT
 .ZVARS = '(cmd,ptype)'
)REINIT
 ...
)PROC
 ...
)END
```

Figure 3-7 Sample)MODEL Section Definition.

As the figure shows, the panel definition up to the)MODEL section is very much the same as before. Text and variables may still be displayed as in the other panels. Any definitions made in the)BODY section are considered permanent, i.e., they will not scroll with the data that is part of the)MODEL section.

The)MODEL header shows that the rows to be displayed will be subject to a match — ROWS(SCAN) — on the search arguments, which should be set somewhere in the application before reaching this point.

In this case, the model for each row to be displayed consists of only one line. Input and output variables (as well as fixed text) may appear on any model line. One input variable is used (the first *z*), while all of the others are strictly output.

Again, please note the .ZVARS assignment in the)INIT section to identify the two place holders ("z") used in the model.

)INIT +)REINIT +)PROC Sections

In these sections, we will be coding some basic logic to control the contents of the panels to be displayed and processed. It must be understood that these sections are *not* intended to replace the purpose of a function. The general intent here is to perform some basic editing and cross-checking of data before allowing the application to continue.

These three sections operate at different times of the panel display process and generally serve three distinct purposes. However, because the syntax of all three sections is basically the same, they will be presented as a unit.

The)INIT section provides logic to be performed just *before* the panel is initially displayed on the screen. The)PROC section provides logic to be performed *after* the panel is displayed, and the user has pressed some key to return control of the terminal to the system. The)REINIT section is processed if errors are detected by the)PROC section causing the ISPF to remain with the same panel on the CRT, or if the dialog function invokes the same display service without a panel name.

Each of these sections is optional, but they will be coded most of the time. This is especially true of the)INIT and the)PROC. Generally, the)REINIT would be coded if one wanted to change the color or a field that might be in error, or highlight some aspect of the screen, or refresh some data field. Otherwise, it is not used as often as the other two sections.

INIT/REINIT/PROC Headers

In each case, the syntax for the section headers is simply the name of the section (no other parameters).

```
⮕  )INIT
⮕  )REINIT
⮕  )PROC
```

INIT/REINIT/PROC Sections

The bodies of these sections may contain any number of logic statements:

- Assignment statements   — Assign values to variables
- VERify statements   — Verify contents of variables
- IF statements   — Conditional execution of logic
- VPUT statements   — Put variables into other pools
- REFRESH statements   — Refresh variables in panel

Before we begin discussing each in detail, let us have a general idea of their formats:

```
⮕  &sappl      = &appl
⮕  &type       = TRUNC(&type, 1)
⮕  &option     = TRANS(&option,  A,ADD,  C,CHANGE,  D,DELETE)
⮕  VER (&ptype,  NONBLANK,  LIST P,S,F,N)
⮕  IF (&option = DELETE)    .CURSOR = del
⮕  VPUT    (var1, var2, var3) PROFILE
⮕  REFRESH (var1, var2)
```

You may notice that the variable names are shown in lowercase. This is strictly for convenience, since ISPF treats them as if they were in uppercase. However, this method will be used in this book so that the dialog variables will stand out more from the rest of the statement.

And now, let us cover each of these types of statements in detail.

Assignment Statements

The syntax for this statement is fairly simple:

```
☞ &varname = value
```

The "value" may be a string of characters, a number, the contents
of another variable, or the result of some function (as we will see in
the next subtopic). The following are some simple examples:

```
☞ &a = 123
☞ &b = SOMESTRING
☞ &c = '''ISPF.PANELS'''
☞ &d = TRUNC(&option, 1)
☞ &e = &d
```

The assignment to variable &c shows the format for a complex
string which may have special characters embedded and/or
apostrophes. It follows the normal convention found in most other
languages of enclosing the string in apostrophes. If these are also
present, use two for every one in the string.

Variable Types. We have already seen that a variable is a named
area whose contents are subject to change. What we have not discussed is the various classes of variables available under ISPF.
These are:

• User variables   — User-selected names: &name
• System variables   — ISPF-selected names: &Zname
• Control variables   — ISPF special purpose: .name

The naming of all these variables follows the same basic rules (1–8
alphanumeric characters, the first of which must be alphabetic —
with the minor exceptions we noted previously). The only difference
is that system variables start with a $Z,$[2] while the control variables
always begin with a period (.).

---

[2]   Older versions of ISPF (while it was still called SPF) did not prefix a system
variable name with a Z, so to ensure compatibility, those variables are still
accepted as system variables. It is recommended, however, that we use the new
format only.

User variables are basically the ones that we have been using up until now. They are names selected by the dialog developer to represent fields directly associated with a particular application. Some simple examples follow:

- &uname
- &room
- &fld1

System variables are of a more general and global nature and contain values such as current date, time, user identification, terminal type, etc. A complete list will be shown in Appendix F, but some of the more commonly used ones are:

- &ZDATE   — Current date in yy/mm/dd format
- &ZTIME   — Present time in hh:mm format
- &ZTERM   — Terminal type
- &ZPF*nn*   — PF*nn* key setting
- &ZCMD   — Command input field
- &ZSEL   — Selection string from selection panel
- &ZPRIM   — Flag panel as primary option menu
- &ZERRMSG — Error message identifier

Control variables are special-purpose variables that can be used only in the logic sections of a panel. They will enable one to control the cursor, to sound the alarm at the terminal, change panel attributes, etc.

Since these are directly related to the current topic, a complete list follows:

- .ALARM   Controls sounding of terminal alarm (if any).
              Ex.: .ALARM = {YES | NO}

- .ATTR   Changes attributes of a panel field.
              Ex.: .ATTR(&varname | .CURSOR) = 'attr-name(value) ...'

- .ATTRCHAR   Changes attributes associated with a particular character.
              Ex.: .ATTRCHAR(character) = 'attr-name(value) ...'

• .AUTOSEL   On table displays, controls whether a row will be selected automatically or not, even if the user does not specifically select it. (This will be discussed in greater detail in Chapter 5.)
Ex.: .AUTOSEL = {YES | NO}

• .CURSOR   Controls placement of the cursor during panel display.
Ex.: .CURSOR = varname

• .CSRPOS   Controls placement of the cursor within a field in the panel.
Ex.: .CSRPOS = {nn | &varname} or &varname = .CSRPOS

• .CSRROW   Controls placement of the cursor in a row of a table display.
Ex.: .CSRROW = {nn | &varname}

• .HELP   Identifies the name of a tutorial panel when HELP is requested.
Ex.: .HELP = panelid

• .MSG   Identifies a particular message to be displayed on the screen.
Ex.: .MSG = messageid

• .PFKEY   Provides the PF key number (as PF*nn* or blank) depending on which key the user pressed.
Ex.: IF (.PFKEY = PF01) ...

• .RESP   Identifies the type of response from the user (End or Return).
Ex.: IF (.RESP = END) ...

• .TRAIL   Provides the remaining string from a TRUNCate operation.
Ex.: &rest = .TRAIL

• .ZVARS   Enables correlation of *z* variables to actual names.
Ex. .ZVARS = '(vname1, vname2, ...)'

Function References. ISPF provides several very useful functions to simplify the coding of our logic:

• The TRUNC function   — Truncate a string
• The TRANS function   — Translate a string
• The PFK function   — Retrieve information on a PF key
• The LVLINE function   — Find last visible line

The *TRUNC function* enables you to TRUNCate a string either at a fixed position or at the occurrence of a given character. In addition, if you wish to retrieve the portion that was truncated, you can simply assign the control variable .TRAIL to whatever variable you wish.
The basic syntax is:

```
⇨ &varname = TRUNC (&variable, {nn | 'char'})
```

It must be noted that when you truncate at a fixed position — TRUNC(&var,1), for example — .TRAIL will contain the remainder of the string. But when you use the character search method, .TRAIL will contain the remainder of the string following the search character, i.e., the character is discarded. Examples:

```
⇨ &x = 'ABC.DEF'        /* &x contains: ABC.DEF */
⇨ &a = TRUNC(&x, 3)     /* &a contains: ABC     */
⇨ &b = .TRAIL           /* &b contains: .DEF    */
⇨ &c = TRUNC(&x, '.')   /* &c contains: ABC     */
⇨ &d = .TRAIL           /* &d contains: DEF     */
```

The *TRANS function* enables you to translate one string into another while at the same time making provisions for an error message if a match cannot be found.
The syntax of this function is:

```
☞ &varname = TRANS (&variable, value,value [...] [MSG=id])

   where: "value,value"  may be:   string,string
                          or:       *,string
                          or:       *,*
```

The mechanism consists of checking the contents of the variable against the first value of each set in the list. If a match occurs, the function returns the second value in the set.

The "*" notation simply indicates "anything else." If the combination "*,string" is coded, it indicates that "any other value is to be translated to the string given." But if the combination "*,*" is coded, it means that "any other value is to be left as is." Examples:

```
☞ &a = TRANS(&opt   A,ADD   C,CHANGE   D,DELETE)
☞ &b = TRANS(&ans   Y,YES   N,NO       MSG=DDSM000)
☞ &c = TRANS(&cod   1,ABC   2,XYZ          *,*)
☞ &b = TRANS(&ans   Y,YES   N,NO           *,'?')
```

Please note that the commas are entirely optional; blanks may be used as well. In the first example, an A in &opt will become ADD, a C will become CHANGE, etc.; if &opt is not A, C, or D, it will become blank. In the second example, if &ans is not Y or N, message DDSM000 will be displayed. In the third example, if not 1 or 2, it will be left as is. In the fourth example, if not Y or N, it will be translated to "?".

These functions may be nested. One very common usage is in selection panels where we often see code similar to the following:

```
☞ &ZSEL = TRANS( TRUNC(&opt, '.')  1,'PGM(ABC)'  2,'CMD(XYZ)')
```

This shows a TRANSlation of whatever &opt contained up to the first "." such that: If it contains a 1, "PGM(ABC)" will be assigned to

&ZSEL; if it contains a 2, "CMD(XYZ)" will be assigned to &ZSEL; anything else will cause blanks to go into &ZSEL.

The *PFK function* allows you to extract information about the settings of any of the Program Function (PF) keys.

The syntax of this function is:

```
☞ &varname = PFK (nn | string)
```

Depending on the format used, the alternate value will be returned. Thus, if "PFK(*nn*)" is used, the *string* that the key represents is returned; if "PFK(string)" is used, the *number* of the key is given. If this string is assigned to more than one PF Key, the first *primary* key with the string will be given.

To illustrate, let us assume the standard PF key assignments on a 24-PF-key terminal, where keys 2 and 14 were assigned the SPLIT command:

```
☞ &pfval = PFK(02)     /*  "SPLIT" will be returned */
☞ &pfnbr = PFK(SPLIT)  /*  "PF14" will be returned */
```

The *LVLINE function* returns the number of the last visible line in this panel for an area defined as DYNAMIC or GRAPHIC. This can vary depending on terminal type and whether a user is in SPLIT screen mode or not.

```
☞ &varname = LVLINE (areaname)
```

VERify Statements. This is one of the most flexible statements available for these logic sections. It enables one to perform some complex data type editing processes on any field with a simple statement. The syntax for this statement is:

```
⊕ VER (&vname [NONBLANK | NB] keyword [value(s)] [MSG=msgid])


where: "keyword" can be:
       ALPHA              (A-Z, a-z, @, #, $)
       NUM                (0-9)
       HEX                (0-9, A-F, a-f)
       BIT                (0, 1)
       PICT 'string'      (C=char, A=alpha, N | 9=numeric,
                           X=hex,  any other character
                           will represent itself)
       NAME               (OS name rules...1-8)
       DSNAME             (OS name rules...1-44)
       FILEID             (CMS rules for LISTFILE names)
       RANGE lower,upper  (Numeric ranges max 16 digits each)
       LIST  val1, val2, ...
```

Each of the parameters may be separated with a blank and/or a comma. The NONBLANK (or NB) indicates that the field is required (it cannot be blank). All the other parameters are self-explanatory, especially considering the comments in the right column.

The VERify process consists of editing the contents of the given field to ensure that it follows the rules for the class of data specified. The only exception allowed is when no entry is made and "NON-BLANK" was not specified, i.e., the entry is optional. In all cases, if the verification should fail, a generic message appropriate to the type of check performed will be issued; if desired, however, the developer may use some other message by specifying the ".MSG=" parameter.

The following examples illustrate some uses of this statement:

```
⊕ VER(&appl, NB, NAME)
⊕ VER(&dtype,    ALPHA)
⊕ VER(&ptype,    LIST P,S,F,N)
⊕ VER(&socsec,   PICT '999-99-9999')
⊕ VER(&length,   RANGE 0,32767  MSG=DDSM110)
```

IF Statements. The IF statement allows conditional execution of other statements within these sections, but in a rather limited fashion. Presently, the IF statement has the following limitations:

- It only permits a check for equal or not equal conditions.
- It does not allow for "ELSE" type logic.
- No "DO-END" groups are allowed. Instead, multiple statements dependent on a given IF condition are recognized by the fact that they must be *indented* from the IF statement!

Several requirements have been submitted to IBM through SHARE (and possibly GUIDE) to improve the function of this particular statement. (SHARE and GUIDE are organizations made up of large IBM customer installations which meet frequently to discuss/resolve/exchange problems/ideas relating to the business of data processing.) In response to those requirements, the newest ISPF release, Version 2.3, removes the first two of the three limitations listed.

It could be argued that extensive logic requiring complex IF statements does not belong in a panel, but rather in a program or command procedure. Nevertheless, the syntax of this statement should be compatible with that of most other languages and consistent with the coding rules of the rest of the statements — not indentation sensitive, as an example.

The general syntax of this statement is:

```
 IF (operand operator operand [,operand ...]) statement

   where:   "operand"    can be a variable or a constant
            "operator"   can be the conditions "=" or "¬="
            "statement"  can be any of the statements given
                         in this section (including other IFs)
```

To better illustrate this, consider the following examples:

```
1    ⇨ IF (&ZTDSELS = 0000) .MSG = DDSM110B

2    ⇨ IF (&option  = D)      VER (&del, NB, LIST  Y,N)

3    ⇨ IF (&option ¬= D)
          VER (&varname, NB, NAME)
          VER (&ptype,   NB, LIST  P,S,F,N)
          ... /* etc. etc. */

4    ⇨ IF (&sappl = ALL,'')  &sappl = *

5    ⇨ IF (&ptype = N)
          IF (&dtype = CHAR, NUMER)
             .MSG = DDSM110C
```

The first example checks the contents of &ZTDSELS against 0000 to see if they are equal; if so, then the assignment of DDSM110B to .MSG will be performed.

The second example is another variation of the same format, this time executing a VERify statement if *&option* equals D. The third example tests for the opposite condition to perform the equivalent of an "ELSE" clause. It also illustrates how to execute several statements within one IF test.

The fourth example illustrates the equivalent of an "OR" condition: IF *&sappl* = ALL *or* *&sappl* = " (null string), then assign "*" to *&sappl*.

The final example illustrates the equivalent of "AND" logic. By nesting the second IF statement within the first one, it will be executed only if the first is true. By further nesting the assignment of DDSM110C to .MSG under the two IF statements, we indicate that this is to be executed only if the first *and* the second IF conditions are both true.

NOTE: Be particularly careful to ensure that the next statement independent of a particular IF is *not* indented from that statement, as this will cause logic errors (which may be very difficult to detect).

VPUT Statements. We have already established that locating needed variables from the various pools for panel displays is performed by scanning the function pool first, then the shared pool, and finally the profile pool. Writing to the pools, however, for anything other than a selection panel, is limited to the function pool.

As such, if one needs to store these variables in the application's shared or profile pool, a VPUT statement is necessary. This process can be performed either by the function or by the logic section of the panel being processed.

The syntax for this statement is:

```
⮑ VPUT   vname-list   [SHARED | PROFILE | ASIS]


   where "vname-list" may be:   vname
                         or:   (vname [vname ...])
```

As indicated, the "variable-name list" consists of a single name or a list of names (without ampersands unless they contain the names that are to be used). If it is a series of names, they must be enclosed in parentheses and separated by blanks and/or commas.

SHARED or PROFILE indicates which of the application pools to address. ASIS (the default) causes the variables to be stored in the shared pool unless a similar name already exists in the profile pool but not in the shared pool as well.

Examples:

```
⮑ VPUT appl SHARED
⮑ VPUT (uname,acct,room,class,pass) PROFILE
```

In the first example, the variable *appl* is being stored in the shared pool so that it will be available to all functions throughout this application. When the application is exited, this pool will be discarded.

In the second example, a list of variables that are to be kept for this user across various sessions is being stored in the profile pool where it will remain until changed.

REFRESH Statements. When a panel is redisplayed, the contents of the various fields in the panel are the same as the user last saw them, even if they should have changed in the meantime. To force ISPF to refetch the values as they are stored, use the REFRESH statement.

Normally, this statement appears in the)REINIT section of a panel, but it may also appear in the)PROC section. Its syntax is:

```
⊜ REFRESH (*  |  vname-list)


  where "vname-list" may be:   vname  [...]
```

The "*" notation indicates that all variables in the panel are to be refreshed; the "variable-name list" follows the same rules as already mentioned for the VPUT statement: if only one name, parentheses are optional.

To illustrate:

```
⊜  REFRESH room
⊜  REFRESH (room, class)
```

INIT/REINIT/PROC Examples

A complete example is provided in Figure 3-8.

)END Section

The)END section of the panel, which is mandatory, consists of only one entry, which physically and logically terminates the panel definition; it is nothing more than the string ")END".

Selection Panel Considerations

At this point, we have discussed the syntax for each of the various sections that may appear on a panel as they apply to either data or table display panels. We have also covered the format of each statement type within each section as well as the various classes of dialog variables that we can use: the user, the system, and the control variables.

We have seen many uses of the user variables, and we discussed all the control variables that can appear on a panel. What we need to discuss now is the use of some special system variables that have

```
)ATTR DEFAULT(%+_)
 /*  % TYPE(TEXT )  INTENS(HIGH)                                   */
 /*  + TYPE(TEXT )  INTENS(LOW )                                   */
 /*  _ TYPE(INPUT)  INTENS(HIGH)  CAPS(ON)  JUST(LEFT)             */
    $ TYPE(INPUT)  INTENS(HIGH)  CAPS(ON)  JUST(LEFT)    PAD(_)
    ! TYPE(INPUT)  INTENS(HIGH)  CAPS(ON)  JUST(RIGHT)   PAD(_)
    ¬ TYPE(INPUT)  INTENS(NON )  CAPS(ON)  JUST(LEFT)


)BODY
%--------------- DDS JOB SUBMISSION PARAMETERS ----------------
%COMMAND ===>_ZCMD
%
+    PLEASE ENTER/VERIFY THE FOLLOWING ITEMS:
+
+    YOUR NAME. . . . . .$uname   +          JOB stmt pgmr's name
+    ACCOUNTING INFO. . .$acct               +Job acct parameters
+    ROOM NUMBER. . . . .$room    +          Room nbr for delivery
+    OUTPUT CLASS . . . .$z+                 Output print classes
+    NUMBER OF COPIES . .$cpy+               Nbr of copies to print
+    ACCESS PASSWORD. . .¬pass    +          Dataset access (if req)


)INIT
 .HELP  = DDSH140
 .ZVARS = class
 &cpy   = 1


)PROC
    VER (&uname, NB, ALPHA)
    VER (&acct,  NB)
    VER (&room,  NB)
    VER (&class, NB, ALPHA)
    IF  (&class = '@', '#', '$')  .MSG = DDSM140A
    VER (&cpy,   NB, RANGE 1,255 .MSG = DDSM140B)
    VPUT(uname,acct,room,class)   PROFILE


)END
```

Figure 3-8   A Complete Panel Definition Example.

particular significance in the context of a selection panel definition.
These are:

- &ZCMD   — Command input field
- &ZSEL   — Select service parameters
- &ZPRIM   — Primary option menu indicator
- &ZPARENT — Parent selection panel name

The following sections describe in detail the usage of these special
system variables.

&ZCMD — Command Input Field

This panel variable normally contains the selection made by the end-
user. Generally, it contains some entry indicating which of the
various choices in the menu was made. It may also be used to enter
some other command which may or may not be related to the panel
currently displayed.

For example, typing the command HELP (or pressing the corresponding PF key) would cause ISPF to suspend the current panel
and fetch the help panel associated with the one that was displayed.
Typing SPLIT (or its PF key) would cause the screen to be split at
the current cursor position.

Some commands can even be passed through to other environments. For example, one might need to inspect the MVS data set
catalog by executing the TSO command LISTCAT. To do this, one
would type "TSO LISTCAT" to indicate that this command is to be
passed to the TSO command processor.

Returning to the case where one is making a choice from the listed
menu, sometimes we are given a second-level menu, and possibly
even a third-level menu. If we travel this path several times, we
begin to remember the exact choices that we need for each specific
menu level. To save time, ISPF allows us to "jump" across several
menus by entering all the known choices at one time.

For example, if we wanted choice 3 on the current menu, followed
by choice 1 on the next menu, followed by choice 2 on the third
menu, we could enter on the command line:[3]

---

[3]   Generally, any input field that is preceded with the sequence "===>" can double
as a command field for the purpose of the jump function.

```
✏ COMMAND ===> 3.1.2
```

This command would allow us to jump to the panel following choices 3, 1, and 2 on the preceding panels without having them displayed.

This jump mechanism can also be used to back up to a higher-level menu and then to traverse through another path from there. This is indicated by prefixing our selections with "="; the "=" indicates that we want to return to the primary option menu before performing the jump function.

For example, entering

```
✏ COMMAND ===> =2.3.1
```

would allow us to return to the primary option menu and then proceed following choices 2, 3, and 1 from that panel and the two subsequent ones.

All these processes are handled automatically by ISPF SELECT service, requiring practically no effort on the developer's side. Normally, the only concern we have is to ensure that we truncate the current command option at the first period so that we can translate it correctly. This is normally performed as:

```
✏ &ZSEL = TRANS (TRUNC (&ZCMD, '.')
          1,'...'
          2,'...'
          etc....)
```

The SELECT service will automatically place the truncated portion of the command into the ZCMD field for the next selection panel.

&ZSEL — SELECT Service Parameters

Unlike DATA or TABLE display panels, SELECTion panels must always assign a value to the system variable &ZSEL to indicate the next selection panel or function to be executed.

Please note that it is not the setting of this variable that makes this a selection panel. A panel becomes a selection panel when it is displayed through the SELECT service. (The other two types of panels already discussed — DATA and TABLE — use the DISPLAY and TBDISPL services, respectively.)

The values assigned to the &ZSEL variable must have one of the following formats:

```
☞ 'PANEL(name)  [OPT(option)]                        [appl-options]'
☞ 'CMD(name    [parms])   [LANG(APL)] [NOCHECK] [appl-options]'
☞ 'PGM(name)   [PARM(parms)]          [NOCHECK] [appl-options]'
☞ EXIT


   where "appl-options" is:  NEWAPPL[[(appl-id)] [PASSLIB]]
                    or:  NEWPOOL
```

The PANEL, CMD, PGM, and EXIT parameters simply indicate whether the next selection will be a panel, a command, a program, or an exit from this panel. Please note that passing parameters is slightly different between the command and the program calls. Coding "OPT(option)" is equivalent to entering that option in the command line of the panel selected.

The "LANG(APL)" parameter indicates that an APL2 environment is to be started.

The NOCHECK parameter, which applies only to CMD or PGM, relates to the jump function already discussed under the &ZCMD topic. Since the SELECT service attempts to follow each of the paths indicated by the user (as in 2.3.1, for example), it cannot proceed when it reaches something other than a selection panel. As a result, it signals an error and remains in the current panel. The NOCHECK option informs the SELECT service to ignore the "error" and to continue with the selection of the given command or program.

In this case, it would be up to the application to extract and then determine what to do with the remainder of the entry. The following sequence could accomplish this:

```
☞ &opt  = TRUNC(&ZCMD, '.')
☞ &rest = .TRAIL
☞ &ZSEL = TRANS(&cmd, 1,'PGM(PRGMX) PARM(&rest.)', 2,... )
```

The NEWAPPL parameter enables you to designate this as the start of a new application, which usually indicates the use of a different set of pools, profiles, and command table. All of these are (or will become) members of a PROFILE library with the following member names:

- Application profile   — *xxxx*PROF
- Edit profile   — *xxxx*EDIT
- Command table   — *xxxx*CMDS

where *xxxx* is the application*id* given to the SELECT service. If no application*id* is given, it will default to the name of "ISP." If this is the first time this application is invoked, the initial values will all be taken from the ISPF default values.

PASSLIB indicates whether you wish to pass libraries that were allocated dynamically for this application. This subject will be discussed more extensively under the LIBDEF service in Chapter 5.

NEWPOOL indicates that although this is not a new application, you wish to begin a new shared variable pool. When finished, the previous shared pool will be reinstated.

Examples:

```
☞ &ZSEL = TRANS(TRUNC(&ZCMD,'.')
          1,'PANEL(DEMP000)          NEWAPPL(DEMO)'
          2,'CMD(DDSC000    &trace.)  NEWAPPL(DDS)'
          T,'PGM(ISPTUTOR) PARM(USRH000)'
          X,'EXIT'
          ' ',' '
          *,'?' )
```

This example shows &ZCMD being truncated at the first period and the result being translated such that:

- When it is a 1, a selection panel called DEMP000 will be displayed while a different set of variable pools, profiles, and a command table will be established. The existing ones will be suspended until this application ends.
- When it is a 2, a command procedure will be called and a new environment will also be established. Please note that an argument is being passed to the procedure (*&trace*) whose value has been established elsewhere.
- When it is a T, a program called ISPTUTOR (ISPF Tutorial) will be selected and the argument USRH000 (a panel name in this case) will be passed to the program. A new application environment is not being requested.
- When it is an X, this panel will be exited and control returned to the point that selected this panel.
- A blank will be "translated" to a blank and have no effect when at a primary option menu. At a lower-level one, an "INVALID OPTION" message will be displayed.
- Anything else will be translated to a "?" causing the "INVALID OPTION" message to appear.

&ZPRIM — Primary Option Menu Indicator

This variable flags a particular selection panel as a "primary option menu." The particular significance of this is to control jump functions as well as exit processes.

Normally, entering END will cause ISPF to return to the previous selection panel. Repeating this process will continually take a user to each higher level until the top one is reached. An alternative is to enter RETURN, which will simulate the effect of repeated ENDs until the top level is reached.

The one problem with this process is that if one is inside lower-level applications and RETURN is entered by mistake, the exiting of the lower levels causes the shared pools to be discarded and the user might have to redo some of the work. To prevent this, it is customary to put stops at critical points (such as the one starting a new application) by coding the following statement:

```
⮕  &ZPRIM = YES
```

&ZPARENT — Parent Selection Panel Name

Normally, selection panels are displayed based on a preestablished hierarchy which is followed downward based on the user's choices, and then returned through the same path upward as the user ENDs each choice (or RETURNs).

It is possible, however, for a developer to override this normal process (called "standard mode") with another one called "explicit chain mode." This mode is indicated when a developer assigns a selection panel name to &ZPARENT. This indicates to the SELECT service that when the current selection is finished, the panel in &ZPARENT is the one to which it must return.

If one must use this option, it should be done with extreme care since it disables the normal process of NEWAPPL and NEWPOOL. One should not mix standard mode with explicit chain mode processes. To do so may invite more problems than anticipated.

When used in a panel, it may be coded in any of the sections as:

```
⮕  &ZPARENT = panelname
```

Figure 3-9 illustrates a complete selection panel.

TUTORIAL Panel Considerations

There are still a few other system variables that have special significance in a TUTORIAL panel definition. These will be discussed extensively in Chapter 7, but for now, a simple listing will round out this chapter.

* &ZHTOP   — Name of tutorial top panel (table of contents)
* &ZCONT   — Name of tutorial continuation panel
* &ZUP   — Name of tutorial parent subject panel
* &ZHINDEX   — Name of tutorial index panel
* &ZIND   — Indicator for tutorial index panel

```
)BODY
%--------------- ISPF USER PRIMARY OPTION MENU  ------------
%COMMAND   ===>_ZCMD
%
%   1 +DEMO        - ISPF Demo/Test of Dialog Management
%   2 +DDS         - Data Dictionary System
%   3 +...         - ... ... ...
%   T +TUTORIAL    - General description of each application
%   X +EXIT        - Terminate User Developed Dialogs


)INIT
  &ZPRIM   = YES      /* PRIMARY OPTION MENU        */
  &ZHTOP   = USRH000  /* TUTORIAL TABLE OF CONTENTS */
  .HELP    = USRH100
  &ZHINDEX = USRH999  /* TUTORIAL INDEX             */


)PROC
  &ZSEL = TRANS(TRUNC(&ZCMD,'.')
                1,'PANEL(DEMP000) NEWAPPL(DEMO)'
                2,'CMD(DDSC000)    NEWAPPL(DDS)'
                3,'... ... ...'
                T,'PGM(ISPTUTOR) PARM(USRH000)'
                X,'EXIT'
                ' ',' '
                *,'?' )


)END
```

Figure 3-9   Sample Selection Panel Definition.

Summary

This concludes the full syntax definition for any type of panel. To summarize, we have seen that a panel can consist of various sections, which are:

-)ATTR   — Optional : Define field attributes for 3270 panel
-)BODY   — Required : Define panel design and contents

-)MODEL   — Optional : Define model for table display process
-)INIT   — Optional : Define logic to perform before displays
-)REINIT   — Optional : Define logic to perform before redisplays
-)PROC   — Optional : Define logic to perform after displays
-)END   — Required : Define end of panel definition

In the logic sections, we saw that we could code several types of statements, which are:

- **Assignment statements**   — Assign values to variables
- **VERify statements**   — Verify contents of variables
- **IF statements**   — Conditional execution of logic
- **VPUT statements**   — Put variables into other pools
- **REFRESH statements**   — Refresh variables in panel

We also showed that several functions may be invoked in assignment statements:

- **The TRUNC function**   — Truncate a string
- **The TRANS function**   — Translate a string
- **The PFK function**   — Retrieve information on a PF key
- **The LVLINE function** — Find last visible line

All the foregoing items operate with variables that fall under one of the following classes:

- **User variables**   — User-selected names: &name
- **System variables**   — ISPF-selected names: &Zname
- **Control variables**   — ISPF-special purpose: .name

Some of the system variables presented were:

- **&ZCMD**   — Command input field
- **&ZSEL**   — SELECT service parameters
- **&ZPRIM**   — Primary option menu indicator
- **&ZPARENT**   — Parent selection panel name
- **&ZCONT**   — Name of tutorial continuation panel
- **&ZHINDEX**   — Name of tutorial index panel
- **&ZHTOP**   — Name of tutorial top panel (table of contents)
- **&ZIND**   — Indicator for tutorial index panel
- **&ZUP**   — Name of tutorial parent subject panel

We also discussed all the control variables, which are:

- .ALARM — Controls sounding of terminal alarm (if any)
- .ATTR — Changes attributes of a panel field
- .ATTRCHAR — Changes attributes for a particular character
- .AUTOSEL — Indicates if a row will be selected automatically
- .CURSOR — Controls placement of the cursor during panel display
- .CSRPOS — Controls placement of the cursor within a field
- .CSRROW — Controls placement of the cursor in a row of a table
- .HELP — Identifies the name of a tutorial panel
- .PFKEY — Provides the PF key number the user pressed
- .MSG — Identifies a particular message to be displayed
- .RESP — Identifies the type of response (END or RETURN)
- .TRAIL — Provides the remaining string after TRUNC function
- .ZVARS — Enables correlation of z variables to actual names

We already know that there are three types of variable pools to control the scope and communication of data:

- **The application profile pool** — Lasts across sessions
- **The shared application pool** — Lasts across functions
- **The function pool** — Lasts for one function

And finally, we also know that selection panels have direct access to the shared application pool, while the other panels only have direct access to the function pool.

4

Message Definitions

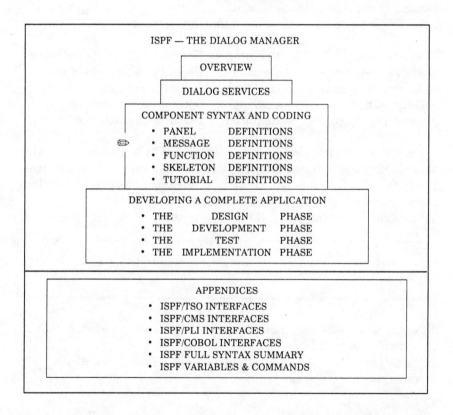

Now that we know how to build panels, the next topic becomes how to *supplement* those panels with other information that may be needed from time to time and which may or may not be related to the panel currently displayed.

This is where the message component comes in. A message may alert a user that an error has been committed, it may confirm that some process has been completed, or it may inform the user of some other unusual situation.

As previously mentioned, whatever the message may be, it will always be displayed in one of two fixed locations depending on whether it is a short message or a long one. If it is a short message, it will appear at the top right corner of the current panel. If it is a long one, it will appear on the third line. Again, it is possible to override these locations by the manner in which the panel body is defined, but this is usually not recommended.

Messages are composed of the following elements:

- **Message ID** — Required : The message identification
- **Short message** — Optional : Up to 24 characters of text
- **Alarm indicator** — Optional : Audible alarm (if available)
- **Help panel** — Optional : Special tutorial section
- **Long message** — Required : Up to 78 characters of text

Each message is coded as a two-line entry in a member of a message library (we will see later how we address this and all the other libraries). The first line will contain all the elements except the "long message" which is entered as the second line of the set.

The general syntax of a full message is then:

```
☞ msg-id ['short msg'] [.HELP={panel | *}] [.ALARM={YES | NO}]
☞ 'long message'
```

A series of these sets make up a message library member such as the one in Figure 4-1.

With these preliminaries established, let us now look at each element in detail.

MESSAGE Identifier

This identifier, which can range from 4 to 8 characters, must be structured as follows:

```
DDSM120A 'TABLE &table LISTED'
'THE FILE TAILORING PROCESS REQUESTED COMPLETED SUCCESSFULLY'

DDSM120B 'UNABLE TO DO FTOPEN'    .ALARM = YES
'UNABLE TO ACCESS THE SKELETON LIBRARY OR THE OUTPUT FILE'

DDSM120C 'UNABLE TO DO FTINCL'    .ALARM = YES
'UNABLE TO PROCESS SKELETON &skel.'

DDSM120D 'UNABLE TO DO FTCLOSE'   .ALARM = YES
'ENQ FAILED: OUTPUT FILE &dsn IS PRESENTLY IN USE'
```

Figure 4-1   Sample Message Library Member.

- One to 5 alphabetic characters (A–Z, $, @, #)
- A 3-digit number
- An optional 1-character alphabetic suffix

From this identifier, a library member name will be derived by truncating the identifier following the second digit. Once the member is retrieved, a sequential search will be performed until the exact message identifier is located in that member.

To illustrate this, consider the following message identifier examples and the resultant library member names where they will be searched:

MESSAGE IDENTIFIER	LIBRARY MEMBER NAME
A123X	A12
A124X	A12
AB123Y	AB12
AB124Y	AB12
$$$123Z	$$$12
$$$124Z	$$$12
DDSM120A	DDSM12
DDSM120B	DDSM12
DDSM130	DDSM13

SHORT MESSAGE

The short message element is optional. If it is not present, the DIS-
PLAY service will automatically use the long message.

When present, it is coded as a character string enclosed in
apostrophes. Again, if the string itself should have apostrophes embedded, for each one desired, code two consecutive ones.

It is also possible to use dialog variables within this string. Substitution will be performed by the service and the resultant string
will be displayed in the short message field with a length of up to 24
characters. Any excess will be truncated.

Examples:

```
☞ DDSM110B 'SELECT LINE OR END'

☞ DDSM120A 'TABLE &table LISTED'

☞ DDSM120B 'UNABLE TO DO FTOPEN'
```

ALARM Indicator

Some terminals have an audible alarm that can be used to alert the
user of some of the more serious difficulties. ISPF also makes this
facility available to us. Of course, if a particular terminal has no
such feature, the request will simply be ignored.

The syntax is simply:

```
☞ .ALARM = {YES | NO}
```

Examples:

```
☞ DDSM110B 'SELECT LINE OR END'

☞ DDSM120A 'TABLE &table LISTED'      [.ALARM=NO]

☞ DDSM120B 'UNABLE TO DO FTOPEN'      .ALARM=YES
```

NOTE: One should take care with the usage of this facility, since an excess can be a source of irritation to the end-user.

HELP PANEL

Generally, SELECT, DATA, or TABLE display panels already have HELP panels associated with each one. It is possible, however, that those help panels might be excessively long in a case where we know exactly where the problem lies.

In this situation, it would be useful to point directly to the topic in the string of help panels otherwise available. This would be analogous to opening a book to a specific paragraph (or small section) rather than instructing someone to read a particular chapter from the beginning until that paragraph (or section) is found.

To accomplish this, we could code:

```
☞ .HELP = {panelid | *}
```

The "*" notation simply indicates that you wish to use whatever help panel was designated in the SELECT, DATA, or TABLE display panel in question (the default).

Examples:

```
☞ DDSM110B 'SELECT LINE OR END'      .HELP=DDSH110B
☞ DDSM120A 'TABLE &table LISTED'     [.ALARM=NO]
```

LONG MESSAGE

The long message element is required. It must contain a message string (which may contain dialog variables) whose length after substitution must not exceed 78 characters (or it will be truncated).

This entry occupies the second line of the two-line message definition, as illustrated:

```
DDSM120A 'TABLE &table LISTED'
'THE FILE TAILORING PROCESS REQUESTED COMPLETED SUCCESSFULLY'


DDSM120D 'UNABLE TO DO FTCLOSE'   .ALARM = YES
'ENQ FAILED: OUTPUT FILE &dsn IS PRESENTLY IN USE'
```

Summary

In conclusion, this is without a doubt an extremely simple component to develop. It is made of several elements, which are:

* Message ID   — Required : The message identification
* Short message   — Optional : Up to 24 characters of text
* Alarm indicator   — Optional : Audible alarm (if available)
* Help panel   — Optional : Special tutorial section
* Long message   — Required : Up to 78 characters of text

These elements are coded in sets of two lines where the long message must occupy the second line. As many of these sets as necessary may be developed provided, of course, that they have unique identifiers.

We also established that these identifiers must meet a certain structure, which is:

* One to 5 alphabetic characters (A–Z, $, @, #)
* A 3-digit number
* An optional 1-character alphabetic suffix

And we saw that ISPF locates these messages by searching the message library for members whose names match the message identifier up to the second digit. From there, it then performs a serial search for the actual identifier.

A *final word:* When you construct these members, be sure that your editing profile reflects the NUMBER OFF option so that you will not have sequence numbers on each line. If you do not observe this restriction, you will not be able to display your messages.

5

Function Definitions

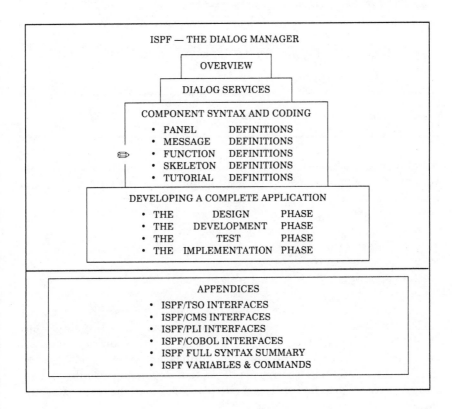

ISPF — THE DIALOG MANAGER

OVERVIEW

DIALOG SERVICES

COMPONENT SYNTAX AND CODING
- PANEL   DEFINITIONS
- MESSAGE   DEFINITIONS
- FUNCTION DEFINITIONS
- SKELETON DEFINITIONS
- TUTORIAL DEFINITIONS

DEVELOPING A COMPLETE APPLICATION
- THE   DESIGN   PHASE
- THE   DEVELOPMENT PHASE
- THE   TEST   PHASE
- THE   IMPLEMENTATION PHASE

APPENDICES
- ISPF/TSO INTERFACES
- ISPF/CMS INTERFACES
- ISPF/PLI INTERFACES
- ISPF/COBOL INTERFACES
- ISPF FULL SYNTAX SUMMARY
- ISPF VARIABLES & COMMANDS

We have established that functions form the logic core that control an application, and that they can be written in a variety of programming or command procedure languages.

These functions will be performing service requests to carry out a number of tasks needed by an application. Considering the large array of services available, and in order to keep this as brief and as simple as possible, we will be discussing and illustrating all services using CLIST (MVS/TSO) command-language syntax and procedures only. At the end, an appendix will be provided to show how any of the services presented can also be coded in other languages.

The general syntax for each service call is:

```
⇨ ISPEXEC service parameter [parameter ...]
```

For example, to display a data panel called DDSP110A, we would code:

```
⇨ ISPEXEC DISPLAY PANEL(DDSP110A)
```

Following each service call, a dialog may have to examine the return code given by each service. Although the exact meanings of each value differ from call to call, the general concept is:

- 0 — Successful completion of service call
- 4 — Informational or Warning conditions detected
- 8 — Possible Error detected
- 12 — (Or higher) : Severe error condition detected

Any return code of 12 or higher normally causes ISPF to exit the dialog. If an application needs to retain control, then the statement "ISPEXEC CONTROL ERRORS RETURN" would allow you to do so. Obviously, when this is the case, the application must be designed to handle these unusual conditions. To avoid repetition of all the possible return codes for each service call, we will be concentrating mostly on the return values of 4 or 8.

When using CLISTs, the syntax to query the return code is as follows:

```
⊜ IF   &LASTCC   operator   value     THEN   statement

   where "operator" may be: <,=,>,<=,>=,¬<,¬=,¬>
     and "value"    may be a constant, variable, or expression
```

For example:

```
⊜ IF   &LASTCC   ¬= 0   THEN EXIT
```

And now, to better understand all these services, we will be covering them in logical groups under the following classes: •

• DISPLAY SERVICES   — To display panels and messages
• TABLE SERVICES   — To process data tables
• FILE TAILORING SERVICES   — To process file skeletons
• VARIABLE SERVICES   — To process variables in any pool
• OTHER SERVICES   — To interface with other products

DISPLAY SERVICES

Display services enable us to display data panels, table panels, and to overlay messages on any panels. The actual service names and their functions are:

• DISPLAY   — Display a data panel
• TBDISPL   — Display a table panel
• SETMSG   — Display a message on a panel

DISPLAY — Display Data Panel

This service displays a data entry panel and/or a message at the terminal. The syntax is:

```
@ ISPEXEC DISPLAY [PANEL(name)]      [MSG(msgid)]
                  [CURSOR(field)]   [CSRPOS(position)]
```

These parameters should be rather obvious. PANEL should contain the name of the panel to be displayed; if not given, it will
default to a redisplay of the current one. MSG provides for a message to be inserted into whatever panel is being displayed.

CURSOR and CSRPOS allow you to indicate where to place the
cursor just in case it was not specified in the panel. (If it was, it will
be ignored here.) If these parameters are not coded anywhere, the
cursor will default to the first input field while the cursor position
will default to 1.

After this service call is made, a dialog should check the return
code for at least a value of 8; this would indicate that the user
responded with END or RETURN.

This service could then be called and checked as follows:

```
@ ISPEXEC   DISPLAY   PANEL(DDSP110A)
@ IF        &LASTCC   ¬= 0  THEN EXIT
```

If, upon returning from the display, you should find the need to
return to the same panel so that the user can be alerted to some
problem with a field, you could code the following:

```
@ ISPEXEC DISPLAY MSG(DDSM110C) CURSOR(fieldx)
```

The same panel would be displayed — with a message, in this case
— and the cursor positioned at &fieldx — the field in question. If the
panel had a)REINIT section, it could be coded so that the attributes
of the field flagged could be changed to further emphasize where the
problem lies. For example:

```
🖙  )REINIT
🖙  .ATTR(.CURSOR) = 'HILITE(REVERSE)'
```

TBDISPL — Display Table Panel

This service provides for a table to be displayed based on a panel definition that contains a)MODEL section detailing the output format for each row selected.
The syntax is:

```
🖙 ISPEXEC TBDISPL tblname [PANEL(name)]      [MSG(msgid)]

                          [CURSOR(field)]    [CSRPOS(position)]

                          [CSRROW(row)]      [AUTOSEL(YES | NO)]

                          [POSITION(vname1)][ROWID(vname2)]
```

The *tblname* parameter obviously indicates the name of the table to be used for this service. The PANEL, MSG, CURSOR, and CSRPOS are exactly the same as the ones for the DISPLAY service previously presented.

The CSRROW parameter tells the service on which of the several rows possibly displayed to place the cursor. The AUTOSEL parameter works closely with the CSRROW. When AUTOSEL(YES) is in effect, that particular row will be treated as if it had been selected by the end-user regardless of the user action (an application might be forcing the user to process a certain row). If the CSRROW is not coded, AUTOSEL will have no effect.

The POSITION parameter will be set, upon return from the display, to the Current Row Pointer (CRP)[1] of the table containing the row that the user selected — if any. If none was selected, it will be set to 0 (TOP of table). The ROWID parameter is an alternate way of identifying the row selected. Its value is such that it can be used

---

[1]   The Current Row Pointer (CRP) is an ISPF internal value used to address a row for a given table in process. This value consists of an ordinal number ranging from 0 to the number of rows in the table; a value of 0, however, indicates the TOP of the table which does not actually contain any data.

subsequently in a TBSKIP service (ROW parameter) to position the table to this exact row.

The major difference between POSITION and ROWID is the identification form of the row in question. POSITION returns a row number which is subject to change as other rows are added or deleted; ROWID, however, returns a temporary internal identifier which will point to this particular row regardless of how many other rows may be added or deleted. This internal identifier is only kept until the table is closed.

Upon return from the TBDISPL call, the 4-character function pool variable &ZTDSELS will indicate the number of rows selected. You will be placed automatically at the first row selected, while all the others will remain pending. As you finish processing one row and wish to proceed to the next pending row, you simply invoke a TBDISPL with no other parameters except the table name. You should repeat this process until &ZTDSELS is decremented down to 1, indicating that you are processing the last row selected.

If you should perform another TBDISPL with a panel name (or message ID), any pending rows will be ignored and &ZTDSELS will be reset. Also, if you should perform another DISPLAY service before completing the TBDISPL process, you should invoke a CONTROL DISPLAY SAVE (before) and a CONTROL DISPLAY RESTORE (after), so that your environment will be preserved for correct processing.

All these concepts will be illustrated in detail in a later section, "Comprehensive Example," but for now, let us look at the highlights of these processes (see Figure 5-1).

SETMSG — Set Message for Display

This service is extremely simple: it enables you to indicate a message identifier so that the next time any panel is displayed, this message will appear. The syntax is:

```
⮕ ISPEXEC SETMSG MSG(msgid)
```

```
      SET        &TBLRC   = 0              /* initialize loop control */
      DO         WHILE    &TBLRC  <   8 /* repeat until END | RETURN */
      ISPEXEC    TBDISPL  &TABLE   PANEL(DDSP110B)
      SET        &TBLRC = &LASTCC         /* save for next loop check */
        DO       WHILE    &ZTDSELS > 0  /* loop for each row sel'd */
        ...
        ISPEXEC  CONTROL  DISPLAY SAVE      /* save TBDISPL controls */
        ISPEXEC  DISPLAY  PANEL(DDSP110C)     /* display data panel */
        SET      &PANRC = &LASTCC         /* save display ret code */
        ISPEXEC  CONTROL  DISPLAY RESTORE  /* restore TBDISPL cntls */
        IF       &PANRC   > 4 THEN GOTO R
        ...
   R:   IF       &ZTDSELS > 1 THEN ISPEXEC TBDISPL &TABLE
        ELSE SET &ZTDSELS = 0             /* force exit of row loop */
        END                              /* end of TBDISPL loop */
      END
```

Figure 5-1   Sample TBDISPL and DISPLAY Service Processing.

For example:

```
⊜ ISPEXEC  FTOPEN
⊜ IF        &LASTCC ¬= 0 THEN DO
⊜           ISPEXEC  SETMSG  MSG(DDSM120B) /* unable to open */
⊜           EXIT
⊜           END
```

Table Services

We have already seen that table services provide us with general operations such as creating, opening, closing, erasing, etc., as well as more detailed operations such as adding, deleting, retrieving, etc., specific rows of a table.

At this time, we need to examine the specifics of each of these services. For each one, we will discuss the syntax and give a brief example. Then, at the end of this section, we will have a more comprehensive example.

Table-wide Operations

These are the services that apply to the table as a whole, i.e., they always operate on the entire table — not just specific rows. Although these could be presented in almost any order, they will be covered in a sequence that reflects (more or less) their logical order of usage.

TBCREATE — Create a Table. This service names the columns for a new table and indicates which of these will be key fields (if any). The syntax is:

```
☞ ISPEXEC TBCREATE tblname [KEYS(list)]          [NAMES(list)]

                           [WRITE | NOWRITE]     [SHARE]

                           [LIBRARY(ddname)]     [REPLACE]
```

Generally, in addition to the table name, you will also provide a list of variable names to be stored in the table. If no names are given, the table will only accept "extension variables" which have to be specifically named each time you write to the table.

The WRITE and NOWRITE parameters indicate whether the file will be permanent (written to disk) or temporary (discarded when closed). The SHARE parameter relates to split-screen processing. Although a table can only be created by one screen, it may be accessed by other logical screens for the same terminal.

The LIBRARY parameter allows you to specify some DDNAME other than the default (ISPTLIB) which controls the input library to search (in connection with the REPLACE parameter). The REPLACE indicates that if a table with the same name already exists, it will be replaced with this new version. This includes any possible core copy.

Unusual conditions to check are: 8 — the table already exists and REPLACE was not specified; 12 — the table is currently in use and the ENQueue process failed.

The following creates a permanent table named DDST000 which will contain three key fields and three data fields:

```
⊜ ISPEXEC TBCREATE DDST000 KEYS(APPL, VARNAME, PTYPE) +
                            NAMES(DTYPE, LENTH, DESCRIPT)
⊜ IF       &LASTCC ¬= 0 THEN DO
⊜           ISPEXEC  SETMSG  MSG(DDSM123A) /* bad tbcreate */
⊜           EXIT
⊜           END
```

TBOPEN — Open a Table for Processing. This service accesses a permanent table on disk (temporary tables must be created each time with TBCREATE) so that processing may begin. The syntax is:

```
⊜ ISPEXEC TBOPEN tblname [WRITE | NOWRITE] [SHARE]
                          [LIBRARY(ddname)]
```

These parameters have the exact same meaning as the ones already described for TBCREATE. Upon return from the service, the function should check the return code for at least one of the following values: 8 — the table does not exist; or 12 — The ENQ failed because the table is already in use.

The following example opens a table (if it exists) or creates one (if it does not exist):

```
⊜ ISPEXEC   TBOPEN   DDST000 WRITE
⊜ IF        &LASTCC  =  8    THEN  DO
⊜           ISPEXEC   TBCREATE DDST000 +
                      KEYS     (APPL, VARNAME, PTYPE) +
                      NAMES    (DTYPE, LENTH, DESCRIPT)
⊜           END
```

TBSORT — Sort a Table. This service not only sorts a table but it also saves the sort information so that the table may be kept in that order as changes take place. It is for this reason that usually one will do a TBSORT immediately after a table is created — this is not only permitted on an empty table, but a common procedure as well. The syntax is:

```
☞ ISPEXEC TBSORT tblname FIELDS(sortlist)


  where "sortlist" is: field, C | N, A | D, ...
```

The "C | N" indicates Character or Numeric, while the "A | D" indicates Ascending or Descending. Multiple sequences of the three entries may be coded. The following example sorts a newly created table on the three key fields (all character) in ascending order:

```
☞ ISPEXEC   TBCREATE &TABLE   KEYS(APPL, VARNAME, PTYPE) +

            NAMES     (DTYPE, LENTH, DESCRIPT)
☞ ISPEXEC   TBSORT    &TABLE +

            FIELDS    (APPL,C,A, VARNAME,C,A, PTYPE,C,A)
```

TBQUERY — Query Information about a Table. This   service   returns general information about a table which presently must be open by the dialog. The syntax is:

```
☞ ISPEXEC TBQUERY tblname [KEYS(vname1)]    [NAMES(vname2)]

                          [KEYNUM(vname3)] [NAMENUM(vname4)]

                          [ROWNUM(vname5)] [POSITION(vname6)]
```

KEYS will return the list of key variable names, while NAMES will return the list of other variable names. KEYNUM will return the number of key variable names, while NAMENUM will return the number of other variable names. ROWNUM will give us the number of rows presently in the table, while POSITION will give us the value of the current row pointer (CRP).

To illustrate, use the example given under TBCREATE for the table DDST000, which presently might be holding five rows of data:

```
  ISPEXEC TBQUERY DDST000 KEYS(vname1)    NAMES(vname2)    +
                          KEYNUM(vname3) NAMENUM(vname4) +
                          ROWNUM(vname5)
```

Following this call, &vname1 through &vname5 would have:

- &vname1 = '(APPL VARNAME PTYPE)'
- &vname2 = '(DTYPE LENTH DESCRIPT)'
- &vname3 = 3
- &vname4 = 3
- &vname5 = 5

TBSTATS — Obtain Statistical Data on a Table. This service returns a variety of statistical data on a table that may or may not be presently open. The syntax for this service is:

```
  ISPEXEC TBSTATS tblname [CDATE(vname1)]     [CTIME(vname2)]
                          [UDATE(vname3)]     [UTIME(vname4)]
                          [USER(vname5)]      [ROWCREAT(vname6)]
                          [ROWCURR(vname7)]   [ROWUPD(vname8)]
                          [TABLEUPD(vname9)]  [SERVICE(vname10)]
                          [RETCODE(vname11)]  [STATUS1(vname12)]
                          [STATUS2(vname13)]  [STATUS3(vname14)]
                          [LIBRARY(ddname)]
```

CDATE and CTIME return the "create" date and time in the forms of *yy/mm/dd* and *hh.mm.ss*. UDATE and UTIME return similar values but based on the last update performed. USER returns the userid of the person who last accessed the table.

ROWCREAT will return the number of rows on initial creation of the table, ROWCURR will give the current number of rows, and ROWUPD will give the number of rows updated. TABLEUPD will return the number of times the table has been updated, SERVICE will return the name of the service last performed on this table, and RETCODE will give the value of the return code for that last service.

STATUS1 will give one of the following values:

- 1 — Table exists in the table input library chain
- 2 — Table does not exist in the table input library chain
- 3 — Table input library is not allocated

STATUS2 will give one of the following values:

- 1 — Table is not open for this logical screen
- 2 — Table is open in NOWRITE mode for this screen
- 3 — Table is open in WRITE mode for this screen
- 4 — Table is open in SHARED NOWRITE mode
- 5 — Table is open in SHARED WRITE mode

STATUS3 will give one of the following values:

- 1 — Table is available for WRITE mode
- 2 — Table is not available for WRITE mode

Finally, LIBRARY can be specified to designate an input library DDNAME other than the default of ISPTLIB.

To illustrate, assume the same DDST000 table illustrated under TBCREATE:

```
☞ ISPEXEC TBSTATS DDST000 CDATE(vname1)   CTIME(vname2)    +
                          UDATE(vname3)   UTIME(vname4)
```

Following this call, &vname1 through &vname4 might have values similar to the following:

- &vname1 = '77/01/31'
- &vname2 = '12.01.59'
- &vname3 = '77/05/22'
- &vname4 = '17.33.40'

TBSAVE — File a Table and Continue. This service allows a table (which must be in WRITE mode) to be saved periodically without closing the table from further processing. The syntax is:

```
☞ ISPEXEC TBSAVE tblname [NAME(name)]    [NEWCOPY | REPLCOPY]
             [PAD(percent)] [LIBRARY(ddname)]
```

The NAME parameter allows you to specify a new member name. NEWCOPY indicates that this member is to be written at the end of the library specified, while REPLCOPY indicates that, if the size permits, this new copy is to be written over the previous one with the same name (if any).

The PAD parameter relates somewhat to REPLCOPY. It enables you to reserve a certain percentage of additional space so that future updates may be possible with the REPLCOPY parameter (to avoid having to compress the library too many times).

The LIBRARY parameter allows you to specify a DDNAME other than the default ISPTABL, indicating the output library where this member will be saved.

The following example shows a typical application of this call:

```
☞ ISPEXEC TBSAVE DDST000 REPLCOPY
```

CAUTION: While the REPLCOPY can save undue maintenance on a library, it does have its dangers. Because it writes the new version over the old one, if the system should fail before completion you will lose both copies. If this is critical, you may prefer not to use this option.

TBCLOSE — File a Table and Disconnect It from Use. This service not only saves a table (which must be in WRITE mode), but it also deletes the core copy, thus terminating process of the table. The call is similar in syntax and meaning to that of the TBSAVE:

```
☞ ISPEXEC TBCLOSE tblname [NAME(name)]    [NEWCOPY | REPLCOPY]
             [PAD(percent)] [LIBRARY(ddname)]
```

A sample call of this service follows:

```
☞ ISPEXEC TBCLOSE DDST000 REPLCOPY
```

TBEND — End Table Processing without Saving. This service terminates processing of a table without saving it. However, if this table should be available in multiple logical screens, it will continue to be available to those screens until the usage count for this table is decremented to 0. The syntax is simply:

```
☞ ISPEXEC TBEND tblname
```

TBERASE — Erase a Table from a Library. This service erases a table from a library, provided that it is not currently in use and in WRITE mode. The syntax is:

```
☞ ISPEXEC TBERASE tblname [LIBRARY(ddname)]
```

The LIBRARY parameter allows you to specify a DDNAME other than the default of ISPTABL. Upon completion, a dialog might check the return code for at least the following two conditions: 8 — the table does not exist in the output library; 12 — the table is presently in use and the ENQ failed.

Single Row Operations

We now begin the table services that operate on specific rows at a time. Since no particular sequence is the right one, we will discuss them in alphabetical order.

TBADD — Add a Row to a Table. Generally, a row will be added at the point immediately following the current row unless the ORDER parameter is specified *and* the table has previously been sorted. In this case, the row will be inserted into the proper place based on the sort sequence specified.

In addition, if the table has keys, a check for possible duplicate entries will also be made and an error returned in that case. The syntax is:

```
⊜ ISPEXEC TBADD tblname [SAVE(namelist)] [ORDER]
```

The SAVE parameter allows you to specify "extension variables," i.e., variables that normally are not found in every row. The ORDER parameter applies to tables that have been previously sorted. Adding a row to a table without this parameter invalidates any sort that might have been done previously.

Generally, the only return code checked after this service is for the value of 8 which indicates that you are trying to add a row with a duplicate key (see also TBMOD).

An example of this call, after the key and name fields have been set, follows:

```
⊜ ISPEXEC TBADD DDST000 ORDER SAVE(remarks)
⊜ IF      &LASTCC = 8 THEN +
          ISPEXEC SETMSG MSG(DDSM234B) /* cannot add */
```

In this example, a row is added to the table in key order, and the contents of an extra field named &remarks will also be stored with this particular row.

TBDELETE — Delete a Row from a Table. For tables without keys, the current row is deleted; for tables with keys, the row that matches the current variables in the function pool will be deleted. The syntax is simply:

```
⊜ ISPEXEC TBDELETE tblname
```

Generally, a dialog might check the return code for at least a value of 8 which would indicate that the row could not be deleted. This would be either because the given key(s) did not exist in the table, or the current row pointer was pointing to the TOP of the table (value of 0).

A simple example for this call, after setting the various key values or pointing to the correct row, would be:

```
☞ ISPEXEC TBDELETE DDST000
☞ IF      &LASTCC = 8 THEN +
          ISPEXEC SETMSG MSG(DDSM345C) /* cannot delete */
```

TBEXIST — Check Existence of a Given Key. This service, which applies only to tables with keys, checks for the existence of a particular row in a table. Its syntax is:

```
☞ ISPEXEC TBEXIST tblname
```

Upon return, the dialog should check the return code for at least a value of 8 which would indicate that the row does not exist, or that this is not a keyed table. In either case, the CRP would be set to 0 (TOP).

Again, assuming that the various key values have been set, we could code:

```
☞ ISPEXEC TBEXIST DDST000
☞ IF      &LASTCC = 8 THEN +
          ISPEXEC SETMSG MSG(DDSM456D) /* not found */
```

TBGET — Get a Row from a Table. This service will reposition you into a particular row of a table and usually retrieve the variables for that row. The syntax is:

```
☞ ISPEXEC TBGET tblname [SAVENAME(vname1)] [NOREAD]
                        [POSITION(vname2)] [ROWID(vname3)]
```

The SAVENAME parameter is now the reverse of the SAVE for TBADD, i.e., you now wish to know the name(s) of any extension variable(s) in this particular row. The NOREAD parameter allows you to be positioned at the needed row but without reading its contents (usually because the function variables already have the new values and you do not wish to lose them with this GET).

The POSITION and the ROWID parameters return the pointer to this row, as already discussed under the TBDISPL service.

Generally, a dialog might check the return code for a value of 8 which would indicate that either the given key(s) do not exist (for keyed tables), or the CRP was pointing to the TOP (for nonkeyed tables).

Assuming that we wanted to retrieve the row that we previously added under TBADD with an extension variable, and assuming also that the key(s) have already been set, we could code:

```
 ISPEXEC TBGET DDST000 SAVENAME(names)
 IF      &LASTCC  = 8 THEN DO
         ISPEXEC SETMSG  MSG(DDSM456D) /* not found */
         GOTO    SHOW                  /* redisplay */
         END
```

And, in this case, &names would receive the string '(REMARKS)'.

TBMOD — Modify/Add a Row to a Table. This service is similar to TBADD, but more flexible. For keyed tables, the row will be added if the key(s) do not yet exist, otherwise the row will be updated (MODified). For nonkeyed tables, a new row will be added. The syntax is exactly the same as for TBADD:

```
 ISPEXEC TBMOD tblname [SAVE(namelist)] [ORDER]
```

Here, a return code of 8 indicates that such a key does not exist and the row was added to the table (instead of MODified). For example:

```
➥ ISPEXEC TBMOD DDST000 ORDER
➥ IF     &LASTCC  = 8 THEN +
         ISPEXEC  SETMSG  MSG(DDSM235B) /* row added */
```

TBPUT — Put a Row into a Table. This service updates a row in a table. For nonkeyed tables, the current row will be written (assuming that its value is not 0); for keyed tables, a search is performed for a match on the key fields. If a return code of 8 is given, the update was not possible for either of the two reasons just given. The syntax is also like that of the TBADD:

```
➥ ISPEXEC TBPUT tblname [SAVE(namelist)] [ORDER]
```

For example:

```
➥ ISPEXEC TBPUT DDST000 ORDER
➥ IF     &LASTCC  = 8 THEN +
         ISPEXEC  SETMSG  MSG(DDSM236B) /* no update */
```

TBSARG — Set Search Arguments for a Scan. This service enables you to define the search arguments to be used when limiting the rows to be processed either for a TBSCAN or for a TBDISPL in conjunction with a)MODEL ROWS(SCAN).

Any dialog variable matching a column name in the table will be used for the search unless it contains a null value. If not, it will be checked for an exact match unless some condition other than "EQ" is specified. Generic searches are possible by providing an "*" following the necessary generic root. For example, specifying ABC* will cause a search on any entry that begins with ABC. However, specifying ABC*DEF* will cause a search on anything beginning with ABC*DEF. In other words, only the last "*" indicates "anything else."

The syntax for this service is:

```
⊜ ISPEXEC TBSARG tblname [ARGLIST(list)] [NEXT | PREVIOUS]
                         [NAMECOND(conditions)]


where "conditions" represents: name,condition, ...
and "condition"      may be: LT | LE | EQ | NE | GE | GT
```

The ARGLIST parameter allows you to scan for "extension variables" in addition to the common table variables. The NEXT or PREVIOUS parameters indicate the direction of the search through the table from the current row: NEXT means forward, PREVIOUS means backward.

The NAMECOND allows you to specify the conditions for satisfaction of the search on each of the variables given. When not specified, the default is always for an equal condition (EQ).

Assume, for example, that a table has three columns — &name, &ptype, and &dtype — representing, perhaps, a variable name, a pool type (P, S, F, or N), and a data type class (CHAR, NUMER, MSG, PANEL, etc.). If we wanted to limit our TBDISPL to only the rows that match a data type of CHAR and a pool type of P or S or F, we could code the following:

```
⊜ SET      NAME   =
⊜ SET      PTYPE  = N
⊜ SET      DTYPE  = CHAR
⊜ ISPEXEC TBSARG  DDST000 NAMECOND(PTYPE,NE)
⊜ ISPEXEC TBDISPL DDST000 PANEL(DDSP110B)
```

In this example, &name would not be considered in the search because it is null; &ptype would be scanned for an "NE" (not equal) value of N (thus getting all others: P, S, or F); and &dtype would be scanned for a match on CHAR ("EQ" by default). All rows that would fit these conditions would be selected and displayed on panel DDSP110B, provided that this panel contained the statement ")MODEL ROWS(SCAN)".

If the search was in relation to a TBSCAN service (next topic), then the search would terminate as soon as a row satisfying the given conditions was found.

Generally, one return code that the dialog might check for would be the value of 8, which would mean that no matches are possible because all search variables are set to nulls.

TBSCAN — Search Table Based on TBSARG. This service combines the TBSEARCH function with a TBGET process. It scans a table based on the TBSEARCH parameters (which can also be set here in TBSCAN), and reads the next row in the table that satisfies the given conditions. The syntax is:

```
☞ ISPEXEC TBSCAN tblname [ARGLIST(list)]     [NEXT | PREVIOUS]
                         [CONDLIST(conditions)]
                         [SAVENAME(vname1)] [NOREAD]
                         [POSITION(vname2)] [ROWID(vname3)]

  where "conditions" represents: name,condition, ...
     and "condition"     may be: LT | LE | EQ | NE | GE | GT
```

ARGLIST, when coded, will cause TBSARG to be ignored. In such a case, it must specify *all* variables to be used in the scan process. NEXT, PREVIOUS, and CONDLIST operate in the exact same fashion as for TBSARG. SAVENAME, NOREAD, POSITION, and ROWID also operate in the same fashion as already indicated for TBGET.

One should check the return code for at least a value of 8 which means: no match found.

If we use the same conditions as already mentioned for TBSARG, this time to find the NEXT row that matches our search, we could code:

```
☞ SET      NAME  =
☞ SET      PTYPE = N
☞ SET      DTYPE = CHAR
☞ ISPEXEC TBSARG  DDST000 NAMECOND(PTYPE,NE)
☞ ISPEXEC TBSCAN  DDST000
☞ IF &LASTCC = 8 THEN ISPEXEC SET MSG(DDSM123) /* no hits */
```

TBVCLEAR — Clear Table Variables to Null. This service provides for a quick way of clearing to null values all dialog variables associated with a table. The syntax is simply:

```
☞ ISPEXEC TBVCLEAR tblname
```

Please note that this clears the variables in the function pool, but not necessarily the contents of the current row in the table (unless, for example, a TBPUT was to be issued).

Row Pointer Operations

Many of the table services already described either refer to whatever the current table row is or will set the current row for you. If you wish to alter this value, you have three additional services.

TBTOP — Point to TOP of Table (Row 0). This service will position you at the TOP of the table — which actually precedes the first row. The syntax is simply:

```
☞ ISPEXEC TBTOP tblname
```

TBSKIP — Skip to the Next Row. This service will position you at a specific row of the table and then perform the equivalent of a TBGET. The syntax is:

```
☞ ISPEXEC TBSKIP tblname [NUMBER(nbr)]      [ROW(rowid)]

                         [SAVENAME(vname1)] [NOREAD]

                         [POSITION(vname2)] [ROWID(vname3)]
```

The NUMBER parameter allows you to specify how many rows to skip. If the value is negative, it will skip backward; otherwise, it will skip forward. The ROW parameter allows an alternate way of skipping to a row: The *rowid* value can be derived from most of the other table services and contains an internal identifier that applies to a specific row, regardless of whether other rows have been added or deleted in the meantime. When neither of these parameters is given, the default is NUMBER(+1).

The SAVENAME, NOREAD, POSITION, and ROWID parameters are the same as for the TBGET service.

The one return code value that a dialog might check for would be a value of 8, which would indicate that you have SKIPped beyond the end of the table.

To illustrate, assume that we have a table that we wish to process as if it were a sequential file. To perform this, we could code:

```
☞ ... ...
☞ ISPEXEC TBOPEN &table        /* leaves us at the TOP */
☞ LOOP: +
☞ ISPEXEC TBSKIP &table        /* move to/get next row */
☞ IF      &LASTCC = 8   THEN   GOTO ENDFILE
☞ ... ...                      /* process the row       */
☞ ... ...
☞ ISPEXEC TBPUT  &table        /* update the row        */
☞ GOTO    LOOP
☞ ENDFILE: +
☞ ISPEXEC TBCLOSE &table       /* close the table       */
☞ ... ...
```

TBBOTTOM — Point to Bottom of Table (Last Row). This service will position you at the last row of a table and then perform the equivalent of a TBGET. The syntax is very similar to that of TBSKIP except that there is no need to specify the row number:

```
☞ ISPEXEC TBBOTTOM tblname [SAVENAME(vname1)] [NOREAD]
                          [POSITION(vname2)] [ROWID(vname3)]
```

The parameters have the exact same meaning as those already described under TBGET. If the table should be empty, this call would return a value of 8 and the CRP would be set to 0 (TOP).

Comprehensive Example

Perhaps because of the number of services available, these functions seem to be the most difficult ones to master. Since it is critical that we understand how all of this works — most dialogs handle one or more tables — we will be examining in detail an example that illustrates most of what has already been covered.

Suppose, for example, that we had the table in Figure 5-2.

Suppose, also, that we wished to display this table with the panel shown in Figure 5-3.

appl id	variable name	pool type	data type	field len	field description and comments
DDS					
DDS	APPL	P	CHAR	4	APPLICATION IDENTIFICATION
DDS	DESCRIPT	F	CHAR	30	FIELD DESCRIPTION
DDS	DTYPE	F	CHAR	5	DATA TYPE (NUMER OR CHAR)
DDS	LENTH	F	NUMER	5	MAXIMUM FIELD LENGTH
DDS	PTYPE	F	CHAR	1	VARIABLE POOL CLASSIFICATION
DDS	VARNAME	F	CHAR	8	FIELD NAME WITHIN APPLICATION

Figure 5-2   Table DDST000.

```
)ATTR DEFAULT(%+_)
 /* % TYPE(TEXT  )  INTENS(HIGH)                              */
 /* + TYPE(TEXT  )  INTENS(LOW )                              */
 /* _ TYPE( INPUT)  INTENS(HIGH)  CAPS(ON )  JUST(LEFT )      */
    ¬ TYPE(OUTPUT)  INTENS(LOW )  CAPS(ON )  JUST(LEFT )
    ! TYPE(OUTPUT)  INTENS(LOW )  CAPS(ON )  JUST(RIGHT)


)BODY
%----------------- DDS TABLE DISPLAY PANEL  --------------------
%COMMAND ===>_ZCMD                            %SCROLL ===>_AMT +
%
+ENTER:  %A+(ADD), %C+(CHANGE), OR %D+(DELETE) COMMAND(s)
+
%CMD APPL VARIABLE POOL  DATA    FIELD  FIELD DESC AND COMMENTS
%CDE  ID    NAME    TYPE  TYPE   LENGTH
+


)MODEL   ROWS(SCAN)
 _z+¬appl¬varname + ¬z+  dtype+!lenth+¬descript             +


)INIT
  .HELP  = DDSH110B
  .ZVARS = '(option ptype)'
  &amt   = &ZSCROLLA


)PROC
  IF (&ZTDSELS = 0000) .MSG = DDSM110B
  VER(&option, LIST, A,C,D)


)END
```

Figure 5-3   Panel DDSP110B.

In addition, as each row is selected, we may wish to expand its data into a separate data entry panel where more detailed information may be available. To do this, we will use panel DDSP110C depicted in Figure 5-4.

```
)ATTR DEFAULT(%+_)
 /*  %  TYPE(TEXT)    INTENS(HIGH)                                      */
 /*  +  TYPE(TEXT)    INTENS(LOW)                                       */
 /*  _  TYPE(INPUT)   INTENS(HIGH)  CAPS(ON)  JUST(LEFT)              */
     $  TYPE(INPUT)   INTENS(HIGH)  CAPS(ON)  JUST(LEFT)   PAD(_)
     !  TYPE(INPUT)   INTENS(HIGH)  CAPS(ON)  JUST(LEFT)   PAD(_)

)BODY
%-------------------- DDS DATA ENTRY PANEL ----------------------
%COMMAND ===>_ZCMD                                                +
%
+    PLEASE ENTER OR VERIFY THE FOLLOWING ITEMS:
+    ACTION TO PERFORM: %&option
+
+    APPLICATION ID . . .$appl+      Maximum 4 alphanumeric chars
+    VARIABLE NAME. . . .$varname +  Maximum 8 alphanumeric chars
+    POOL TYPE. . . . . .$z+         P=Prof,S=Shr,F=Funct,N=N/A
+
+    DATA TYPE. . . . . .$dtype+     CHAR,NUMER,PANEL,MSG,TABLE..
+    FIELD LENGTH . . . .$lenth+     Maximum field length (32767)
+    DESCRIPTION. . . . .$descript             + Max 30
+
+    DELETE CONFIRMATION.$del+       Enter Yes/No for DELETE opt

)INIT
 .HELP  = DDSH110C
 .ZVARS = ptype
 &option= TRANS(&option A,ADD C,CHANGE D,DELETE)
 if (&option ¬= DELETE) .CURSOR = varname
 if (&option  = DELETE) .CURSOR = del

)PROC
   &option =  TRUNC (&option,1)
   &del    =  TRUNC (&del,   1)
   VER (&appl,   NB, NAME)
   IF  (&option ¬= D)
       VER (&varname,NB, NAME)
       VER (&ptype,  NB, LIST, P,S,F,N)
       VER (&dtype,  NB, ALPHA)
       VER (&lenth,  NB, NUM)
   IF  (&option = D)
       VER (&del, NB, LIST, Y,N)

)END
```

Figure 5-4   Panel DDSP110C.

```
)ATTR DEFAULT(%+_)
  /*  % TYPE(TEXT)    INTENS(HIH)                              */
  /*  + TYPE(TEXT)    INTENS(LOW)                             */
  /*  _ TYPE(INPUT)   INTENS(HIGH)  CAPS(ON)  JUST(LEFT)       */
     $ TYPE(INPUT)   INTENS(HIGH)  CAPS(ON)  JUST(LEFT)   PAD(_)
     ! TYPE(INPUT)   INTENS(HIGH)  CAPS(ON)  JUST(RIGHT)  PAD(_)


)BODY
%--------------- DDS APPLICATION SELECTION PANEL ---------------
%COMMAND ===>_ZCMD                                              +
%
+    TO ISOLATE A GIVEN SUBSET, ENTER MATCHING PARAMETERS:
+    APPLICATION ID . . .$appl+      (no entry processes all appls)
+    POOL TYPE. . . . . .$z+         (no entry processes all types)
+    DATA TYPE. . . . . .$dtype+     (no entry processes all types)


)INIT
  .HELP  = DDSH110A
  .ZVARS = ptype


)PROC
    VER (&appl,  NAME)
    VER (&ptype, LIST, P,S,F,N)
    VER (&dtype, ALPHA)


)END
```

Figure 5-5   Panel DDSP110A.

Finally, as this table grows, the user may become tired of scrolling through large numbers of entries to find the desired ones. To avoid this, we will provide the user with a third panel (see Figure 5-5) where table selection parameters will be asked before we actually begin the table processing.

Now all that we need is a function (see Figure 5-6) to "thread" and control all these components in the following manner:

1. Display the options panel DDSP110A.
2. Open the table DDST000 for update.

```
PROC       0
CONTROL    NOLIST    NOCONLIST    MSG    NOFLUSH
ISPEXEC    CONTROL   ERRORS    RETURN
SET        TABLE =   DDST000
ISPEXEC    DISPLAY   PANEL(DDSP110A)                                    1
IF         &LASTCC   ¬= 0      THEN    EXIT                             2
IF         &APPL     ¬=        THEN    ISPEXEC VPUT (APPL) PROFILE      3
ELSE SET   &APPL =   &STR(*)                                           4
ISPEXEC    TBOPEN    &TABLE    WRITE                                    5
IF         &LASTCC   < 8       THEN    GOTO   P                         6
ISPEXEC    TBCREATE  &TABLE    KEYS(APPL, VARNAME, PTYPE) +             7
           NAMES     (DTYPE, LENTH, DESCRIPT)
ISPEXEC    TBSORT    &TABLE    +                                       8
           FIELDS    (APPL,C,A, VARNAME,C,A, PTYPE,C,A)
/*----------------------------------------------------------------*/
P: SET        &TBLRC    = 0
ISPEXEC    TBSARG    &TABLE                                            9
ISPEXEC    TBSCAN    &TABLE                                            10
IF         &LASTCC   < 8       THEN    GOTO   L                        11
SET        &VARNAME =
SET        &PTYPE   =
ISPEXEC    TBADD     &TABLE    ORDER                                   12
L: DO         WHILE     &TBLRC    < 8                                     13
ISPEXEC    TBDISPL   &TABLE    PANEL(DDSP110B) AUTOSEL(NO)             14
SET        &TBLRC =  &LASTCC                                          15
DO         WHILE     &ZTDSELS > 0                                      16
IF         &OPTION   = A       THEN    SET    &VARNAME =               17
ISPEXEC    CONTROL   DISPLAY SAVE                                      18
ISPEXEC    DISPLAY   PANEL(DDSP110C)                                   19
SET        &PANRC =  &LASTCC
ISPEXEC    CONTROL   DISPLAY RESTORE                                   20
IF         &PANRC    > 4       THEN    GOTO    R                       21
IF         &OPTION   = A       THEN    ISPEXEC TBADD &TABLE ORDER      22
IF         &OPTION   = C       THEN    ISPEXEC TBMOD &TABLE ORDER
IF         &OPTION   = D       THEN    ISPEXEC TBDELETE &TABLE
R: SET        &OPTION   =
SET        &DEL      =
IF         &ZTDSELS > 1        THEN    ISPEXEC TBDISPL  &TABLE         23
ELSE SET   &ZTDSELS = 0
END                                                                   24
END                                                                   25
/*----------------------------------------------------------------*/
ISPEXEC    TBCLOSE   &TABLE                                            26
END
```

Figure 5-6   CLIST DDSC110: Display table DDST000 on panel DDSP110B.

3. Display the table panel DDSP110B.
4. Display the data entry panel DDSP110C for each row selected.
5. Loop back to step 3 until the user responds with END.
6. Close the table and exit.

This process would work as follows:

1. We begin by displaying a simple data entry panel (DDSP110A) where the user will be asked whether to limit the table processing to a specific application identifier (*&appl*), a specific pool type (*&ptype*), and/or a specific data type (*&dtype*). The user is instructed that if no entry is made for a particular item, it will default to selecting all variations of that item.

2. Following this data panel display, we check the return code to ensure that the user did not press END or RETURN. If so, then we simply exit, thus returning to the point that called us.

3. If the user did make an entry in *&appl* (not null), we save it in the profile pool, since the user is very likely to remain with this application for some period of time.

4. On the other hand, if no entry has been made in *&appl*, we set the search argument to "*" (which means all variations of this field) but do not alter the value of this variable in the profile pool.

   We do not have to set the other two search arguments (*&ptype*, *&dtype*) because, if they have a null value, they will not be used in a search. Only one variable must have a value even if it is an asterisk (*).

5. At this point we open the table (DDST000) for processing in WRITE mode, since we anticipate that the user will want to make changes, additions, and/or deletions.

6. We now check the return code from the open process. If the value is less than 8, we consider this a successful open and proceed to point P.

7. If unsuccessful, we assume that the table does not yet exist and we create it now indicating the names of the key fields (*&appl*, *&varname*, *&ptype*) as well as the names of the other data fields (*&dtype*, *&lenth*, *&descript*).

8. Since we wish to maintain this table in alphabetical order by key fields, we now perform a table sort. Although this seems silly at this point (the table is empty), the effect is to store information with the table that indicates the order in which we

wish to maintain the data. As we add entries to the table, this order will be observed (unless, of course, we decide later to sort it some other way).

9. We are now ready to inform ISPF to set the search arguments for the table based on the values in the table variables (*&appl*, *&varname*, *&ptype*, *&dtype*, *&lenth*, *&descript*). Since these are function variables, and since only three of them can possibly have any values at this time, we will be searching on any or all of the three fields (*&appl*, *&ptype*, *&dtype*).

10. We now tell ISPF to actually perform the table scan, thus limiting the table entries to only those that match the search arguments. Normally we would not have to do this if the only purpose were to control what goes into the table display panel. ROWS(SCAN) would accomplish this. However, we need to ensure that at least one entry is available so that an empty panel will not be displayed.

11. Following the table scan, we check the condition code. If the value is less than 8, we find some matches and we proceed to label L. Otherwise, the search has been unsuccessful and we have nothing to display. In this case, we initialize a "header" entry with the current *&appl*, while *&varname* and *&ptype* are set to null.

12. We now add this application "header" to the table so that a minimum of one entry will show on the panel.

13. With this prologue finished, we now enter the main process loop which will continue until such time as the user presses END or RETURN.

14. At this point we are ready to perform the table display for table DDST000 (*&table*) using panel DDSP110B with the AUTOSEL option set to NO.

15. This step simply saves the return code from the table display service so that later we can determine whether to remain in the loop or not. We do not check it at this time because the user might have selected some rows *and* pressed END or RETURN as well. We will allow this combination.

16. Upon returning from the table display, the function pool variable &ZTDSELS will contain the number of rows selected by the user. Since we will be processing one row at a time, we will begin a loop for as long as &ZTDSELS is greater than 0.

    Please note that regardless of how many rows were selected by the user, ISPF will only give us the values for one row at a time. Any other rows that the user may also have chosen are called "pending selected rows." To access the next pending row (and decrement the value in &ZTDSELS), issue a TBDISPL service with no parameters other than the table name. Nothing will be displayed on the screen, but it will advance the process to the next row.

Should you issue a TBDISPL with a panel or message name, then any pending selected rows will be discarded and control will return to the user.

Our panel could have been designed so that the user could modify any of the table fields directly on that panel. In that case, and depending on the user's command code entered, we would simply perform a TBPUT (update a row in the table), a TBDELETE (delete a row), or a TBADD (add a row) as we process each selected row.

As the panel is, however, we will be going to a separate data entry panel so that more complex service combinations can be exercised with this example.

17. This brings us to the next command line which simply clears the &varname for an addition to the table, thus forcing the user to enter some value on the panel that we are about to display.

18. *This is an important step.* Anytime that you interrupt a TBDISPL (and sometimes others as well), you should request ISPF to save the current environment so that you can resume where you left off. This is what the CONTROL DISPLAY SAVE call does.

19. Now we display a data entry panel with all the details for the table entry requested. The user will be able to modify any field, while at the same time receiving more detailed instructions as to what each field might be.

20. When we return from the data entry panel, we save the return code and restore the TBDISPL environment so that we may proceed with the current row processing.

21. If the user pressed END or RETURN while in the data entry panel, we assume that the user decided to cancel that particular selection, but we will continue with any remaining ones. In this case, we branch to the R statement where some row "clean-up" process will be performed.

22. At this point, the user has entered the data for a selected row and we proceed with the action request: a TBADD for additions, a TBMOD for modifications (or addition, if the user changed the key), and a TBDELETE for deletions.

23. We have now finished processing one selected row and we have also cleared the work variables &option and &del. Now we check for any "pending selected rows" remaining and, if so, perform a TBDISPL with only the table name. This will get us the next row without actually going to the terminal. If &ZTDSELS is 1, that means that we have processed the last selected row. If there are no more rows, then we force 0 into &ZTDSELS so that we will exit the DO loop and go to the user with a new display.

24. This END statement closes out the DO loop for the &ZTDSELS. Thus, either we will go to the next row, if any, or we will exit into the next statement.

25. This END statement closes out the DO loop for user table displays, thus repeating this whole process all over again. Eventually, the user will press END or RETURN, which will give us a return code of 8 and take us out of this loop into the next statement.

26. When that happens, we close the table and we exit this function, thus returning to the point that called us.

FILE TAILORING Services

As previously indicated, file tailoring consists of creating an output file, reading an input skeleton with data and control statements that dictate the contents of the output file, then closing the created file and, if necessary, erasing it when no longer needed.

It is not important, at this time, that we know the details of how a file skeleton is developed or how it controls the output. This will be discussed in the next chapter. In this section, we will discuss the services that "trigger" the file skeleton process. The services available for this type of process, in the order of normal process, are:

- FTOPEN   — Create an output file for file tailoring
- FTINCL   — Include a skeleton to control output

- FTCLOSE   — Close out the file tailoring process
- FTERASE   — Erase the created output file

FTOPEN — Create an Output File

This service begins the file tailoring process by opening the intended output file in anticipation of writing to it. This file will be designated through the DDNAME of ISPFILE, which can be overridden, and must be allocated some time before this call. The syntax for this service is:

```
⇨ ISPEXEC FTOPEN [TEMP]
```

The TEMP parameter simply indicates that you wish to use a temporary file (rather than the one specified by ISPFILE). In this case, ISPF will create the file for you and make its name available in the system variable &ZTEMPF.

Two possible return values to check might be: 8 — file tailoring already in progress; or 12 — the output file is presently in use.

The following illustrates this service:

```
⇨ ALLOCATE   FI(ISPFILE) DA(DDS.FTOUTPUT)   OLD
⇨ ISPEXEC    FTOPEN
⇨ IF         &LASTCC   ¬= 0   THEN DO
⇨            ISPEXEC   SETMSG   MSG(DDSM120B)
⇨            FREE      FI(ISPFILE)
⇨            END
```

FTINCL — Include a Skeleton to Control Output

This is the service that actually reads the skeleton to determine what to write to the output file. The syntax is:

```
⇨ ISPEXEC FTINCL skelname [NOFT]
```

The NOFT parameter simply indicates that the skeleton is to be copied to the output file with no other process whatsoever.

Two possible return codes to check would be: 8 — the skeleton cannot be found; 12 — the skeleton or the table are in use.

Example:

```
⇨ ISPEXEC    FTINCL    &SKEL
⇨ IF         &LASTCC   ¬= 0      THEN  DO
⇨            ISPEXEC   SETMSG    MSG(DDSM120C)
⇨            ISPEXEC   FTCLOSE   NOREPL
⇨            EXIT
⇨            END
```

FTCLOSE — Close Out the Process

This service terminates the file tailoring and closes the output file. The syntax is:

```
⇨ ISPEXEC FTCLOSE [NAME(member)] [NOREPL] [LIBRARY(ddname)]
```

The NAME parameter is to be used whenever the file is partitioned (the output file may be sequential as well). The NOREPL indicates that if such a member already exists, this process is to be aborted. The LIBRARY parameter allows you to specify a DDNAME other than the default of ISPFILE. This would not apply if the FTOPEN indicated a TEMP option.

The possible return code values to check might be: 4 — REPL was specified and the member already exists; 8 — no FTOPEN performed prior to this service; 12 — the output file is in use.

To show a simple example:

```
⇨ ISPEXEC    FTCLOSE
⇨ IF   &LASTCC   ¬= 0 THEN   ISPEXEC SETMSG MSG(DDSM120D)
```

FTERASE — Erase the Output File

This service enables you to purge file tailoring output that is no longer needed. The syntax is:

```
⇨ ISPEXEC FTERASE member [LIBRARY(ddname)]
```

The LIBRARY parameter is the same as for FTCLOSE. Upon completion, you might check the return code for either: 8 — the file does not exist; or 12 — the file is in use.

Example:

```
⇨ ISPEXEC   FTERASE   DDSO120
```

Comprehensive Example

The command procedure shown in Figure 5-7 provides a complete file tailoring process example. It reads a skeleton called DDSS120 and writes the output on a sequential data set named 'userid.DDS.FTOUTPUT'. Since the file is accessed with a disposition of OLD, any previous output is simply overlaid.

Variable Services

We know, by now, that we have three classes of variable pools: the application profile pool, the application shared pool, and the function pool. Reading variables from these pools to any *panel* is an automatic feature of ISPF. When it needs a value, it will search the function pool first, then the shared pool, and finally the profile pool.

Writing these variables to the pools, however, is somewhat different: only selection panels read and write directly to the shared and/or profile pools. Any other component accesses only the function pool.

To transfer data from one pool to another, we can use the VGET and VPUT services that follow.

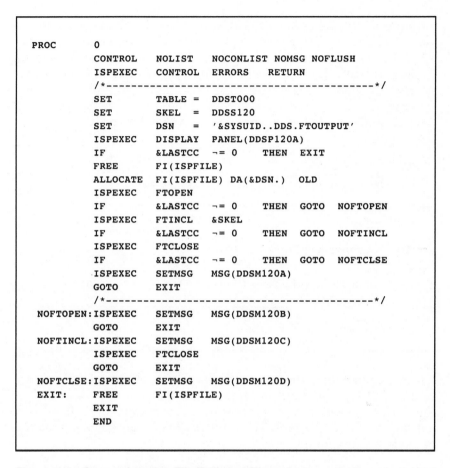

Figure 5-7 Comprehensive File Tailoring Example.

VGET — Get Variable from Shared or Profile Pool

This service will retrieve any number of variables from the shared or profile pool into the current function pool. The syntax is:

```
⇨ ISPEXEC VGET (list) [SHARED | PROFILE | ASIS]
```

The "list" entry indicates that you may specify as many names as you wish. If only one name is given, the parentheses are optional. The other parameters indicate from which pool the variable is to be fetched. If ASIS is given, you are indicating that it will come from the SHARED pool if found there, otherwise from the PROFILE pool.

Upon return, you may wish to check the return code for a value of 8 which would indicate that the variable was not found.

Example:

```
☞ ISPEXEC VGET (uname,acct,room,class) PROFILE
```

VPUT — Put Variable in Shared or Profile Pool

This service performs the reverse of the VGET. The syntax is:

```
☞ ISPEXEC VPUT (list) [SHARED | PROFILE | ASIS]
```

The parameters operate similarly to those of the VGET. In the case of ASIS, you are indicating that the variable is to be stored in the SHARED pool unless that variable is already in the PROFILE but not the SHARED pool. The return code of 8 also means that the variable was not found.

```
☞ ISPEXEC VPUT (uname,acct,room,class) PROFILE
```

Other Services

This brings us to the last class of services — those that provide some miscellaneous ISPF services or those that generally interface with other products outside of the dialog manager. Since no particular order is best, they will be presented in alphabetical sequence.

BROWSE — Invoke the BROWSE Program from a Dialog

This service allows you to access the BROWSE program which is part of the PDF program product. The syntax is:

```
⊜ ISPEXEC BROWSE DATASET(dsname)   [VOLUME(vol)]
                  [PASSWORD(pass)] [PANEL(name)]
```

Each parameter is self-explanatory. The PANEL entry allows for a customized panel other than the one normally used by BROWSE. The following illustrates a typical call:

```
⊜ ISPEXEC BROWSE DATASET(DDS.FTOUTPUT)
```

CONTROL — Specify Screen and Error-Handling Options

This service specifies special processing requirements for a given function. The syntax is:

```
⊜ ISPEXEC CONTROL {DISPLAY   {LOCK                } }
                  {          {LINE                } }
                  {          {REFRESH             } }
                  {          {SAVE    | RESTORE}  }
                  {                                }
                  {NONDISPL [ENTER  | END]        }
                  {                                }
                  {ERRORS   [CANCEL | RETURN]     }
                  {                                }
                  {SPLIT    {ENABLE | DISABLE}  }
                  {                                }
                  {NOCMD                          }
```

The DISPLAY option controls the display mode:

- LOCK will lock up the terminal for the next display only so that the function may continue without interruption. It may be useful to display a message such as "PLEASE WAIT."
- LINE alerts ISPF that some line-mode output may have taken place and the entire screen needs to be rewritten on the next display.
- REFRESH is similar to LINE. It applies to other products that use full-screen write operations.
- SAVE will store critical control information about the current logical screen. This is critical when a TBDISPL process is "interrupted" with another DISPLAY process.
- RESTORE reinstates the information stored with the SAVE.

The NONDISPL indicates that for the next panel display only, no output is to be sent to the terminal. The response simulated is based on its associated subparameters of ENTER or END.

The ERRORS parameter alerts ISPF as to what to do when a service returns a code of 12 or more. CANCEL, generally, will cancel the dialog, while RETURN will give control back to the function.

The SPLIT allows you to ENABLE or DISABLE the user to enter split-screen mode. The NOCMD indicates that for the next display only, any command entered on the command line is not to be honored.

Some common examples:

```
⇨ ISPEXEC CONTROL ERRORS RETURN
⇨ ...
⇨ ISPEXEC TBDISPL DDST000 PANEL(DDSP110B)
⇨     ...
⇨     ISPEXEC CONTROL DISPLAY SAVE
⇨     ISPEXEC DISPLAY PANEL(DDSP110C)
⇨     ISPEXEC CONTROL DISPLAY RESTORE
```

EDIT — Invoke the EDIT Program from a Dialog

This service allows you to access the EDIT program which is part of the PDF program product. The syntax is:

```
⏏ ISPEXEC EDIT DATASET(dsname)   [VOLUME(vol)]
               [PASSWORD(pass)] [PANEL(name)]
               [MACRO(mname)]    [PROFILE(pname)]
```

The first four parameters are the same as for the BROWSE service. The MACRO parameter allows you to indicate a macro to be executed immediately after the data is fetched, while the PROFILE allows you to name a special profile to be used.

The following illustrates a typical call:

```
⏏ ISPEXEC EDIT DATASET(DDS.FTOUTPUT)
```

EDREC — EDIT Recovery Table Processing

This service can initialize an EDIT recovery table or determine if recovery is pending or take some other action. Detailed discussion of this item is more appropriate under the PDF services; consequently, only its syntax will be presented here:

```
⏏ ISPEXEC EDREC {INIT      [CMD(cmdname)]                      }
                {QUERY                                         }
                {PROCESS [DATAID(id)]   [PASSWORD(word)]}
                {CANCEL                                        }
                {DEFER                                         }
```

GETMSG — GET Information on a Particular Message

This service retrieves a message from the library and provides information on its contents. The syntax is:

```
⏏ ISPEXEC GETMSG MSG(id) [SHORTMSG(vname1)] [LONGMSG(vname2)]
                          [ALARM(vname3)]    [HELP(vname4)]
```

Each parameter is self-explanatory, and each *&vnamex* will receive the contents of that item as found in the message specified. A return code of 12 would indicate that the message was not found.

Assume, for example, that message DDSM120B existed as follows:

```
DDSM120B 'UNABLE TO DO FTOPEN'   .ALARM = YES
'UNABLE TO ACCESS THE SKELETON LIBRARY OR THE OUTPUT FILE'
```

To request information on this message, we could code:

```
☞ ISPEXEC GETMSG MSG(DDSM120B) SHORTMSG(short) ALARM(tone)
```

This would return "UNABLE TO DO FTOPEN" in *&short,* and "YES" in *&tone.*

GR*xxxxxx* — Establish GDDM Interface Processes

These services cannot be called from a command procedure — only a programming language. Consequently, their syntax will be discussed at that point.

ISREDIT — Invoke EDIT Macros from a Dialog

This service enables you to interface with EDIT macros for the PDF EDIT program (which is outside the scope of this book). Each macro definition can be found in the *Edit Macros* manual published by IBM, so only the general syntax will be shown here:

```
☞ ISPEXEC ISREDIT macro [parm ...]
```

LIBDEF — Define ISPF Libraries for a Dialog

This is one of the most important and useful additions made to ISPF with Version 2.2 of this product. It allows us to allocate dynamically new ISPF dialog libraries, thus removing the restriction of having to allocate every possible library needed by every possible application before the session begins.

The general syntax is:

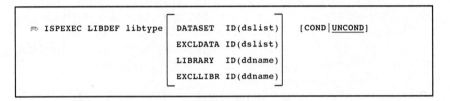

```
⇨ ISPEXEC LIBDEF libtype ┌                    ┐
                         │ DATASET  ID(dslist) │  [COND|UNCOND]
                         │ EXCLDATA ID(dslist) │
                         │ LIBRARY  ID(ddname) │
                         │ EXCLLIBR ID(ddname) │
                         └                    ┘
```

The parameter *libtype* can designate one of the following:

- ISPLLIB — The load module library
- ISPPLIB — The panel library
- ISPMLIB — The message library
- ISPTLIB — The table input library
- ISPTABL — The table output library
- ISPSLIB — The skeleton library
- ISPFILE — The file tailoring output file
- *xxxxxxx* — Any other ddname specified in a LIBRARY parameter

The basic difference between specifying DATASET or LIBRARY is that DATASET performs the equivalent of an ALLOCATE command, whereas LIBRARY simply uses a previous allocation. In both cases, the libraries specified will be searched ahead of any other libraries currently in use by ISPF. This process will remain in effect until a new LIBDEF for the same library is established, the current application is suspended for a lower-level one (and no PASSLIB given), or it terminates.

It is possible to have still a third level of libraries that would be searched ahead of those in the LIBDEF statements. Those libraries would have to be allocated by the user *before* the corresponding LIBDEFs and would have the following DDNAMEs:

- ISPLUSR — The user load module library
- ISPPUSR — The user panel library
- ISPMUSR — The user message library
- ISPTUSR — The user table input library
- ISPTABU — The user table output library
- ISPSUSR — The user skeleton library
- ISPFILU — The user file tailoring output file

The EXCLDATA and EXCLLIBR parameters apply *only* to ISPLLIB definitions. They indicate that any other definitions are to be EXCLuded from the search while this LIBDEF is in effect.

The COND/UNCOND parameters indicate whether this LIBDEF is/is not conditional on whether a LIBDEF for this library type has already been established or not.

If none of the primary parameters — DATASET, EXCLDATA, LIBRARY, EXCLLIBR — are coded in a given LIBDEF statement, the current LIBDEF for this library type is cancelled. Cancelling a LIBDEF automatically disconnects any USER libraries as well for that library type.

To illustrate this important service, let us assume that we wish to begin a new application whose libraries are not in the existing search sequence. In order to make them available, the new application might call a function that would issue the necessary LIBDEFs as follows:

```
☞ &ZSEL = 'CMD(DDSC000) NEWAPPL(DDS)'
```

where the DDSC000 function might be as shown in Figure 5-8.

When this application terminates, these LIBDEFs will be released automatically and the environment that existed when it started will be reinstated. In other words, as NEWAPPLs begin, any new LIBDEFs supersede the previous ones (stacked) until the NEWAPPL exits and the old ones are reinstated (popped).

LM*xxxxxx* — Use PDF Library Access Services

This series of services enable you to interface with the Library Management Facility of the PDF product, the details of which are

```
... ...
ISPEXEC  LIBDEF ISPLLIB DATASET ID(DDS.LOAD)
ISPEXEC  LIBDEF ISPPLIB DATASET ID(DDS.PANELS)
ISPEXEC  LIBDEF ISPMLIB DATASET ID(DDS.MSGS)
ISPEXEC  LIBDEF ISPTLIB DATASET ID(DDS.TABLES)
ISPEXEC  LIBDEF ISPTABL DATASET ID(DDS.TABLES)
ISPEXEC  LIBDEF ISPSLIB DATASET ID(DDS.SKELS)
... ...
ISPEXEC  SELECT PANEL(DDSP100)  /* DDS primary option panel */
... ...
```

Figure 5-8 Sample LIBDEF Application.

outside the scope of this book. Each service description can be found in the *ISPF/PDF Services Manual* published by IBM, so only the general syntax will be shown here:

```
☞ ISPEXEC LMxxxxx DATAID(id) [MEMBER(name)] [parm ...]
```

LOG — Write Dialog Messages to a Log File

This service will cause a message to be written to the log file. This can be useful as it provides an audit trail of special events that may have taken place. The syntax is:

```
☞ ISPEXEC LOG MSG(messageid)
```

PQUERY — Obtain Information on a Panel Area

This service retrieves information about a DYNAMIC or GRAPHIC panel area. The syntax is:

```
☞ ISPEXEC PQUERY   PANEL(panelname)    AREANAME(name)
                   [AREATYPE(vname1)]
                   [WIDTH(vname2)]      [DEPTH(vname3)]
                   [ROW(vname4)]        [COLUMN(vname5)]
```

PANEL and AREANAME are self-explanatory. AREATYPE
returns DYNAMIC or GRAPHIC. WIDTH and DEPTH return the
number of columns and lines based on the appearance of the panel
on the current physical screen. ROW and COLUMN return the row
and column numbers of the top left corner of the area.

A simple example might be:

```
☞ ISPEXEC PQUERY PANEL(ABCP123) AREANAME(PIC) DEPTH(depth)
```

SELECT — Display Selection Panel

This service provides the equivalent of the SELECT process performed by selection panels. The syntax is:

```
☞ ISPEXEC SELECT sel-options   [appl-options]

   where "sel-options" is one of the following:
   ♦   PANEL(name) [OPT(option)]
   ♦   CMD(name    [parms])        [LANG(APL)]
   ♦   PGM(name)   [PARM(parms)]

   and "appl-options" is:   NEWAPPL[[(appl-id)] [PASSLIB]]
                       or:   NEWPOOL
```

All these parameters have already been discussed in Chapter 3,
"ISPF Panel Definitions." Consequently, only a brief example follows:

```
☞ ISPEXEC SELECT PANEL(DDSP100)
```

Summary

As you have seen, ISPF provides a rich assortment of services to enable the coding of complex processes within any function with a simple call. The number of services may appear intimidating to anyone just starting, but as you begin to use them, you will find that they are fairly simple to use — with the exception, perhaps, of the table display process. But even that one, if you follow the example given carefully, should not cause you any major difficulty in developing an application of your own.

As you search for the right service, you may find it useful to remember the class under which that service falls:

- DISPLAY SERVICES — To display panels and messages
- TABLE SERVICES — To process data tables
- FILE TAILORING SERVICES — To process file skeletons
- VARIABLE SERVICES — To process variables in any pool
- OTHER SERVICES — To interface with other products

To further assist you, the Table of Contents has been designed to show you each service available under these classes as well as a very brief description of what each service does for you.

You must remember that all these services are requested through one common point — the Dialog Manager — and that the general format of each call is:

```
☞ ISPEXEC service parameter [parameter ...]
```

6

Skeleton Definitions

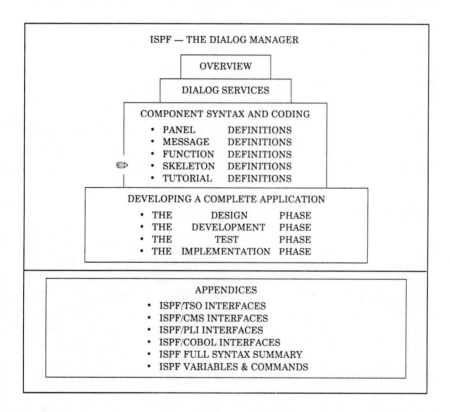

```
ISPF — THE DIALOG MANAGER

        ┌─────────────────────────┐
        │        OVERVIEW         │
      ┌─┴─────────────────────────┴─┐
      │       DIALOG SERVICES       │
    ┌─┴─────────────────────────────┴─┐
    │   COMPONENT SYNTAX AND CODING    │
    │      • PANEL      DEFINITIONS    │
    │      • MESSAGE    DEFINITIONS    │
    │      • FUNCTION   DEFINITIONS    │
    │      • SKELETON   DEFINITIONS    │
    │      • TUTORIAL   DEFINITIONS    │
  ┌─┴──────────────────────────────────┴─┐
  │    DEVELOPING A COMPLETE APPLICATION  │
  │      • THE      DESIGN       PHASE    │
  │      • THE      DEVELOPMENT  PHASE    │
  │      • THE      TEST         PHASE    │
  │      • THE  IMPLEMENTATION   PHASE    │
  └───────────────────────────────────────┘

  ┌───────────────────────────────────────┐
  │              APPENDICES                │
  │      • ISPF/TSO INTERFACES             │
  │      • ISPF/CMS INTERFACES             │
  │      • ISPF/PLI INTERFACES             │
  │      • ISPF/COBOL INTERFACES           │
  │      • ISPF FULL SYNTAX SUMMARY        │
  │      • ISPF VARIABLES & COMMANDS       │
  └───────────────────────────────────────┘
```

At this point, you already have the knowledge to build the most important components of any dialog: the panels, the messages, and the functions that control the application (and build tables as well). In many applications, this will be better than 90 percent of your effort in developing a new dialog. There may be cases, however, when you will find that the usage of file skeletons will enhance considerably the simplicity of developing your application. This is what we will be discussing in this chapter.

As previously mentioned, file skeletons are preformatted files where the basic structure of the desired output is established, but the variable data has to be inserted on demand. This process, which is called *file tailoring*, enables you to construct job streams, create some simple output reports, and any other file that may be used for some other process.

You already know that you have up to four services to perform this file tailoring process:

- FTOPEN — Create an output file for file tailoring
- FTINCL — Include a skeleton to control output
- FTCLOSE — Close out the file tailoring process
- FTERASE — Erase the created output file

What you need to know now is how to construct a skeleton so that when you invoke the FTINCL service you will get the desired results.

File Specifications

The input file (the skeleton library member) consists of any number of logical records whose lengths may range from 80 to 255 bytes each and whose format may be of a fixed or variable length.

The output file may also contain records of fixed-length or variable-length format whose lengths range from 80 to 255 bytes each. The contents of this output file will be totally dependent on the contents of the input (skeleton) file as described in the next topic. In the event that an output record generated exceeds the specified length for that file, the file tailoring process terminates immediately.

SKELETON File

When fixed-length records are used, ISPF treats the last eight columns as a sequence field which has no significance to file tailoring. In addition, if the column preceding this sequence field should contain a special character ("?" by default), this record is understood to be continued onto the next one. Any other character in this column is treated as part of the input statement.

The skeleton file is understood to contain two types of statements:

- **Control Statements** — Those with a control character in column 1 (a ")" by default) immediately followed by a control word. Generally, these are the statements that inform the file tailoring process how to interpret the contents of this skeleton.
- **Data Statements** — All others (including those that begin with a ")" but are immediately followed by a blank). These are the statements that contain the actual data that is to appear in the output file, depending on the conditions established by the control statements.

Control Statements

These, then, are the statements that inform the file tailoring process how to interpret the contents of this skeleton. The complete list of control statements is:

-)DEFAULT   — Establish control characters
-)TB   — Establish tab positions
-)CM   — Comment line
-)BLANK   — Generate blank line(s)
-)SET   — Set values in variables
-)SEL   — Conditional selection of data
-)ENDSEL   — End conditional selection
-)DOT   — Do-loop for a table
-)ENDDOT   — End a do-loop for table
-)IM   — Imbed another skeleton

Each of these statements will be presented in detail in the following topics.

)DEFAULT — Establish Control Characters.   File tailoring is conditioned to recognize seven special characters that may be used for special functions such as tabbing data, indicating the continuation character, indicating conditional logic, etc. By default, these seven characters and their meanings are:

1.)   — The control statement identifier
2. &   — The variable symbol identifier
3. ?   — The continuation character
4. !   — The tab character
5. <   — The left character for conditional strings
6. | — The center character for conditional strings
7. >   — The right character for conditional strings

Obviously, if you should have these characters as part of the actual data, you would have to change something. ISPF allows you to change these defaults through the)DEFAULT statement whose syntax is:

```
⇨ )DEFAULT abcdefg


      where "abcdefg" are the characters to substitute
      for ")&?!<|>"
```

These new values become effective with the next statement read from the skeleton file. For example:

```
⇨ )DEFAULT $&?!<|>
⇨ $CM  This line is now read as a control statement (COMMENT)
⇨ $DEFAULT )&?!<|>
⇨ )CM  This line is now read as a control statement
```

)TB — Establish Tab Positions. In order to simplify positioning data at predetermined columns, ISPF allows you to use a tab character ("!" by default). When this character is found in a data statement, file tailoring will advance the data to the next tab position available.

These positions are established through the)TB statement as follows:

```
⇨ )TB position1 [ ... [ position16 ] ]
```

Up to sixteen different tab positions may be specified, indicating a value from 1 to the maximum logical record size being used. For example,

```
⇨ )TB   2 8 19 25 32 41
⇨ !&appl !&varname !&ptype !&dtype !&lenth !&descript
```

would cause the contents of &appl to begin in column 2, those of &varname to appear in column 8, etc.

)CM — Comment Line. This statement allows you to document your skeleton with comments to assist future readers of this skeleton. It will not be copied into the output file. Its syntax is simply:

```
⇨ )CM any comment desired
```

)BLANK — Generate Blank Line(s). This statement enables you to generate any number of blank lines into the output file. This might be useful when you are generating a report where you wish to separate various sections of that report. The syntax is:

```
)BLANK [nn]


where  nn is the number of blank lines needed (default 1)
```

The following example shows a portion of a report skeleton that contains carriage control characters in column 1 of each data statement. However, since each report detail line will be single-spaced except for the one immediately following the page headings, an extra blank line will be generated in this case:

```
)CM            ------------------------------- start heading routine
1DDS TABLE ENTRIES FOR: APPL=&sappl.,PTYPE=&spool.,DTYPE=&sdata.
0APPL   VARIABLE   POOL    DATA    FIELD      FIELD DESC AND COMMENTS
  ID      NAME     TYPE    TYPE    LENGTH
)BLANK
```

)SET — Set Values in Variables.

This statement allows you to assign the results of some simple arithmetic expressions to a variable. The only operations allowed are "+" or "-". The syntax is:

```
)SET vname = op1 [ ± op2 [ ± ... [ ± op15 ] ] ]


where "op1" ... "op15" may be variables or constants
  and ± may be "+" or "-"
```

For example:

```
)SET LINES = 5
...
)SET LINES = &LINES + 1
```

)SEL +)ENDSEL — Conditional Selection of Data. This pair of statements allows you to either process or skip sections of the skeleton depending on the outcome of specified conditions. The syntax is:

```
⟳ )SEL exp1 [ op exp2 [ ... [ op exp8 ] ] ]

⟳ ... ...

⟳ )ENDSEL


    where "exp" may be a logical expression
      and "op"  may be a logical condition: "|" (OR), "&&" (AND)


    further, "logical expression" may be: operand operator operand
    where  "operator" may be: NL | LT | LE | EQ | NE | GE | GT | NG
                          or: ¬< | <  | <= | =  | ¬= | >= | >  | ¬>
```

This may appear complicated, but it really isn't. To illustrate, consider the following example:

```
)SEL &LINES > 50
1DDS TABLE ENTRIES FOR: APPL=&sappl.,PTYPE=&spool.,DTYPE=&sdata.
0APPL  VARIABLE  POOL   DATA   FIELD     FIELD DESC AND COMMENTS
  ID     NAME    TYPE   TYPE   LENGTH
)BLANK
)SET LINES = 5
)ENDSEL
```

In this example, the entire sequence forms one select group that will be executed if the contents of &LINES should be greater than 50; if not, every statement from this)SEL up to its corresponding)ENDSEL will be skipped.

It is possible to "nest" (totally contain) one)SEL within other)SEL — *up to eight levels deep.* In such cases, you will be performing the equivalent of "AND" logic for each of the inner)SEL groups. Each)SEL group must be terminated with a corresponding)ENDSEL which is matched in reverse sequence to the)SEL statement. Example:

```
)SEL     &sappl = *         |      &sappl = &appl
)SEL     &spool = *         |      &spool = &ptype
   &appl !&varname !&ptype !&dtype !&lenth !&descript
)SET LINES = &LINES + 1
)ENDSEL
)ENDSEL
```

In this case, we have a)SEL group nested in another)SEL group where the total meaning is: "IF ((*&sappl*=* OR *&sappl=&appl*) AND (*&spool*=* OR *&spool=&ptype*)) THEN . . ." execute the next statement(s) until their)ENDSELs are detected.

)DOT +)ENDDOT — Do-loop for a Table. This pair of statements allows you to repeat a given process for as many times as there are rows in a particular table. The syntax is:

```
⇨  )DOT &tablename
⇨  ...
⇨  )ENDDOT
```

Many functions are performed automatically with this particular group. The table will be open (if not already so), the next row will be fetched and the contents stored into dialog variables, any statements within this group are then executed, and the process is repeated until no more rows remain to be processed.

The following illustrates the writing into the output file of every row in a table:

```
)TB   2  8  19  25  32  41
)DOT &table
!&appl !&varname !&ptype !&dtype !&lenth !&descript
)ENDDOT
```

For each row in &*table*, one output line (in this example) would be generated where the identified fields would be positioned based on the tabs given —)TB.

)IM — Imbed Another Skeleton. It is also possible for one skeleton to have other skeletons imbedded which, in turn, may still have others imbedded — *up to three levels deep*. As a skeleton is imbedded, it is treated as if it actually resided where the)IM statement is found. The syntax for this statement is:

```
⇨ )IM skeleton [NT] [OPT]
```

The NT parameter indicates that this skeleton is not to undergo file tailoring; instead, it is to be copied to the output file in its entirety regardless of the logic it contains.

The OPT parameter indicates that this may be optional, i.e., if the skeleton is found then proceed, but if not, do not raise an error condition.

Suppose, for example, that you had a variety of small job-stream skeletons that you could use to compile and/or link edit some program. Suppose, also, that you had a dialog which, based on user parameters, developed the exact job stream required. The overall logic for these skeletons might be:

```
☞  ...
☞  )SEL  &compile = YES
☞  )IM   COMPILE
☞  )ENDSEL
☞  )SEL  &link    = YES
☞  )IM   LINKEDIT
☞  )ENDSEL
☞  ...
```

Data Statements

Generally, these statements are simply copied into the output file after variable substitution and tab positioning (if any). If we should end up with a totally blank record, it will be ignored and will not be written to the output file.

It is possible to specify some additional logic within these data statements as it relates to variable substitution. For example, we can indicate that if a particular variable should be null, we wish to use some other variable. The format for this would be:

```
... [text]  ...  <&varname | string>  ...  [text]  ...
```

To illustrate, assume that we wanted to show either the contents of &descript or the string "-- NONE --" if &descript should have a null value. We would code:

```
... [text]  ...  <&descript |-- NONE -->  ...  [text]  ...
```

The meaning here would be: copy the data statement to the output file observing any variable substitution desired up to the point of replacing &descript. At this point, if this field should have a value, then use it, but if it should be null, then use the second string "-- NONE --" instead. Continue with the remainder of the statement.

Please note that the second string could be a variable as well. You will also note that the conditional string was not enclosed in quotes. This is because anything entered on a data statement is treated as data *except* for the characters: &, !, <, |, >.

The reason for this should be obvious: these are the control characters that instruct ISPF on how to interpret and substitute variables in your data statement. If you should need to code any of these as text, then you have a choice: either (1) you can code a)DEFAULT statement with new symbols, or (2) you can use two consecutive control characters for each one needed as text.

For example, assuming that &name contained "test," and &descript was null, the following statements

```
)TB 10 20
 &name.&& !<&descript |NONE!!> !Need <<&&||&&>>
```

would give

```
test&    NONE!    Need <&|&>
```

Comprehensive Example

Let us assume that we wish to produce a listing that shows the contents of the table DDST000 already illustrated in previous chapters (see Figure 5-2). As we did before, we wish to give the user the

```
)ATTR DEFAULT(%+_)
        $ TYPE(INPUT)  INTENS(HIGH)  CAPS(ON)  JUST(LEFT)   PAD(_)

)BODY
%----------------- DDS FILE TAILORING OPTIONS -----------------
%COMMAND ===>_ZCMD
%
+   INDICATE FIELDS TO MATCH  (NO ENTRY = SELECT ALL)
+
+   APPLICATION ID . . .$z   +        Maximum 4 alphanumeric chars
+   POOL TYPE. . . . . .$z+           P=Prof,S=Shared,F=Funct,N=N/A
+   DATA TYPE. . . . . .$z   +        CHAR,NUMER,PANEL,MSG,CMS,etc.
+

)INIT
  .HELP = DDSH120
  .ZVARS = '(sappl spool sdata)'
  &sappl = &appl

)PROC
   VER (&sappl, NAME)
   VER (&spool, LIST, P,S,F,N)
   VER (&svarn, ALPHA)
   IF  (&sappl = '')  &sappl = *
   IF  (&spool = '')  &spool = *
   IF  (&sdata = '')  &sdata = *

)END
```

Figure 6-1   Panel DDSP120A.

ability to limit the output based on application name and/or data type class and/or pool type code. We will need a data entry panel as shown in Figure 6-1.

Once we know the selection parameters, we then want to process the table and produce the desired listing using a skeleton as in Figure 6-2.

```
)DEFAULT   )&?!<|>
)TB   2 8 19 25 32 41
)SET  LINES = 255
)CM ---------------------------- start loop for all table rows
)DOT &table
)CM   ---------------------------- start row selection process
)SEL    &sappl = *       |      &sappl = &appl
)SEL    &spool = *       |      &spool = &ptype
)SEL    &sdata = *       |    &sdata = &dtype
)CM     - row selected if all 3 true -
)SEL         &LINES > 50
)CM     ----------------------------- start heading routine
1DDS TABLE ENTRIES FOR: APPL=&sappl.,PTYPE=&spool.,DTYPE=&sdata.
0APPL   VARIABLE  POOL   DATA   FIELD    FIELD DESC AND COMMENTS
   ID     NAME    TYPE   TYPE   LENGTH
)BLANK
)SET LINES = 5
)CM           ----------- end heading routine/resume row processing
)ENDSEL
   &appl !&varname !&ptype !&dtype !&lenth !&descript
)SET LINES = &LINES + 1
)ENDSEL
)ENDSEL
)ENDSEL
)CM    --------------------------------- end selection process
)ENDDOT
)CM --------------------------------- end loop for table rows
```

Figure 6-2   Skeleton DDSS120.

Now, all that is left is to develop a function that "connects" these various components as follows:

1. Display the selection options panel (DDSP120A).
2. Open the file tailoring output file (ISPFILE).
3. Include the skeleton to control output (DDSS120).
4. Close the file tailoring output file.
5. Set up completion message (DDSM120A).
6. Release output file allocation and exit.

```
PROC      0
          CONTROL    NOLIST    NOCONLIST NOMSG NOFLUSH
          ISPEXEC    CONTROL   ERRORS    RETURN
          /*-----------------------------------------------*/
          SET        TABLE =   DDST000
          SET        SKEL  =   DDSS120
          SET        DSN   =   '&SYSUID..DDS.FTOUTPUT'
          ISPEXEC    DISPLAY   PANEL(DDSP120A)
          IF         &LASTCC   ¬= 0      THEN   EXIT
          FREE       FI(ISPFILE)
          ALLOCATE   FI(ISPFILE) DA(&DSN.)  OLD
          ISPEXEC    FTOPEN
          IF         &LASTCC   ¬= 0      THEN   GOTO   NOFTOPEN
          ISPEXEC    FTINCL    &SKEL
          IF         &LASTCC   ¬= 0      THEN   GOTO   NOFTINCL
          ISPEXEC    FTCLOSE
          IF         &LASTCC   ¬= 0      THEN   GOTO   NOFTCLSE
          ISPEXEC    SETMSG    MSG(DDSM120A)
          GOTO       EXIT
          /*-----------------------------------------------*/
NOFTOPEN:ISPEXEC     SETMSG    MSG(DDSM120B)
          GOTO       EXIT
NOFTINCL:ISPEXEC     SETMSG    MSG(DDSM120C)
          ISPEXEC    FTCLOSE
          GOTO       EXIT
NOFTCLSE:ISPEXEC     SETMSG    MSG(DDSM120D)
EXIT:     FREE       FI(ISPFILE)
          EXIT
          END
```

Figure 6-3   Command DDSC120.

Figure 6-3 shows the command procedure to perform all our needed processes:

This particular example has already been broadly explained in Chapter 1. In addition, each segment of this function was used to illustrate the various file tailoring service calls involved. Consequently, there is no point in repeating a full explanation of this function.

The result from this process would be a file containing the desired report in a format similar to the one in Figure 6-4.

Please note that the file was generated with ANSI (American National Standards Institute) carriage control characters in position 1

```
1DDS TABLE ENTRIES FOR:   APPL=*,POOLTYPE=*,DATATYPE=*
0APPL  VARIABLE  POOL   DATA   FIELD  FIELD DESCRIPTION AND COMMENTS
   ID    NAME    TYPE   TYPE   LENGTH


AAA
AAA    TEST       F    CHAR    0     TESTING MULTIPLE APPLICATIONS
DDS
DDS    ACCT       P    CHAR   15     USER ACCOUNT DATA FOR JOB STMT
DDS    APPL       P    CHAR    4     APPLICATION IDENTIFICATION
DDS    CLASS      P    CHAR    1     PREFERRED OUTPUT CLASS ON JOBS
DDS    CPY        F    NUMER   3     NUMBER OF COPIES TO PRINT
...    ...
...    ...      (50 lines per page)
...    ...
1DDS TABLE ENTRIES FOR:   APPL=*,POOLTYPE=*,DATATYPE=*
0APPL  VARIABLE  POOL   DATA   FIELD   FIELD DESCRIPTION AND COMMENTS
   ID    NAME    TYPE   TYPE   LENGTH

DDS    ROOM       P    CHAR    8     USER ROOM/OFFICE NBR FOR JOBS
DDS    SAPPL      F    CHAR    4     SELECTED APPLICATION ID OR *
DDS    SDATA      F    CHAR    5     SELECTED DATA TYPE OR *
DDS    SKEL       F    CHAR    8     NAME OF SKELETON IN A FUNCTION
DDS    SPOOL      F    CHAR    1     SELECTED POOL TYPE OR *
DDS    TABLE      F    CHAR    8     NAME OF TABLE IN THIS FUNCTION
DDS    UNAME      P    CHAR    8     USER'S LAST NAME FOR JOB STMT
DDS    VARNAME    F    CHAR    8     FIELD NAME WITHIN APPLICATION
...    ...
...    ...
```

Figure 6-4   Output Generated through DDSS120 Skeleton.

of each line, so that when we print this later we will have the correct vertical spacing. Their meanings are:

- 1 — New page
- + — No spacing (overprint)
-   — Single spacing
- 0 — Double spacing
- - — Triple spacing
- etc.

Summary

It has been established that there are four Dialog Management services connected with file tailoring, which are:

- **FTOPEN** — Create an output file for file tailoring
- **FTINCL** — Include a skeleton to control output
- **FTCLOSE** — Close out the file tailoring process
- **FTERASE** — Erase the created output file

We then saw that FTINCL causes the inclusion and processing of a file skeleton, which is made up of two classes of statements:

- **Control statements** — Control skeleton process logic
- **Data statements** — Data for output generation

We saw that there are seven types of control statements:

- **)DEFAULT** — Establish control characters
- **)TB** — Establish tab positions
- **)CM** — Comment line
- **)BLANK** — Generate blank line(s)
- **)SET** — Set values in variables
- **)SEL** — Conditional selection of data
- **)ENDSEL** — End conditional selection
- **)DOT** — Do-loop for a table
- **)ENDDOT** — End a do-loop for table
- **)IM** — Imbed another skeleton

7

Tutorial Definitions

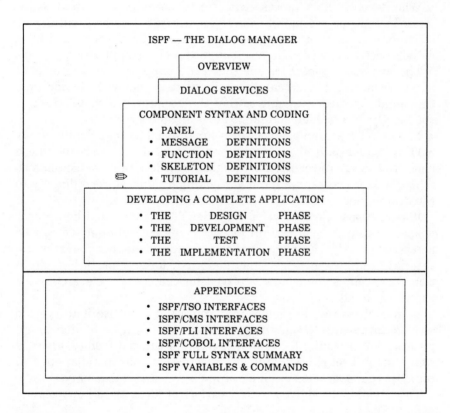

ISPF — THE DIALOG MANAGER

OVERVIEW

DIALOG SERVICES

COMPONENT SYNTAX AND CODING
- PANEL   DEFINITIONS
- MESSAGE   DEFINITIONS
- FUNCTION   DEFINITIONS
- SKELETON   DEFINITIONS
- TUTORIAL   DEFINITIONS

DEVELOPING A COMPLETE APPLICATION
- THE   DESIGN   PHASE
- THE   DEVELOPMENT PHASE
- THE   TEST   PHASE
- THE IMPLEMENTATION PHASE

APPENDICES
- ISPF/TSO INTERFACES
- ISPF/CMS INTERFACES
- ISPF/PLI INTERFACES
- ISPF/COBOL INTERFACES
- ISPF FULL SYNTAX SUMMARY
- ISPF VARIABLES & COMMANDS

TUTORIAL Concepts

You now have the basic tools with which to construct an interactive application. The only element left is to determine what type of assistance (if any) the users might need as they take advantage of your new application.

Clearly, this is not an absolute requirement for an application to function properly. As a matter of fact, when the application is fairly simple, you may not even take time to develop any help panels.

For more complex dialogs, however, it is highly recommended that tutorials be provided along the way, particularly for the more complicated functions. Not only will this availability make the application self-teaching and user-friendly, but it will also avoid much inconvenience and possible interruptions to answer questions.

Whether this help process consists of nothing more than a few "loose" panels or a comprehensively structured document with table of contents, "chapters," indices, etc., is entirely up to you and is usually dictated by the size and complexity of the application.

The important aspect here is that ISPF supports the development of a tutorial facility that can be as complete as you wish. In addition, commands are also available so that the user can "navigate" through the facility in a fashion similar to accessing a book.

You can, for example, structure your tutorial so that the user may read it sequentially from end to end just as if you were reading a book from cover to cover. You can also provide a table of contents so that the user can examine the various topics and proceed directly to the desired one.

It is also possible to develop an index facility so that when a user wishes to search on a certain keyword, the relevant section can be accessed quickly. Finally, you can structure your application-to-tutorial interfaces in such a manner that, for any particular situation, the user is immediately placed on the "page" relevant to the process at hand.

So flexible is this ISPF tool that you could even use it to provide on-line documents for anything that may not even be related to applications. You could, for example, create a tutorial facility which is really the full set of standards and practices at your installation. You could, perhaps, develop on-line courses also using this facility.

This should provide you with a variety of ideas as to how you can exploit this very interesting facet of ISPF.

COMMAND	ABV	FUNCTION	VARIABLE	LOCATION
HELP	n/a	Enter tutorial	.HELP	)INIT, etc.
TOP INDEX	T I	Table of contents Index	&ZHTOP &ZHINDEX	)INIT)INIT
UP SKIP	U S	Parent topic Next topic	&ZUP n/a	)PROC (automatic)
enter BACK	n/a B	Next page Previous page	&ZCONT n/a	)PROC (automatic)

Figure 7-1   Tutorial Commands and Variables.

TUTORIAL Commands and Variables

To assist the user in navigating through a tutorial, ISPF provides a series of commands which, when coupled with properly placed system variables, will achieve the desired effect. The full list of commands, their abbreviations and their corresponding variables is shown in Figure 7-1.

Each of these commands and variables will be discussed in detail in the following sections. In the meantime, however, please refer to Figure 7-2 for a broad overview of the meaning and usage of these commands in relation to a tutorial structure.

The HELP Command and .HELP Variable

This is the command that triggers the tutorial process. It is usually activated by pressing the PF key which has been equated to this string — normally PF1 or PF13. Once the tutorial mode is entered, all commands listed become active.

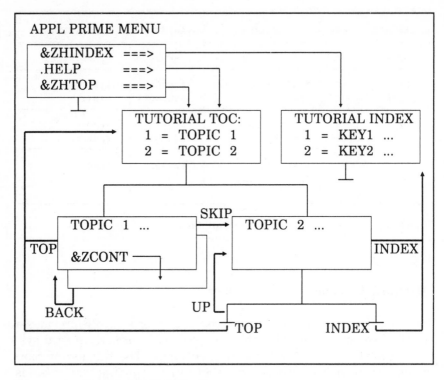

Figure 7-2   Structured HELP Facility.

The first concern for the tutorial processor is to determine which help panel to display. This value is generally set in the)INIT section of the menu, data entry, or table display panel that was presented to the user just before HELP was requested. That is accomplished by simply assigning a panel name to the control variable ".HELP". It is also possible to set (or reset) this value in the)PROC or)REINIT section.

Figure 7-3 shows a selection panel being associated with the help panel named DDSH100. If the user should request HELP at the time that panel is displayed, it would be suspended while the tutorial facility displays panel DDSH100 and proceeds from there. Eventually, the user would press END, the tutorial would terminate, and ISPF would return to the terminal with the suspended panel back on the screen.

```
)BODY
%---------------- DDS PRIMARY OPTION MENU  ------------------
%SELECTION ===>_ZCMD
+
+  ... ... ...


)INIT
  &ZHTOP    = DDSH000      /* Tutorial Table of Contents */
  .HELP     = DDSH100      /* HELP panel for this menu   */
  &ZHINDEX  = DDSH999      /* Tutorial Index "pages"     */


)PROC
  ... ... ...
  ... ... ...
)END
```

Figure 7-3 Identifying HELP Panels.

The one other place where a help panel may also be designated is in a message definition. This case would be more appropriate for help topics that are rather lengthy. In this case, instead of simply showing the user the first panel for the long topic in question until the appropriate "page" is found, it would be more helpful to point to the relevant page directly, thus saving the user valuable time.

If the tutorial is properly designed, pointing directly to a small section of a large topic would not preclude the user from "leafing" through adjacent pages of a given topic. All of this is controlled with the placement of the correct tutorial variables in the various panels.

If the tutorial is defined as a hierarchical structure, you will probably want to provide panels where a list of selections is given. This is accomplished by assigning values to the system variable &ZSEL.

Although this concept is similar to that already defined for the application menus, the syntax is much simpler:

```
☞ &ZSEL = [*]panelid
```

```
)BODY
 %TUTORIAL ---------- DATA DICTIONARY SYSTEM ----------- TUTORIAL
 %SELECTION ===>_ZCMD                                   +
 %
 %              -------------------------------------
                |     TABLE OF CONTENTS             |
                -------------------------------------
 + ... ... ...
 + ... ... ...

       The following are the available topics:

       %0+ GENERAL INFO        General system description
       %1+ UPDATE TABLE        Update/create master dictionary
       %2+ LIST   TABLE        List full dictionary or a subset
       %3+ VIEW   OUTPUT       View listing at the terminal
       %4+ PRINT OUTPUT        Send listing to the printer


 )PROC
       &ZSEL = TRANS (&ZCMD
                     0, DDSH100
                     1,*DDSH110
                     2,*DDSH120
                     3,*DDSH130
                     4,*DDSH140
                     *,'?')
 )END
```

Figure 7-4   HELP Selection Panels.

You will note that the keyword PANEL is omitted in this case because of the context of this variable. Since we are in tutorial mode, the only process involved is to display panels; consequently, it would be redundant to continually enter that keyword.

The option "*" indicates whether selection of this item is to be automatic or not. The absence of an "*" indicates automatic topic selection; its presence indicates that the item will be selected only if explicitly requested by the end-user (see Figure 7-4).

The example illustrates that, although one normally would have to enter a 0 in order to see panel DDSH100, in this case selection of

```
)BODY
%TUTORIAL ---------- DATA DICTIONARY SYSTEM ---------- TUTORIAL
%SELECTION ===>_ZCMD                                      +
%
+ ... ... ...


The following topics may be viewed in sequence or by selection:

    %1+ UPDATE TABLE        Update/create master dictionary
    %2+ LIST   TABLE        List full dictionary or a subset
    %3+ VIEW   OUTPUT       View listing at the terminal
    %4+ PRINT OUTPUT        Send listing to the printer
```
```
)PROC
      &ZUP  = DDSH000
      &ZSEL = TRANS (&ZCMD
             1,DDSH110
             2,DDSH120
             3,DDSH130
             4,DDSH140
             *,'?')
)END
```

Figure 7-5   Automatic Topic Selection.

this item will be automatic by simply pressing the ENTER key. All the other items, however, must be requested by entering the appropriate code.

NOTE: In this particular application, DDSH100 (Figure 7-5) also has a similar list of items (1–4) where the selection is automatic. Thus, the user has a choice of entering the needed topic directly from DDSH000, or from DDSH100. This will control the serial presentation to the user if the ENTER key is continually pressed — without repeating any topics.

The TOP Command and &ZHTOP Variable

This command takes you to the table of contents (if any) of a structured tutorial, provided that &ZHTOP has been given a value.

Generally, this value is assigned once in the)INIT section of the application primary option menu. Once this is done (and unless it is changed), ISPF will know that any TOP (T) command is to proceed to that panel. Figure 7-3 also illustrates this assignment.

The INDEX Command and &ZHINDEX Variable

This command takes you to the index (if any) of a structured tutorial provided that &ZHINDEX has been given a value. Like &ZHTOP, &ZHINDEX is normally assigned a value in the)INIT section of the application primary option menu. Thereafter, ISPF will know that the INDEX (I) command is to proceed to that panel.

The same Figure 7-3 illustrates this assignment as well.

NOTE: Coding "&ZIND = YES" in the)PROC section of a tutorial panel triggers *index mode* processing. While in index mode, entering any command abbreviation will not be recognized, because a single letter is generally understood to be the index letter desired. Consequently, the full command must be entered.

The UP Command and &ZUP Variable

As you proceed down the established hierarchy, you may wish to "pop" back up to the last tutorial selection panel. This is where the UP (U) command and the &ZUP variable come into play.

It is not imperative that you assign a value to &ZUP. This is actually unnecessary for cases where the tutorial process is progressing through the hierarchy, because ISPF remembers the path taken. There may be cases, however, where the application panel may have entered a help panel deep in the hierarchy directly. In this situation, ISPF does not know which is the parent topic unless &ZUP is set. If it isn't, ISPF will use the &ZHTOP value as the parent topic.

To set &ZUP, simply code an assignment statement in the)PROC section of the help panel in question as shown in Figure 7-6.

The SKIP Command

You may have chosen a topic from the last tutorial selection panel which you have decided not to continue. Of course, you could always

```
)BODY
%TUTORIAL ----------  DATA DICTIONARY SYSTEM  ----------- TUTORIAL
%SELECTION ===>_ZCMD                                      +
%
%                 ------------------------------------
                  |        LIST DICTIONARY           |
                  ------------------------------------
+
This option allows a developer to list the contents of the
dictionary either for more extensive browsing capabilities
or for hard-copy print, or both.

The dictionary can be processed in its entirety, or it may be
selected by%(1)+application identifier,%(2)+by variable pool type,
and/or%(3)+by data type class.  These three entries may be used in
any combination to provide a very selective listing of the desired
items.

For a detailed explanation of each of the three entries, press the
ENTER key.

)PROC
      &ZUP    = DDSH100       /* higher selection panel */
      &ZCONT = DDSH120A       /* continuation panel */
)END
```

Figure 7-6   Identifying Parent Topics and Continuations.

enter the UP (U) command and make the other selection. But, if you already know that you want to proceed to the next selection available, entering the SKIP (S) command will have the same effect.

Determining the next path topic is an automatic process performed by ISPF as you travel "down" the hierarchy. You do not need to set any variables. However, if you have made a direct entry from an application panel to a tutorial panel deep in the hierarchy, entering the SKIP (S) command is the same as entering UP (U).

The ENTER Key and &ZCONT Variable

For lengthy tutorials, you will need more than one panel to explain a given topic. To inform ISPF that the panel is continued onto another one, simply assign the name of that continuation panel into the variable &ZCONT in the)PROC section of the panel to be continued. Once this is done, the user can proceed by simply pressing the ENTER key.

Figure 7-6 also illustrates the usage of this variable. If a panel is not continued, then obviously &ZCONT should not be assigned a value. In that case, even if the user should press the ENTER key, ISPF will automatically bring the user "up" to the next higher panel that ISPF knows (through &ZUP or &ZHTOP).

The BACK Command

This command simply indicates that you wish to review the panel previously displayed (regardless of the logical relationship to the one presently on the screen). This process is an automatic feature of the tutorial facility and does not depend on the settings of any variables.

If there is no previous panel, requesting BACK (B) will simply leave you on the current panel.

Comprehensive Examples

To "thread" a complete structure, let us see how we would code a series of panels that integrate all these concepts just discussed.

The following six figures will show how to:

• develop a table of contents
• code a second-level selection panel
• provide a short topic panel
• use a longer topic needing continuation
• create a general index panel
• utilize a detailed index panel

```
)BODY
%TUTORIAL ---------- DATA DICTIONARY SYSTEM ----------- TUTORIAL
%SELECTION ===>_ZCMD                                        +
%
%            ------------------------------------
             |       TABLE OF CONTENTS          |
             ------------------------------------

You may "navigate" throughout this tutorial facility as if it were
a normal book, i.e., you may proceed sequentially through each of
the topics offered, or you may go directly to the desired one
shown based on the one-character designators associated with each
entry.

Once in a topic, you may go from one "page" to the next (if any)
by pressing the%ENTER+key, you may back up with the%B(ack)+command,
you may skip to the next topic with the%S(kip)+command, you may go
up to the higher topic with the%U(p)+command, or you may go to the
index (the%I(ndex)+command) or the table of contents (the%T(op)+
command).

The following are the available topics:

    %0+ GENERAL INFO      General system description
    %1+ UPDATE TABLE      Update/create master dictionary
    %2+ LIST  TABLE       List full dictionary or a subset
    %3+ VIEW  OUTPUT      View listing at the terminal
    %4+ PRINT OUTPUT      Send listing to the printer

)PROC
       &ZSEL = TRANS (&ZCMD
                      0, DDSH100
                      1,*DDSH110
                      2,*DDSH120
                      3,*DDSH130
                      4,*DDSH140
                      *,'?')
)END
```

Figure 7-7   The Tutorial Table of Contents.

```
)BODY
%TUTORIAL ---------- DATA DICTIONARY SYSTEM ----------- TUTORIAL
%SELECTION ===>_ZCMD                                           +
%
+ ... ... ...

The following topics may be viewed in sequence or by selection:

    %1+ UPDATE TABLE         Update/create master dictionary
    %2+ LIST   TABLE         List full dictionary or a subset
    %3+ VIEW   OUTPUT        View listing at the terminal
    %4+ PRINT OUTPUT         Send listing to the printer


)PROC
     &ZUP  = DDSH000
     &ZSEL = TRANS (&ZCMD
                 1,DDSH110
                 2,DDSH120
                 3,DDSH130
                 4,DDSH140
                 *,'?')
)END
```

Figure 7-8   A General Selection Panel.

```
)BODY
%TUTORIAL ---------- DATA DICTIONARY SYSTEM ----------- TUTORIAL
%SELECTION ===>_ZCMD                                           +
%
 ... ...


)PROC
     &ZUP  =  DDSH110
)END
```

Figure 7-9   A Topic without Continuation.

```
)BODY
%TUTORIAL ---------- DATA DICTIONARY SYSTEM ----------- TUTORIAL
%SELECTION ===>_ZCMD                                       +
%
 ... ... ...
For a detailed explanation of each of the three entries, press the
ENTER key.
```

```
)PROC
      &ZUP   = DDSH100      /* higher selection panel */
      &ZCONT = DDSH120A     /* continuation panel */
)END
```

Figure 7-10   A Longer Topic with Continuation.

```
)BODY
%TUTORIAL ---------- DATA DICTIONARY SYSTEM ----------- TUTORIAL
%COMMAND ===>_ZCMD                                        +
%
%          ------------------------------------
           |              INDEX               |
           ------------------------------------
+
To use the index, enter the first letter of the topic of interest.
The index page containing subjects starting with that letter is
displayed.  While on an index page, any subject can be selected by
entering the option code preceding that selection.

The index pages are presented in sequence if you press the ENTER
key.  You can also access any index page directly by simply typing
the desired letter.
```

```
)PROC
      &ZIND = YES                    /* THIS IS AN INDEX PANEL */
      &ZCMD = TRUNC (&ZCMD,1)
      VER(&ZCMD, ALPHA)
      IF (&ZCMD ¬= ' ') &ZSEL  = DDSH999&ZCMD
      IF (&ZCMD  = ' ') &ZCONT = DDSH999A
)END
```

Figure 7-11   A General Index Panel.

```
)BODY
%TUTORIAL ---------- DATA DICTIONARY SYSTEM ----------- TUTORIAL
%COMMAND ===>_ZCMD                                          +
%
%              ------------------------------------
               |           INDEX:  'A'            |
               ------------------------------------
+
+To select a topic, enter code (letter and number) in cmd fld:
+
%A1 +-                                    %A16+-
%A2 +-ACCOUNTING                          %A17+-
%A3 +-                                    %A18+-
%A4 +-ACTION                              %A19+-
%A5 +-                                    %A20+-
%A6 +-ADD                                 %A21+-
%A7 +-                                    %A22+-
%A8 +-ANALYZE (Display)                   %A23+-
%A9 +-ANALYZE (Listing)                   %A24+-
%A10+-                                    %A25+-
%A11+-APPLICATION                         %A26+-
   ... ...                                %A27+-
```

```
)PROC
      &ZIND = YES                    /* THIS IS AN INDEX PANEL */
      &ZSEL = TRANS(&ZCMD
                  A2,*DDSH140
                  A4,*DDSH110C
                  A6,*DDSH110B
                  A8,*DDSH110A
                  A9,*DDSH120A
                  A11,*DDSH110A
                  )
      IF  (&ZSEL  = ' ')
      &ZCMD = TRUNC(&ZCMD,1)
      IF (&ZCMD ¬= ' ')          &ZSEL  = DDSH999&ZCMD
      IF (&ZCMD  = ' ')          &ZCONT = DDSH999B
)END
```

Figure 7-12   Index Panel for Letter A.

Summary

We have now seen how flexible and simple it is to use the ISPF tutorial. It can be used for a variety of items ranging from simple isolated panels to comprehensive documents fully structured.

We also saw that navigation through the tutorial is enhanced with the use of several commands, which are:

- **HELP**   — Enter tutorial
- **TOP** (T)   — Table of contents
- **INDEX** (I)   — Index
- **UP** (U)   — Parent topic
- **SKIP** (S)   — Next topic
- **enter**   — Next page
- **BACK** (B)   — Previous page

And we saw that these commands work closely with the setting of system and control variables, which are:

- **.HELP**   — Identify associated help panel
- **&ZHTOP**   — Identify tutorial table of contents
- **&ZHINDEX**   — Identify tutorial index entry
- **&ZUP**   — Identify parent topic
- **&ZCONT**   — Identify continuation panel
- **&ZIND**   — Identify current panel as index item

Chapter

8

Designing a New Application

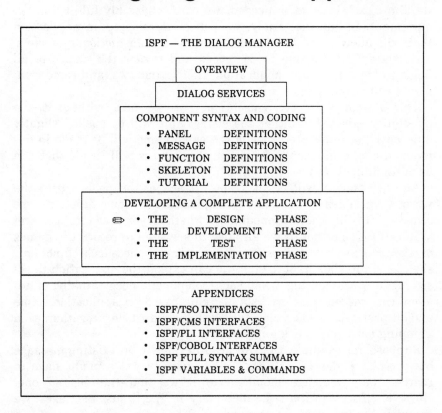

```
ISPF — THE DIALOG MANAGER

    OVERVIEW

   DIALOG SERVICES

COMPONENT SYNTAX AND CODING
  • PANEL      DEFINITIONS
  • MESSAGE    DEFINITIONS
  • FUNCTION   DEFINITIONS
  • SKELETON   DEFINITIONS
  • TUTORIAL   DEFINITIONS

DEVELOPING A COMPLETE APPLICATION
  • THE      DESIGN       PHASE
  • THE      DEVELOPMENT  PHASE
  • THE      TEST         PHASE
  • THE      IMPLEMENTATION PHASE

      APPENDICES
  • ISPF/TSO INTERFACES
  • ISPF/CMS INTERFACES
  • ISPF/PLI INTERFACES
  • ISPF/COBOL INTERFACES
  • ISPF FULL SYNTAX SUMMARY
  • ISPF VARIABLES & COMMANDS
```

We now have all the theoretical knowledge needed to build any of the ISPF dialog components. We should, therefore, be able to develop any interactive application by applying this knowledge.

To assist you in getting started, we will be stepping through the various phases involved in designing, developing, testing, and implementing a complete application. You can then follow these exact steps to develop any other application of your own.

Defining a New Application

The first step is to define the purpose for the new application. Unless we know exactly what is needed, we cannot possibly fulfill that requirement. In our case study, we will be developing an application that will allow us to build and maintain a *data dictionary system*. This system will enable us to record and review the names of all fields to be used in any application, their attributes, and some comments as to their usage.

This system will serve a useful purpose because, without it, the possibility exists that either the same name will be spelled slightly differently, or duplicate usage of the same name will be made in different dialog components. In either case, errors will result that can be quite difficult to trace.

Another benefit will be in keeping track of the pools where the various variables will reside. Then, as the various functions are coded, you will know immediately whether you need to perform VGETs/VPUTs or not. If we also use this system to record the names of the components themselves (i.e., panels, messages, functions, skeletons, tutorials, tables, etc.), we can exploit the application to assist us in documenting what each component does. Finally, if we allow the system to select lists of items based on application name and/or pool type and/or element class, we can bring together each grouping for a very quick analysis.

Suppose, for example, that we need to refer to an existing message but forgot its identifier. Without this dictionary, we might have to search many message members until we find the desired one. However, if we can limit the dictionary listing to just messages, we can view the complete list at a glance.

As long as we are at it, let us also make it possible to provide for the ability to extract hardcopy listings from this dictionary.

Developing the Structure

Once the needed processes have been defined, the next step is to develop a hierarchical structure that will show how our new application will work. Based on the requirements given earlier, we could structure our Data Dictionary System (DDS) as shown in Figure 8-1.

Naming the Components

The next step is to begin assigning names to the components that will be performing the necessary processes for our application. The more names we develop and the more common the libraries for our components, the more careful we will have to be with the selected identifiers. Failure to do so may destroy similarly named items in those libraries.

Many schemes can be developed to generate unique identifiers for each component. As a matter of fact, some installations may already have very rigid standards that developers may have to follow. However, if none exist, you may consider the one that I found to work very well for me.

Each component name is made up of four parts — *xxxy999z*:

• *xxx* — This is a three-letter designator for the application being developed. Any three-letter code not yet in use will immediately isolate any names that we develop from those that any other application may have. Two designators that should *never* be used are: ISP and ISR. These prefixes represent ISPF and PDF components, respectively, which trigger special handling within ISPF.
• *y* — This is a one-letter designator for the type of component that we are naming. Although any code could be used, you may wish to consider the following set:

P	= Panels	S	= Skeletons
M	= Messages	T	= Tables
C	= Command procedures	O	= File tailoring output
G	= Programs	H	= Help panels (tutorials)

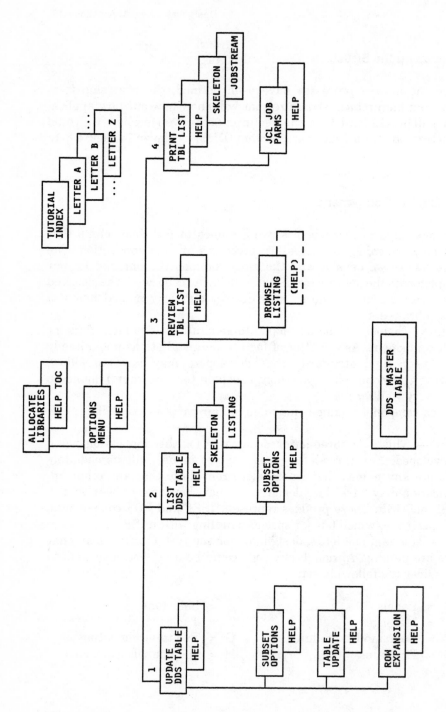

Figure 8-1 The DDS Processes.

• 999 — This is a three-digit number that automatically indicates the logical placement within the hierarchical structure. Each digit represents a logical level in the structure, thus allowing us to go as far as four levels deep. (Deeper nesting is not recommended.) To illustrate, we could number our components as follows:

- Level 0 — 000
- Level 1 — *1*00, 200, 300, 400, etc. (option 1, 2, 3,...)
- Level 2 — *11*0, 120, 130, 140, etc. (option 1.1, 1.2,...)
- Level 3 — *111*, 112, 113, 114, etc. (option 1.1.1,...)

• *z* — This is a suffix for multiple items within the same function and at the same level. For example, DDSP110A, DDSP110B, DDSP110C could be three different panels being driven by the function DDSC110.

To apply this naming process to the structure that we defined before, please refer to Figure 8-2.

Developing a Data Dictionary

Once we decide what to call each of our application components, we should begin to construct a data dictionary. This process may be as informal as simply writing those names on a piece of paper, or they may be so formalized as to use some computerized process that an installation may have developed.

If you do not yet have such a process, the application that we are now developing will do that for you. To keep it uncomplicated, only a few attributes for each name are maintained by this application; however, once you understand it, there is no reason why you could not expand it to track other attributes beyond the ones given here.

Figure 8-3 shows all the names used by this application. You will note that names for entries other than dialog components did not have to follow the naming conventions that were suggested in the preceding section. The reason is that all other data names are *internal* to this application, thus "insulating" them from similar names in other applications. Component names, however, often reside in common libraries and therefore require special rules.

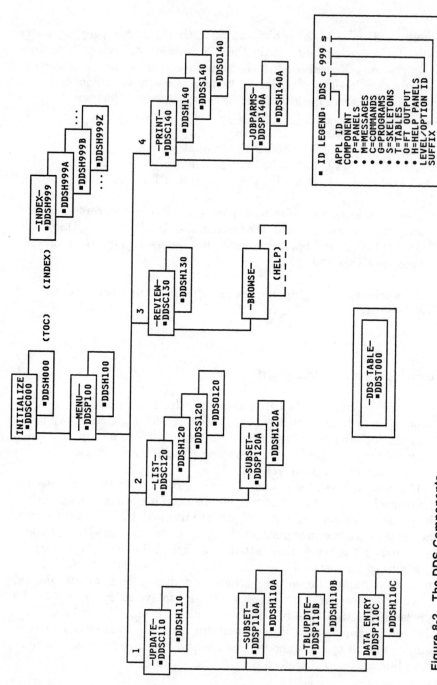

Figure 8-2 The DDS Components.

APPL ID	VARIABLE NAME	POOL TYPE	DATA TYPE	FIELD LENGTH	FIELD DESCRIPTION AND COMMENTS
DDS					
DDS	ACCT	P	CHAR	15	USER ACCOUNT DATA FOR JOB STMT
DDS	APPL	P	CHAR	4	APPLICATION IDENTIFICATION
DDS	CLASS	P	CHAR	1	PREFERRED OUTPUT CLASS ON JOBS
DDS	CPY	F	NUMER	3	NUMBER OF COPIES TO PRINT
DDS	DDSC000	N	CMD	0	APPLICATION START-UP COMMAND
DDS	DDSC110	N	CMD	0	TABLE UPDATE DRIVER COMMAND
DDS	DDSC120	N	CMD	0	FILE TAILORING PROCESSING CMD
DDS	DDSC130	N	CMD	0	VIEW LISTED FILE COMMAND
DDS	DDSC140	N	CMD	0	PRINT LISTED TABLE COMMAND
DDS	DDSH000	N	PANEL	0	TUTORIAL TABLE OF CONTENTS
DDS	DDSH100	N	PANEL	0	TUTORIAL PRIMARY OPTION MENU
DDS	DDSH110	N	PANEL	0	TUTORIAL ON DICTIONARY UPDATE
DDS	DDSH110A	N	PANEL	0	TUTORIAL ON SUBSETTING OPTIONS
DDS	DDSH110B	N	PANEL	0	TUTORIAL ON TBL DISPLAY PANEL
DDS	DDSH110C	N	PANEL	0	TUTORIAL ON DATA ENTRY PANEL
DDS	DDSH120	N	PANEL	0	TUTORIAL ON DICTIONARY LISTING
DDS	DDSH120A	N	PANEL	0	TUTORIAL ON SELECT PARAMETERS
DDS	DDSH130	N	PANEL	0	TUTORIAL ON REVIEWING LISTING
DDS	DDSH140	N	PANEL	0	TUTORIAL ON PRINT LISTING
DDS	DDSH140A	N	PANEL	0	TUTORIAL ON PRINT JOB PARMS
DDS	DDSH999	N	PANEL	0	TUTORIAL START OF INDEX PANELS
DDS	DDSH999A	N	PANEL	0	TUTORIAL INDEX FOR LETTER A
DDS	DDSM110B	N	MSG	0	SELECT LINE OR END
DDS	DDSM120A	N	MSG	0	TABLE &TABLE LISTED
DDS	DDSM120B	N	MSG	0	UNABLE TO DO FTOPEN
DDS	DDSM120C	N	MSG	0	UNABLE TO DO FTINCL
DDS	DDSM120D	N	MSG	0	UNABLE TO DO FTCLOSE
DDS	DDSM140A	N	MSG	0	LISTING PRINTED
DDS	DDSO120	N	FTOUT	0	FILE TAILORING OUTPUT LIST
DDS	DDSP100	N	PANEL	0	DDS APPL PRIMARY OPTION PANEL
DDS	DDSP110A	N	PANEL	0	SUBSET SELECTION FOR UPDATES
DDS	DDSP110B	N	PANEL	0	TABLE DISPLAY FOR UPDATES
DDS	DDSP110C	N	PANEL	0	DATA ENTRY PANEL FOR UPDATES
DDS	DDSP120A	N	PANEL	0	FILE TAILORING PARAMETERS
DDS	DDSP140A	N	PANEL	0	LISTING PRINTING PARAMETERS
DDS	DDSS120	N	SKEL	0	SKELETON FOR TABLE LISTING
DDS	DDSS140	N	SKEL	0	JOB SKELETON FOR LIST PRINTING
DDS	DDST000	N	TABLE	0	DDS MASTER TABLE

Figure 8-3   The DDS Element Names.

APPL ID	VARIABLE NAME	POOL TYPE	DATA TYPE	FIELD LENGTH	FIELD DESCRIPTION AND COMMENTS
DDS	DESCRIPT	F	CHAR	30	FIELD DESCRIPTION
DDS	DTYPE	F	CHAR	5	DATA TYPE (NUMER OR CHAR)
DDS	LENTH	F	NUMER	5	MAXIMUM FIELD LENGTH
DDS	PASS	F	CHAR	8	DATASET PASSWORD ACCESS CNTL
DDS	PTYPE	F	CHAR	1	VARIABLE POOL CLASSIFICATION
DDS	ROOM	P	CHAR	8	USER ROOM/OFFICE NBR FOR JOBS
DDS	SAPPL	F	CHAR	4	SELECTED APPLICATION ID OR *
DDS	SDATA	F	CHAR	5	SELECTED DATA TYPE OR *
DDS	SKEL	F	CHAR	8	NAME OF SKELETON IN A FUNCTION
DDS	SPOOL	F	CHAR	1	SELECTED POOL TYPE OR *
DDS	TABLE	F	CHAR	8	NAME OF TABLE IN THIS FUNCTION
DDS	UNAME	P	CHAR	8	USER'S LAST NAME FOR JOB STMT
DDS	VARNAME	F	CHAR	8	FIELD NAME WITHIN APPLICATION

Figure 8-3   (continued from previous page)

Please note, also, that it is *not* important for you to develop all the names at this point. What is important is that, as you need a new element, the name of that element be added to the dictionary at that time.

Prototyping the DDS Application

So far we have defined the purpose of our application, designed its structure, and named its components. The next step is to begin designing the inputs and outputs for our application. This is where prototyping comes into play.

Rather than simply sketching the various formats on a piece of paper, with today's tools we can be designing, coding, and simulating — all at once — our intended application. Using the simplicity of panel development, we can sit with the user(s) and interactively design the full application. The user is not concerned with the internal mechanisms of how we do this, only with the final results.

We will be covering the coding sequence in the next chapter. As such, for now let us concentrate on the product design and examine it from an external point of view.

```
DDSP100 -------------  DDS PRIMARY OPTION MENU  -------------
SELECTION ===> 1

SELECT ONE OF THE FOLLOWING OPTIONS:

1  UPDATE TABLE      Update/create master dictionary
2  LIST   TABLE      List full dictionary or a subset
3  VIEW   OUTPUT     View listing at the terminal
4  PRINT  OUTPUT     Send listing to the printer
X  EXIT              Exit this application
```

Figure 8-4 Primary Option Menu.

```
DDSP110A -----------  DDS APPLICATION SELECTION PANEL  ------------
COMMAND ===>

TO ISOLATE AND PROCESS A GIVEN SUBSET, ENTER MATCHING PARAMETERS:

APPLICATION ID . . . .  DDS_        (No entry processes all appl.)
POOL TYPE. . . . . . .  _           (No entry processes all types)
DATA TYPE. . . . . . .  ____        (No entry processes all types)
```

Figure 8-5 Table Update Parameters.

ENTER: A (ADD), C (CHANGE), OR D (DELETE) COMMAND(s) ON THE DESIRED LINE(s)

CMD CDE	APPL ID	VARIABLE NAME	POOL TYPE	DATA TYPE	FIELD LENGTH	FIELD DESCRIPTION AND COMMENTS
	DDS	ACCT	P	CHAR	15	USER ACCOUNT DATA FOR JOB STMT
	DDS	APPL	P	CHAR	4	APPLICATION IDENTIFICATION
	DDS	CLASS	P	CHAR	1	PREFERRED OUTPUT CLASS ON JOBS
	DDS	CPY	F	NUMBER	3	NUMBER OF COPIES TO PRINT
	DDS	DDSC000	N	CMD	0	APPLICATION START-UP COMMAND
	DDS	DDSC110	N	CMD	0	TABLE UPDATE DRIVER COMMAND
	DDS	DDSC120	N	CMD	0	FILE TAILORING PROCESSING CMD
	DDS	DDSC130	N	CMD	0	VIEW LISTED FILE COMMAND
	DDS	DDSC140	N	CMD	0	PRINT LISTED TABLE COMMAND
	DDS	DDSH000	N	PANEL	0	TUTORIAL TABLE OF CONTENTS
	DDS	DDSH100	N	PANEL	0	TUTORIAL PRIMARY OPTION MENU
	DDS	DDSH110A	N	PANEL	0	TUTORIAL ON DICTIONARY UPDATE
	DDS	DDSH110B	N	PANEL	0	TUTORIAL ON SUBSETTING OPTIONS
	DDS	DDSH110C	N	PANEL	0	TUTORIAL ON TBL DISPLAY PANEL
	DDS	DDSH120	N	PANEL	0	TUTORIAL ON DATA ENTRY PANEL
	DDS	DDSH120A	N	PANEL	0	TUTORIAL ON DICTIONARY LISTING
	DDS	DDSH130	N	PANEL	0	TUTORIAL ON SELECT PARAMETERS
	DDS	DDSH130	N	PANEL	0	TUTORIAL ON REVIEWING LISTING

Figure 8-6   Table Display.

ENTER: A (ADD), C (CHANGE), OR D (DELETE) COMMAND(s) ON THE DESIRED LINE(s)

CMD CDE	APPL ID	VARIABLE NAME	POOL TYPE	DATA TYPE	FIELD LENGTH	FIELD DESCRIPTION AND COMMENTS
c	DDS	ACCT	P	CHAR	15	USER ACCOUNT DATA FOR JOB STMT
	DDS	APPL	P	CHAR	4	APPLICATION IDENTIFICATION
	DDS	CLASS	P	CHAR	1	PREFERRED OUTPUT CLASS ON JOBS
	DDS	CPY	F	NUMER	3	NUMBER OF COPIES TO PRINT
	DDS	DDSC000	N	CMD	0	APPLICATION START-UP COMMAND
	DDS	DDSC110	N	CMD	0	TABLE UPDATE DRIVER COMMAND
	DDS	DDSC120	N	CMD	0	FILE TAILORING PROCESSING CMD
	DDS	DDSC130	N	CMD	0	VIEW LISTED FILE COMMAND
	DDS	DDSC140	N	CMD	0	PRINT LISTED TABLE OF CONTENTS
	DDS	DDSH000	N	PANEL	0	TUTORIAL TABLE OF CONTENTS
	DDS	DDSH100	N	PANEL	0	TUTORIAL PRIMARY OPTION MENU
	DDS	DDSH110	N	PANEL	0	TUTORIAL ON DICTIONARY UPDATE
	DDS	DDSH110A	N	PANEL	0	TUTORIAL ON SUBSETTING OPTIONS
	DDS	DDSH110B	N	PANEL	0	TUTORIAL ON TBL DISPLAY PANEL
	DDS	DDSH110C	N	PANEL	0	TUTORIAL ON DATA ENTRY PANEL
	DDS	DDSH120	N	PANEL	0	TUTORIAL ON DICTIONARY LISTING
	DDS	DDSH120A	N	PANEL	0	TUTORIAL ON SELECT PARAMETERS
	DDS	DDSH130	N	PANEL	0	TUTORIAL ON REVIEWING LISTING

Figure 8-7 Table Row Selection.

```
DDSP110C -------------------- DDS DATA ENTRY PANEL --------------------------
COMMAND ===>

   PLEASE ENTER OR VERIFY THE FOLLOWING ITEMS:

   ACTION TO PERFORM:   CHANGE

   APPLICATION ID . . . :  DDS_          Maximum 4 alphanumeric chars
   VARIABLE NAME. . . . :  ACCT_         Maximum 8 alphanumeric chars
   POOL TYPE. . . . . . :  P             P=Prof,S=Shared,F=Funct,N=N/A

   DATA TYPE. . . . . . :  CHAR_         CHAR,NUMER,PANEL,MSG,TABLE,etc
   FIELD LENGTH . . . . :  15            Maximum field length (32767)
   DESCRIPTION. . . . . :  USER ACCOUNT DATA  FOR JOB STMT  Max 30 characters

   DELETE CONFIRMATION. . ___            Enter Yes/No for DELETE option
```

Figure 8-8 Data Entry Panel.

```
DDSP100 -------------- DDS PRIMARY OPTION MENU --------------
SELECTION ===> 2

   SELECT ONE OF THE FOLLOWING OPTIONS:

   1  UPDATE TABLE    Update/create master dictionary
   2  LIST   TABLE    List full dictionary or a subset
   3  VIEW OUTPUT     View listing at the terminal
   4  PRINT OUTPUT    Send listing to the printer
   X  EXIT            Exit this application
```

Figure 8-9 Selecting Option 2.

```
DDSP120A ------------ DDS FILE TAILORING OPTIONS ------------
COMMAND ===>

INDICATE FIELDS TO MATCH FOR LISTING PURPOSES  (NO ENTRY = SELECT ALL)

APPLICATION ID . . . . DDS_          Maximum 4 alphanumeric chars
POOL TYPE. . . . . . _               P=Prof,S=Shared,F=Funct,N=N/A
DATA TYPE. . . . . . ____            CHAR,NUMER,PANEL,MSG,CMS,etc
```

Figure 8-10 Table Listing Parameters.

```
DDSP100 -------------- DDS PRIMARY OPTION MENU ----- TABLE DDST000 LISTED
SELECTION ===> 3

SELECT ONE OF THE FOLLOWING OPTIONS:

1  UPDATE TABLE     Update/create master dictionary
2  LIST   TABLE     List full dictionary or a subset
3  VIEW   OUTPUT    View listing at the terminal
4  PRINT  OUTPUT    Send listing to the printer
X  EXIT             Exit this application
```

Figure 8-11 Selecting Option 3.

```
BROWSE -- userid.DDS.FTOUTPUT -------------------  LINE 000000 COL  001 080
COMMAND ===>                                               SCROLL ===> CSR
=========================================================================
1DDS TABLE ENTRIES FOR:   APPL=DDS,POOLTYPE=*,DATATYPE=*
================================= TOP OF DATA ===========================
0APPL VARIABLE POOL DATA   FIELD   FIELD DESCRIPTION AND COMMENTS
 ID   NAME     TYPE TYPE   LENGTH
```

APPL ID	VARIABLE NAME	POOL TYPE	DATA TYPE	FIELD LENGTH	FIELD DESCRIPTION AND COMMENTS
DDS	ACCT	P	CHAR	15	USER ACCOUNT DATA FOR JOB STMT
DDS	APPL	P	CHAR	4	APPLICATION IDENTIFICATION
DDS	CLASS	P	CHAR	1	PREFERRED OUTPUT CLASS ON JOBS
DDS	CPY	F	NUMBER	3	NUMBER OF COPIES TO PRINT
DDS	DDSC000	N	CMD	0	APPLICATION START-UP COMMAND
DDS	DDSC110	N	CMD	0	TABLE UPDATE DRIVER COMMAND
DDS	DDSC120	N	CMD	0	FILE TAILORING PROCESSING CMD
DDS	DDSC130	N	CMD	0	VIEW LISTED FILE COMMAND
DDS	DDSC140	N	CMD	0	PRINT LISTED TABLE COMMAND
DDS	DDSH000	N	PANEL	0	TUTORIAL TABLE OF CONTENTS
DDS	DDSH100	N	PANEL	0	TUTORIAL PRIMARY OPTION MENU
DDS	DDSH110	N	PANEL	0	TUTORIAL ON DICTIONARY UPDATE
DDS	DDSH110A	N	PANEL	0	TUTORIAL ON SUBSETTING OPTIONS
DDS	DDSH110B	N	PANEL	0	TUTORIAL ON TBL DISPLAY PANEL
DDS	DDSH110C	N	PANEL	0	TUTORIAL ON DATA ENTRY PANEL
DDS	DDSH120	N	PANEL	0	TUTORIAL ON DICTIONARY LISTING
DDS	DDSH120A	N	PANEL	0	TUTORIAL ON SELECT PARAMETERS
DDS	DDSH130	N	PANEL	0	TUTORIAL ON REVIEWING LISTING
DDS	DDSH140	N	PANEL	0	TUTORIAL ON PRINT LISTING
DDS	DDSH140A	N	PANEL	0	TUTORIAL ON PRINT JOB PARMS

Figure 8-12 Browsing Table Listing.

```
DDSP100 ------------  DDS PRIMARY OPTION MENU  ------------
SELECTION ===> 4

SELECT ONE OF THE FOLLOWING OPTIONS:

1  UPDATE TABLE      Update/create master dictionary
2  LIST  TABLE       List full dictionary or a subset
3  VIEW  OUTPUT      View listing at the terminal
4  PRINT OUTPUT      Send listing to the printer
X  EXIT              Exit this application
```

Figure 8-13 Selecting Option 4.

```
DDSP140A ------------ DDS JOB SUBMISSION PARAMETERS  ------------------
COMMAND ===>

  PLEASE ENTER/VERIFY THE FOLLOWING ITEMS:

  YOUR NAME. . . . . : AZEVEDO___        For JOB statement pgmr's name
  ACCOUNTING INFO. . : ABC-XYZ87_        Job accounting parameters
  ROOM NUMBER. . . . : 1234____          Room/office nbr for delivery
  OUTPUT CLASS . . . : A                 Message/report print classes
  NUMBER OF COPIES . : 1__               Number of copies to print
  ACCESS PASSWORD. . :                   Dataset access (if required)
```

Figure 8-14 Job Submission Parameters.

```
DDSP100  --------------- DDS PRIMARY OPTION MENU  ------------ TABLE PRINTED
SELECTION ===> x

   SELECT ONE OF THE FOLLOWING OPTIONS:

   1  UPDATE TABLE     Update/create master dictionary
   2  LIST   TABLE     List full dictionary or a subset
   3  VIEW  OUTPUT     View listing at the terminal
   4  PRINT OUTPUT     Send listing to the printer
   X  EXIT             Exit this application
```

Figure 8-15 Exiting the Application.

```
DDSH000 -------------- DATA DICTIONARY SYSTEM -------------- TUTORIAL
SELECTION ===>

            |---------------------------------|
            |        TABLE OF CONTENTS         |
            |---------------------------------|

You may "navigate" throughout this tutorial facility as if it were a
normal book, i.e., you may proceed sequentially through each of the
topics offered, or you may go directly to the desired one shown based
on the one-character designators associated with each entry.

Once in a topic, you may go from one "page" to the next (if any) by
pressing the ENTER key, you may back up with the B(ack) command, you
may skip to the next topic with the S(kip) command, you may go up to
the higher topic with the U(p) command, or you may go to the index
(the I(ndex) command) or the table of contents (the T(op) command).

The following are the available topics:

0 GENERAL INFO      General system description
1 UPDATE TABLE      Update/create master dictionary
2 LIST TABLE        List full dictionary or a subset
3 VIEW OUTPUT       View listing at the terminal
4 PRINT OUTPUT      Send listing to the printer
```

Figure 8-16   Tutorial Table of Contents.

```
DDSH100  ------------  DATA DICTIONARY SYSTEM  --------------------  TUTORIAL
SELECTION ===>

                       |-------------------------|
                       |      PRIMARY OPTIONS     |
                       |-------------------------|

The DATA DICTIONARY SYSTEM (DDS) is designed to assist a dialog developer
with the tracking and maintenance of all the VARIABLE NAMES required for
a given application.  To further assist the developer, facilities have
been incorporated to allow also the names of PANELS, MESSAGES, TABLES,
SKELETONS, TUTORIALS, PROGRAMS, COMMANDS, etc.

The following topics may be viewed in sequence or selected directly:

1  UPDATE TABLE      Update/create master dictionary
2  LIST   TABLE      List full dictionary or a subset
3  VIEW OUTPUT       View listing at the terminal
4  PRINT OUTPUT      Send listing to the printer
```

Figure 8-17 Primary Options Tutorial.

```
DDSH110 ------------- DATA DICTIONARY SYSTEM ------------- TUTORIAL
SELECTION ===>

               ------------------------------------
               |                                    |
               |          UPDATE DICTIONARY         |
               |                                    |
               ------------------------------------

This option allows a developer either to create a master dictionary (if
none yet exists), or to update an existing one. Within this dictionary,
entries are "partitioned" by application identifiers which logically
should match the id given to ISPF. This "partitioning" allows one to
subset the dictionary display so that scrolling for the needed data may
be minimized.

This subsetting concept can also be used to reduce the display to names
associated with a particular variable pool type and/or data type classes.

The following topics are presented in sequence, or may be selected by
number:

1  SUBSET SELECTION    Dictionary subsetting parameters
2  TABLE DISPLAY       Dictionary entry selection
3  DATA ENTRY          Dictionary data entry
```

Figure 8-18 Update Option Tutorial.

```
DDSH110A ----------- DATA DICTIONARY SYSTEM ------------ TUTORIAL
SELECTION ===>

            |---------------------------------------|
            |          SUBSETTING OPTIONS           |
            |                                       |
            |---------------------------------------|

This option allows a developer to work with a subset of the complete
dictionary. Normally, a developer is only concerned with a portion
of the full dictionary either because it relates to the application
being developed, or because he/she wishes to examine all of the names
that fit a particular class.

By selecting specific classes, it should become easier to analyze the
various names and to determine patterns and/or abnormalities.
Selections may be performed based on (1) application id, (2) pool type
and/or (3) data type.

For example, if one wanted to see all of the names that relate to
the components of a dialog (PANELS, MESSAGES, TABLES, etc), one
could give the dialog name and a pool of "N" (N/A). If a developer
wanted to review all of the messages available for any application,
the data type parameter of "MSGS", by itself, would accomplish this.
```

Figure 8-19 Subsetting Parms Tutorial.

```
DDSH110B ------------- DATA DICTIONARY SYSTEM ------------- TUTORIAL
SELECTION ===>


                    |-------------------------|
                    |   TABLE DISPLAY PANEL    |
                    |-------------------------|


This option display the dictionary contents based on the subsetting
parameters (if any) given in the preceding panel.

Preceding each entry, provisions are made to accept a command code
to allow additions (A), changes (C), or deletions (D).  As many lines
as necessary may be selected with one of these codes; for each line
selected, an expanded panel display will be provided to allow the user
to add/change/delete the selected entries.
```

Figure 8-20 Table Display Tutorial.

```
DDSH110C -------------  DATA DICTIONARY SYSTEM  -------------  TUTORIAL
SELECTION ===>


                |-------------------------------|
                |       DATA ENTRY PANEL        |
                |-------------------------------|
```

This panel is displayed whenever a valid command code is detected
on any line displayed by the table display panel. Depending on the
command action (displayed at the top of the panel), the user may then
add, change, or delete the entry.

For a delete action, one only needs to confirm it by entering a Yes or
No on the last entry of the screen (the cursor will be placed there
automatically.

For a change or add action, all fields (except the description) are
required. For maximum flexibility, field checking has been limited
to simple data type checks such as numeric, alphabetic, or name rules.
The only entry which is checked for specific codes is the pool type
which must contain a "P", "S", "F", or "N" (for N/A).

It should also be noted that the combination of APPLICATION ID, VARIABLE
NAME, and POOL TYPE form a composite key which should yield a unique value
when adding a new entry.

Figure 8-21 Data Entry Tutorial.

```
DDSH120 ------------- DATA DICTIONARY SYSTEM ------------- TUTORIAL
SELECTION ===>

                 |------- LIST DICTIONARY -------|
                 |                               |
                 |                               |
                 |-------------------------------|

This option allows a developer to list the contents of the dictionary
either for more extensive browsing capabilities or for hard-copy print,
or both.

The dictionary can be processed in its entirety, or it may be selected
by (1) application identifier, (2) by variable pool type, and/or (3)
by data type class. These three entries may be used in any combination
to provide a very selective listing of the desired items.

For a detailed explanation of each of the three entries, press the
ENTER key.
```

Figure 8-22 Dictionary Listing Tutorial.

```
DDSH120A ------------- DATA DICTIONARY SYSTEM ------------- TUTORIAL
SELECTION ===>

            |---------------------------------------------|
            |         LIST SELECTION PARAMETERS           |
            |---------------------------------------------|
```

This panel enables one to identify the selection parameters to control
the contents of the dictionary listing about to be produced.

By selecting specific classes, it should become easier to analyze the
various names and to determine patterns and/or abnormalities.
Selections may be performed based on (1) application id, (2) pool type
and/or (3) data type.

For example, if one wanted to see all of the names that relate to
the components of a dialog (PANELS, MESSAGES, TABLES, etc), one
could give the dialog name and a pool of "N" (N/A). If a developer
wanted to review all of the messages available for any application,
the data type parameter of "MSGS", by itself, would accomplish this.

An absence of a selection parameter indicates that no test is to be
made, i.e., all variations of that entry are to be accepted. As such,
to list the entire dictionary, leave all entries blank.

Figure 8-23 Listing Parameters Tutorial.

```
DDSH130 ------------ DATA DICTIONARY SYSTEM ------------ TUTORIAL
SELECTION ===>

              | ----------------------------------- |
              |    REVIEW DICTIONARY LISTING        |
              | ----------------------------------- |

    This option allows a developer to review the selected dictionary listing
    either for more extensive browsing capabilities or for a hard-copy print,
    or both.

    The full capabilities of the BROWSE command will allow the developer
    to scan the contents of the listing for any field or word that one
    may need to locate.  Any of the BROWSE commands may be used while in
    this option.
```

Figure 8-24 Review Listing Tutorial.

```
DDSH140 -------------- DATA DICTIONARY SYSTEM -------------- TUTORIAL
SELECTION ===>

                    |-----------------------------|
                    |                             |
                    |   PRINT DICTIONARY LISTING  |
                    |                             |
                    |-----------------------------|

This option allows a developer to print the selected dictionary listing
on any printer available through the system using any of the output
classes desired and for any number of copies allowed.

User profile data is maintained for each person so that the same data
will not have to be repeated each time this service is requested. Of
course, the first time that this is used, this profile will not exist.

For a detailed explanation of these user profile items, press the
ENTER key.
```

Figure 8-25 Print Listing Tutorial.

```
DDSH140A --------------- DATA DICTIONARY SYSTEM --------------- TUTORIAL
SELECTION ===>

                      |-----------------------------|
                      |    PRINT JOB PARAMETERS     |
                      |-----------------------------|


This panel enables one to review/provide the necessary job control
parameters in order to submit a job which will print the listing
produced from a previous process.

All of the entries indicated are required except for the ACCESS
PASSWORD which will depend on the security attached to the data
set that holds the dictionary listing.

All parameters will be "remembered" across sessions except for
the number of output copies which will always default to 1. The
actual contents of each entry will depend on the installation
requirements.
```

Figure 8-26 Job Parameters Tutorial.

```
DDSH999 ---------------- DATA DICTIONARY SYSTEM ---------------- TUTORIAL
COMMAND ===>

                          |----------------------------------|
                          |             INDEX                |
                          |                                  |
                          |----------------------------------|

Selected topics discussed in the tutorial can be found in this index.

To use the index, enter the first letter of the topic of interest. The
index page containing subjects starting with that letter is displayed.
On an index page, any subject can be selected by entering the two
character option preceding that selection.

When you are on one index page, you can access any other index page by
entering its letter identification. If you are in the tutorial but not
on an index page, you can get to the index by entering INDEX or I in
the command field.

The index pages are presented in sequence if you press the ENTER key.
```

Figure 8-27 General Tutorial Index.

```
DDSH999A --------------- DATA DICTIONARY SYSTEM --------------- TUTORIAL
COMMAND ===>

                                   |-----------------------|
                        INDEX: 'A' |                       |
                                   |-----------------------|

To select a topic, enter code (letter and number) in the option field:

A1  -ACCOUNTING           A16 --
A2  --ACCOUNTING          A17 --
A3  --ACTION              A18 --
A4  --ACTION              A19 --
A5                        A20 --
A6  --ADD                 A21 --
A7                        A22 --
A8  --ANALYZE (Display)   A23 --
A9  --ANALYZE (Listing)   A24 --
A10                       A25 --
A11 --APPLICATION         A26 --
A12 --                    A27 --
A13 --                    A28 --
A14 --                    A29 --
A15 --                    A30 --
```

Figure 8-28 Index for "A" Keywords.

Summary

Thus, to develop a new application, we must consider various phases, such as:

• Defining the application requirements
• Designing the application structure
• Developing the application code
• Testing the application components
• Implementing the application dialog

We also saw that, before we begin the application development, we should:

• Develop a naming strategy
• Assign names to each component
• Enter the names into a data dictionary
• Prototype the application

It was also recommended that one possible naming strategy could be to name the dialog components as $xxxy999z$, where:

• xxx is the application identifier
• y is the application component code
• 999   is the level/option identifier
• z is a suffix for multiple items

Finally, it was suggested that a possible list of component codes to use could be:

• P = Panels
• M = Messages
• C = Command procedures
• G = Programs
• S = Skeletons
• T = Tables
• O = File tailoring output
• H = Help panels (tutorials)

9

Developing a New Application

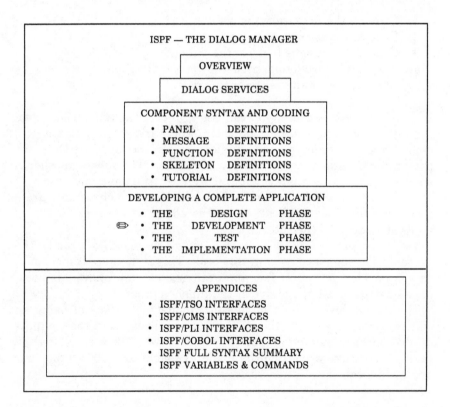

We are now ready to discuss the actual coding phase. At this point, we have a thorough understanding of what the application requires, and we have all the theoretical knowledge necessary to address those requirements. All that we need now is to apply that knowledge by starting to code our solution to the problem at hand.

The Coding Sequence

Considering the large number of components needed for our application, we should develop a plan as to the proper sequence for coding these components. The one that should work best for everyone is the following:

1. Code all the necessary panels.
2. Code any messages as you progress.
3. Code the functions to drive the panels.
4. Add any file skeletons needed by the application.
5. Conclude with any relevant tutorials.

If you follow this order, you can begin to exercise the various components as soon as you develop them. The panels, for example, will enable you to prototype the application for the user — thus the reason for placing them at the top of the list. The messages should also be in place so that when you exercise the functions, most of what is needed will be available. The skeletons, which usually are a small portion of an application, can be added as needed. Finally, if applicable, develop the tutorials.

You may have noticed that the list given matches exactly the presentation sequence used in this book. This is no mere coincidence; as you develop your first few applications, you can follow this book, page by page, until you arrive at the finished product.

The actual development of these components consists of using an edit program — such as the PDF EDIT — to construct the contents of the various members. These members will then be stored in various libraries, which will be made available to ISPF so that our application can execute successfully.

The Basic ISPF Libraries

Generally, all ISPF dialogs require a certain minimum number of libraries which should meet the specifications shown in Figure 9-1.

In addition to these basic ones, you may also need libraries for:

COMPONENT	DATASET	TYPES	RECFM	LRECL
Panels	PANEL	PANELS	F/V	80-160
Messages	MESSAGE	MSGS	F	80
Commands	CLIST		F	80
Tables	TABLE	TABLES	F/V	80-5280
Skeletons	SKELETON	SKELS	F/V	80-255
File Tailoring	any		F/V	80-255

Figure 9-1   ISPF Dialog Libraries.

- PL/I programs   (data set type: PLI)
- COBOL programs   (data set type: COBOL)
- Object modules   (data set type: OBJ)
- Load modules   (data set type: LOAD)

For the DDS application that we are about to construct, we will allocate the data sets listed in Figure 9-2.

You should note that the data set types given are not an absolute requirement — the data sets may actually have any name. However, there are many advantages in selecting the correct data set type, ranging from uniquely appropriate editing profiles to proper selection of MODELS when constructing ISPF elements.

COMPONENT	DATASET NAMES	RECFM	LREC/BLKSZ
Panels	userid.DDS.PANELS	FB	80/6160
Messages	userid.DDS.MSGS	FB	80/6160
Commands	userid.DDS.CLIST	FB	80/6160
Tables	userid.DDS.TABLES	FB	80/6160
Skeletons	userid.DDS.SKELS	FB	80/6160
File Tailoring	userid.DDS.FTOUTPUT	FBA	80/6160

Figure 9-2   DDS Application Libraries.

Using ISPF Element Models

With each copy of the ISPF/PDF product, IBM provides a series of syntax models for each element of a dialog component. This enables a developer to have access to a quick syntax reference while constructing these components, without having to search manuals constantly.

The mechanism for using these models is very simple. While editing one of your dialog components, if you should need a quick reference to the syntax of a particular element, follow these steps:

1. Type MODEL in the command line of the edit panel in use.
2. Enter a line prefix of "A" (after) or "B" (before) at the point where you wish the model to be placed.
3. Make a selection from the menu presented to you.

When you finish this sequence, you will have *in your component* a model statement for whatever element you have selected. You will also have a series of comment lines (these will have the string "=NOTE=" as a prefix) which will not be kept with your component. These lines will assist you in customizing the model statement given. To remove these lines, type RESET in the command line.

To illustrate, suppose that you were developing a command procedure and you needed a model statement for a SELECT service. Typing MODEL on the command line along with an A/B as a prefix at the needed location, you would be given the menu as shown in Figure 9-3.

Assuming, then, that you would choose M1 for the SELECT service, you would be returned to the member that you were editing with the model lines now inserted as shown in Figure 9-4. Having read the comments given, you would modify the model statement based on your needs, then type RESET to clear the NOTEs, and proceed with your next statement.

Creating Your Own Models

This same mechanism exists for panels, messages, skeletons, etc. As you gain experience in developing your dialogs, there may come a time when you may wish to develop your own models. This would

```
----------------------- COMMAND MODELS -----------------------
OPTION  ===>

   VARIABLES            MISCELLANEOUS           LIBRARY ACCESS
   V1   VGET            M1   SELECT             L6    LMMADD
   V2   VPUT            M2   CONTROL            L7    LMMDEL
                        M3   BROWSE             L8    LMMFIND
   FILE TAILORING       M4   EDIT               L9    LMMLIST
   F1   FTOPEN          M5   LOG                L10   LMMREN
   F2   FTINCL          M6   GETMSG             L11   LMMREP
   F3   FTCLOSE         M7   EDREC              L12   LMOPEN
   F4   FTERASE         M8   LIBDEF             L13   LMPROM
                                               L14   LMPUT
   DISPLAY              LIBRARY ACCESS          L15   LMQUERY
   D1   DISPLAY         L1   LMCLOSE            L16   LMRENAME
   D2   TBDISPL         L2   LMERASE
   D3   SETMSG          L3   LMFREE             TABLES
   D4   PQUERY          L4   LMGET              T1    TABLES
                        L5   LMINIT

   Enter END command to cancel MODEL command.
```

Figure 9-3   Menu for Command Models.

```
EDIT ---- userid.DDS.CLIST(TEST1) - 01.00 -------- COLUMNS 001 072
COMMAND ===>                                       SCROLL ===> CSR
====== ==================== TOP OF DATA =========================
=NOTE= TO SELECT A PANEL:
000100 ISPEXEC SELECT  PANEL(PANELNAM) OPT(INIT-OPT) NEWPOOL +
000200                 NEWAPPL(APPLID)
=NOTE= PANELNAM  - NAME OF A SELECTION MENU TO BE DISPLAYED.
=NOTE= INIT-OPT  - OPTIONAL, VALID OPTION ON THE PANEL TO BYPASS
=NOTE=             ITS INITIAL DISPLAY.
=NOTE= NEWPOOL   - OPTIONAL, CREATE A NEW SHARED VARIABLE POOL
=NOTE= NEWAPPL   - OPTIONAL, NEW APPLICATION IS TO BE INVOKED.
=NOTE= APPLID    - OPTIONAL, ID OF THE NEW APPL BEING INVOKED.
=NOTE= EXAMPLE: ISPEXEC SELECT PANEL(PANEL70) OPT(OPT002) +
=NOTE=                  NEWAPPL(ID44)
 ...   ...
```

Figure 9-4   Model for SELECT Service.

```
VAR = TRANS(VARIABLE   VALUE,RESULT VALUE,RESULT  .... MSG=MSG-ID)
)N VAR          -  NAME OF THE VARIABLE TO GET THE RESULT
)N VARIABLE     -  NAME OF THE VARIABLE TO BE TRANSLATED
)N VALUE        -  A POSSIBLE VALUE OF THE VARIABLE
)N              -  * = ANYTHING ELSE
)N RESULT       -  THE TRANSLATED RESULT TO PUT IN THE VARIABLE
)N              -  * = NO TRANSLATION
)N MSG-ID       -  OPTIONAL, NAMES MESSAGE TO DISPLAY IF ANYTHING
)N                 ELSE IS FOUND (DON'T USE IF VALUE IS *)
)N EXAMPLE:  &REPL = TRANS (&MOD Y,YES N,NO *,'?')
```

Figure 9-5   Contents of TRANS Model Member.

enable any user to develop many different processes while in the
PDF EDIT program without having to activate a special application.

The process to develop models is a very simple one. It involves
nothing more than creating, in a file tailoring skeleton library
(ISPSLIB), members containing the desired model line(s) as data
lines, and "=NOTE=" lines which are recognized by a ")N" in position
1.

The skeleton in Figure 9-5 shows how the model for the
TRANSlate function exists in the PDF library released by IBM.

Once these models are developed, you then provide the necessary
selection panels so that the user can be guided into the various
models available. The top-level model selection panel must be called
"ISREMCLS"; thereafter, you may call them anything you like.

An example of the ISREMCLS panel as provided by IBM is shown
in Figure 9-6. This is the element model-classes menu which points
to all available models. If you were to choose selection 1, for example, you would see a second-level model selection panel, IS-
REMCMD in this case, which is shown in Figure 9-7.

From this second-level selection panel, the actual model has now
been identified, and the model processing program ISRECMBR is now
called with a parameter of ISREMCM1 which, in this case, is the
"skeleton" name for the SELECT service model. If you were to look
into the member ISREMCM1 in the library accessed through the
ddname of ISPSLIB, you would see the model shown in Figure 9-8.

```
)BODY
%-------------------- MODEL   CLASSES  --------------------------
%OPTION  ===>_ZCMD                                         %
%
%    1 +CLIST      - ISPF services in CLIST commands
%    2 +COBOL      - ISPF services in COBOL programs
%    3 +EXEC       - ISPF services in EXEC commands
%    4 +FORTRAN    - ISPF services in FORTRAN programs
%    5 +MSGS       - Message format
%    6 +PANELS     - Panel formats and statements
%    7 +PLI        - ISPF services in PLI programs
%    8 +SKELS      - File tailoring control statements
%    9 +PASCAL     - ISPF services in PASCAL programs
  ... ... ...
)PROC
  &ZSEL = TRANS(TRUNC (&ZCMD,'.')
           1,'PANEL(ISREMCMD)'
       CLIST,'PANEL(ISREMCMD)'
  ... ... ...
)END
```

Figure 9-6   IBM's ISREMCLS Model Classes Selection Panel.

```
%-------------------- COMMAND MODELS  ---------------------------
%OPTION  ===>_ZCMD                                             +
%
% VARIABLES              MISCELLANEOUS           LIBRARY ACCESS
% V1  +VGET              %M1  +SELECT            %L6  +LMMADD
% V2  +VPUT              %M2  +CONTROL           %L7  +LMMDEL
  ... ... ...
)PROC
  &ZSEL = TRANS(TRUNC (&ZCMD,'.')
  ... ... ...
       M1,'PGM(ISRECMBR) PARM(ISREMCM1)'
    SELECT,'PGM(ISRECMBR) PARM(ISREMCM1)'
  ... ... ...
)END
```

Figure 9-7   IBM's ISREMCMD Command Selection Panel.

```
)N   TO SELECT A PANEL:
     ISPEXEC SELECT  PANEL(PANELNAM) OPT(INIT-OPT) NEWPOOL +
                     NEWAPPL(APPLID)
)N   PANELNAM    - NAME OF A SELECTION MENU TO BE DISPLAYED.
)N   INIT-OPT    - OPTIONAL, VALID OPTION ON THE PANEL TO BYPASS
)N                 ITS INITIAL DISPLAY.
)N   NEWPOOL     - OPTIONAL, CREATE A NEW SHARED VARIABLE POOL
)N   NEWAPPL     - OPTIONAL, NEW APPLICATION IS TO BE INVOKED.
)N   APPLID      - OPTIONAL, ID OF THE NEW APPL BEING INVOKED.
)N   EXAMPLE:  ISPEXEC SELECT  PANEL(PANEL70) OPT(OPT002) NEWPOOL +
)N                             NEWAPPL(ID44)
)N
)N   TO SELECT A COMMAND:
...  ...  ...
```

Figure 9-8   IBM's ISREMCM1 Model for SELECT Service Command.

Depending on how you wanted your new application to operate,
you could develop your own version of the ISREMCLS panel or you
could add an entry into IBM's version to point to your own selection
panel, which would then point to the various elements you created.

The DDS Application Code

Understanding these concepts for developing new dialog components,
we should now be ready to code the complete Data Dictionary System (DDS), which has been used in fragmented illustrations
throughout this book.

The next several pages contain the complete list of the various
components that make up this application. The components are
shown in the following order:

• The DDS Panels   — For coding details refer to Chapter 3.
• The DDS Messages   — For coding details refer to Chapter 4.
• The DDS Functions — For coding details refer to Chapter 5.
• The DDS Skeletons — For coding details refer to Chapter 6.
• The DDS Tutorial   — For coding details refer to Chapter 7.

```
EDIT ---- userid.DDS.PANELS(DDSP100) - 01.16 ------------------------ COLUMNS 001 080
COMMAND ===>                                                            SCROLL ===> CSR
=====  ===================================== TOP OF DATA ======================================
000001 )ATTR DEFAULT(%+_)
000002        /* % TYPE(TEXT)  INTENS(HIGH)                          */
000003        /* + TYPE(TEXT)  INTENS(LOW)                           */
000004        /* _ TYPE(INPUT) INTENS(HIGH) CAPS(ON) JUST(LEFT)      */
000005 )BODY
000006 %------------------------ DDS PRIMARY OPTION MENU ------------------------
000007 %SELECTION ===>_ZCMD
000008 +
000009 +     SELECT ONE OF THE FOLLOWING OPTIONS:
000010 +
000011 +     %1+ UPDATE TABLE      Update/create master dictionary
000012       %2+ LIST   TABLE      List full dictionary or a subset
000013       %3+ VIEW   OUTPUT     View listing at the terminal
000014       %4+ PRINT  OUTPUT     Send listing to the printer
000015       %X+ EXIT              Exit this application
000016 )INIT
000017     &ZPRIM   = YES
000018     &ZHTOP   = DDSH000
000019     .HELP    = DDSH100
000020     &ZHINDEX = DDSH999
000021 )PROC
000022     &ZSEL   = TRANS (TRUNC (&ZCMD, '.')
000023                     1,'CMD(DDSC110)'
000024                     2,'CMD(DDSC120)'
000025                     3,'CMD(DDSC130)'
000026                     4,'CMD(DDSC140)'
000027                     X, EXIT
000028                     *,'?')
000029 )END
=====  ==================================== BOTTOM OF DATA ====================================
```

Figure 9-9   Panel DDSP100.

195

```
EDIT ---- userid.DDS.PANELS(DDSP110A) - 01.05 -------------------- COLUMNS 001 080
COMMAND ===>                                                        SCROLL ===> CSR
====== ========================================= TOP OF DATA =================================
000001 )ATTR DEFAULT(%+_)
000002   /* % TYPE(TEXT)    INTENS(HIGH)                                                  */
000003   /* + TYPE(TEXT)    INTENS(LOW)                                                   */
000004   /* _ TYPE(INPUT)   INTENS(HIGH)  CAPS(ON)  JUST(LEFT)                            */
000005      $ TYPE(INPUT)   INTENS(HIGH)  CAPS(ON)  JUST(LEFT)   PAD( )
000006      ! TYPE(INPUT)   INTENS(HIGH)  CAPS(ON)  JUST(RIGHT)  PAD(_)
000007 )BODY
000008 %------------------- DDS APPLICATION SELECTION PANEL ------------------------+
000009 %COMMAND ===>_ZCMD
000010 %
000011 +     TO ISOLATE AND PROCESS A GIVEN SUBSET, ENTER MATCHING PARAMETERS:
000012 +
000013 +     APPLICATION ID . . . .$appl+        (No entry processes all appl.)
000014 +     POOL TYPE. . . . . . .$z+           (No entry processes all types)
000015 +     DATA TYPE. . . . . . .$dtype+       (No entry processes all types)
000016 +
000017 )INIT
000018   .HELP  = DDSH110A
000019   .ZVARS = ptype
000020 )PROC
000021   VER (&appl, NAME)
000022   VER (&ptype, LIST, P,S,F,N)
000023   VER (&dtype, ALPHA)
000024 )END
====== ========================================== BOTTOM OF DATA =================================
```

Figure 9-10   Panel DDSP110A.

```
===== ================================= TOP OF DATA ================================
000001 )ATTR DEFAULT(%+_)
000002 /* % TYPE(TEXT )      INTENS(HIGH)                                         */
000003 /* + TYPE(TEXT )      INTENS(LOW )                                         */
000004    _ TYPE( INPUT)     INTENS(HIGH)     CAPS(ON )  JUST(LEFT )
000005    = TYPE(OUTPUT)     INTENS(LOW )     CAPS(ON )  JUST(LEFT )
000006    ! TYPE(OUTPUT)     INTENS(LOW )     CAPS(ON )  JUST(RIGHT)
000007 /*---------|--------------------------------------------------|--------*/
000008 )BODY
000009 %-----------------------|     DDS TABLE DISPLAY PANEL    |------------------
000010 %COMMAND ===>_ZCMD                                  %SCROLL ===>_z +
000011 %
000012 +ENTER:  %A+(ADD),  %C+(CHANGE),  OR %D+(DELETE) COMMAND(s) ON THE DESIRED LINE(s)
000013 +
000014 %CMD     APPL    VARIABLE   POOL     DATA     FIELD     FIELD DESCRIPTION AND COMMENTS
000015 %CDE     ID       NAME      TYPE     TYPE     LENGTH
000016 +
000017 )MODEL ROWS(SCAN)
000018   _z+    ~appl+~varname + ~z+   ~dtype+!lenth+  ~descript                    +
000019 )INIT
000020   .HELP  = DDSH110B
000021   .ZVARS = '(ZSCROLLA, option ptype)'
000022 )PROC
000023   IF (&ZTDSELS = 0000) .MSG = DDSM110B
000024   VER(&option, LIST, A,C,D)
000025 )END
===== =============================== BOTTOM OF DATA ==============================
```

Figure 9-11 Panel DDSP110B.

```
EDIT ---- userid.DDS.PANELS(DDSP110C) - 01.14 --------------------------------- COLUMNS 001 080
COMMAND ===>                                                              SCROLL ===> CSR
====== ========================================= TOP OF DATA =================================
000001 )ATTR DEFAULT(%+_)
000002        /*  % TYPE(TEXT)     INTENS(HIGH)                                            */
000003        /*  + TYPE(TEXT)     INTENS(LOW)                                             */
000004        /*  _ TYPE(INPUT)    INTENS(HIGH)   CAPS(ON)  JUST(LEFT)  PAD(_)             */
000005        /*  $ TYPE(INPUT)    INTENS(HIGH)   CAPS(ON)  JUST(LEFT)  PAD(_)             */
000006        /*  ! TYPE(INPUT)    INTENS(HIGH)   CAPS(ON)  JUST(LEFT)                      */
000007 )BODY
000008 %--------------------------  DDS DATA ENTRY PANEL  --------------------------------  +
000009 %COMMAND ===>_ZCMD
000010 %
000011 +      PLEASE ENTER OR VERIFY THE FOLLOWING ITEMS:
000012 +
000013 +      ACTION TO PERFORM: %&option
000014 +
000015 +      APPLICATION ID . . . .$appl+           Maximum 4 alphanumeric chars
000016 +      VARIABLE NAME. . . . .$varname +        Maximum 8 alphanumeric chars
000017 +      POOL TYPE. . . . . . .$z+               P=Prof,S=Shared,F=Funct,N=N/A
000018 +
000019 +      DATA TYPE. . . . . . .$dtype+           CHAR,NUMER,PANEL,MSG,TABLE,etc
000020 +      FIELD LENGTH . . . . .$lenth+           Maximum field length (32767)
000021 +      DESCRIPTION. . . . . .$descript         + Max 30 characters
000022 +
000023 +      DELETE CONFIRMATION.$del+               Enter Yes/No for DELETE option
000024 +
000025 )INIT
000026  .HELP = DDSH111C
000027  .ZVARS = ptype
000028  &option=TRANS(&option A,ADD C,CHANGE D,DELETE)
000029  if (&option ¬= DELETE) .CURSOR = varname
000030  if (&option  = DELETE) .CURSOR = del
000031 )PROC
000032  &option = TRUNC (&option,1)
000033  &del    = TRUNC (&del, 1)
000034  VER (&appl, NB, NAME)
000035  IF (&option ¬= D)
000036    VER (&varname,NB, NAME)
000037    VER (&ptype, NB, LIST, P,S,F,N)
000038    VER (&dtype, NB, ALPHA)
000039    VER (&lenth, NB, NUM)
000040  IF (&option = D)
000041    VER (&del, NB, LIST, Y,N)
000042 )END
====== ============================================ BOTTOM OF DATA ============================
```

```
EDIT ---- userid.DDS.PANELS(DDSP120A) - 01.08 -------------------- COLUMNS 001 080
COMMAND ===>                                                        SCROLL ===> CSR
====== ========================================= TOP OF DATA ====================================
000001 )ATTR DEFAULT(%+_)
000002   /*  % TYPE(TEXT)      INTENS(HIGH)                                              */
000003   /*  + TYPE(TEXT)      INTENS(LOW)                                               */
000004   /*  _ TYPE(INPUT)     INTENS(HIGH)                                              */
000005       $ TYPE(INPUT)     INTENS(HIGH)   CAPS(ON)  JUST(LEFT)
000006       ! TYPE(INPUT)     INTENS(HIGH)   CAPS(ON)  JUST(LEFT)    PAD(_)
000007                                        CAPS(ON)  JUST(RIGHT)   PAD(_)
000008 )BODY
000009 %-------------------- DDS FILE TAILORING OPTIONS ---------------------+
000010 %COMMAND ===>_ZCMD
000011 %
000012 +       INDICATE FIELDS TO MATCH FOR LISTING PURPOSES   (NO ENTRY = SELECT ALL)
000013 +
000014 +      APPLICATION ID . . . .$z     +       Maximum 4 alphanumeric chars
000015 +      POOL TYPE. . . . . . .$z+    +       P=Prof,S=Shared,F=Funct,N=N/A
000016 +      DATA TYPE. . . . . . .$z     +       CHAR,NUMER,PANEL,MSG,CMS,etc
000017 )INIT
000018   .HELP = DDSH120
000019   .ZVARS = '(sappl spool sdata)'
000020   &sappl = &appl
000021 )PROC
000022   VER (&sappl, NAME)
000023   VER (&spool, LIST, P,S,F,N)
000024   VER (&svarn, ALPHA)
000025   IF (&sappl = '')    &sappl = *
000026   IF (&spool = '')    &spool = *
000027   IF (&sdata = '')    &sdata = *
000028 )END
====== ========================================= BOTTOM OF DATA ==================================
```

Figure 9-13 Panel DDSP120A.

```
EDIT ---- userid.DDS.PANELS(DDSP140A) - 01.01 ------------------- COLUMNS 001 080
COMMAND ===>                                                      SCROLL ===> CSR
=====================================  TOP OF DATA ============================
000001 )ATTR DEFAULT(%+_)
000002   /* % TYPE(TEXT)   INTENS(HIGH)                                        */
000003   /* + TYPE(TEXT)   INTENS(LOW)                                         */
000004   /*   TYPE(INPUT)  INTENS(HIGH)                                        */
000005   $ TYPE(INPUT)  INTENS(HIGH)   CAPS(ON)  JUST(LEFT)
000006   ! TYPE(INPUT)  INTENS(HIGH)   CAPS(ON)  JUST(LEFT)    PAD(_)
000007   - TYPE(INPUT)  INTENS(NON)    CAPS(ON)  JUST(RIGHT)   PAD(_)
000008 )BODY                                      CAPS(ON)  JUST(LEFT)
000009 %------------------ DDS JOB SUBMISSION PARAMETERS ------------------ +
000010 %COMMAND ===>_ZCMD
000011 %
000012 +     PLEASE ENTER/VERIFY THE FOLLOWING ITEMS:
000013 +
000014 +     YOUR NAME. . . . .$uname   +        For JOB statement pgmr's name
000015 +     ACCOUNTING INFO. .$acct    +        +Job accounting parameters
000016 +     ROOM NUMBER. . . .$room    +        Room/office nbr for delivery
000017 +     OUTPUT CLASS . . .$z+                Message/report print classes
000018 +     NUMBER OF COPIES .$cpy+              Number of copies to print
000019 +     ACCESS PASSWORD. .-pass    +        Dataset access (if required)
000020 +
000021 )INIT
000022   .HELP = DDSH140
000023   .ZVARS = class
000024   &cpy = 1
000025 )PROC
000026   VER (&uname, NB)
000027   VER (&acct,  NB)
000028   VER (&room,  NB)
000029   VER (&class, NB)
000030   VER (&cpy,   NB, NUM)
000031 )END
=================================== BOTTOM OF DATA ============================
```

Figure 9-14   Panel DDSP140A.

200

```
EDIT ---- userid.DDS.MSGS(DDSM11) - 01.01 ------------------------------ COLUMNS 001 080
COMMAND ===>                                                              SCROLL ===> CSR
====== ============================== TOP OF DATA ==============================
000001 DDSM110B 'SELECT LINE OR END'
000002 'ENTER A(DD), C(HANGE), OR D(ELETE) ON THE APPROPRIATE LINE(S) OR END COMMAND'
====== ============================= BOTTOM OF DATA =============================



EDIT ---- userid.DDS.MSGS(DDSM12) - 01.07 ------------------------------ COLUMNS 001 080
COMMAND ===>                                                              SCROLL ===> CSR
====== ============================== TOP OF DATA ==============================
000001 DDSM120A 'TABLE &table LISTED'
000002 'THE FILE TAILORING PROCESS REQUESTED COMPLETED SUCCESSFULLY'
000003
000004 DDSM120B 'UNABLE TO DO FTOPEN' .ALARM = YES
000005 'UNABLE TO ACCESS THE SKELETON LIBRARY OR THE OUTPUT FILE'
000006
000007 DDSM120C 'UNABLE TO DO FTINCL' .ALARM = YES
000008 'UNABLE TO PROCESS SKELETON &skel.'
000009
000010 DDSM120D 'UNABLE TO DO FTCLOSE' .ALARM = YES
000011 'ENQ FAILED; OUTPUT FILE &dsn IN USE'
====== ============================= BOTTOM OF DATA =============================



EDIT ---- userid.DDS.MSGS(DDSM14) - 01.01 ------------------------------ COLUMNS 001 080
COMMAND ===>                                                              SCROLL ===> CSR
====== ============================== TOP OF DATA ==============================
000001 DDSM140A 'TABLE PRINTED'
000002 'A JOB STREAM HAS BEEN CREATED TO PRINT THE LISTED TABLE'
====== ============================= BOTTOM OF DATA =============================
```

Figure 9-15 Message Members DDSM11 DDSM12 DDSM14.

```
======= ========================= TOP OF DATA =========================
000100 PROC  0
000200 /* ------------------------------------------------------------ */
000300 /*    ESTABLISH PRIMARY LIBRARIES REQUIRED FOR DDS APPLICATION   */
000400 /* ------------------------------------------------------------ */
000500 CONTROL  NOLIST NOCONLIST  MSG NOFLUSH
000600 ISPEXEC  LIBDEF ISPPLIB DATASET ID(DDS.PANELS)
000700 ISPEXEC  LIBDEF ISPMLIB DATASET ID(DDS.MSGS)
000800 ISPEXEC  LIBDEF ISPTLIB DATASET ID(DDS.TABLES)
000900 ISPEXEC  LIBDEF ISPTABL DATASET ID(DDS.TABLES)
001000 ISPEXEC  LIBDEF ISPSLIB DATASET ID(DDS.SKELS)
001100 ISPEXEC  LIBDEF ISPLLIB DATASET ID(DDS.LOAD)
001200 /* needed:  LIBDEF SYSPROC DATASET ID(DDS.CLIST)                 */
001300 /* since...  LIBDEF SYSPROC not supported, need special handling:*/
001400 CONTROL  NOLIST NOCONLIST NOMSG NOFLUSH
001500 FREE     FILE  (DD1, DD2, DD3)
001600 SET      DS1  = '&SYSUID..DDS.CLIST'
001700 ALLOCATE FI(DD1) DA(&DS1) SHR             /* APPL  CLIST? */
001800 IF       &LASTCC NE 0  THEN SET DS1 =
001900 SET      DS2  = '&SYSUID..USER.CLIST'
002000 ALLOCATE FI(DD2) DA(&DS2) SHR             /* USER  CLIST? */
002100 IF       &LASTCC NE 0  THEN SET DS2 =
002200 SET      GRPUID= &SUBSTR(1:5,&SYSUID)$
002300 SET      DS3  = '&GRPUID..GROUP.CLIST'
002400 ALLOCATE FI(DD3) DA(&DS3) SHR             /* GROUP CLIST? */
002500 IF       &LASTCC NE 0  THEN SET DS3 =
002600 FREE     FI(DD1  DD2 DD3 SYSPROC)
002700 ALLOC    FI(SYSPROC) DA(&DS1 &DS2 &DS3 'SYS1.CLIST') SHR
002800 /* ------------------------------------------------------------ */
002900 /*     BEGIN DDS (DATA DICTIONARY SYSTEM) APPLICATION            */
003000 /* ------------------------------------------------------------ */
003100 ISPEXEC  SELECT PANEL(DDSP100)
003200 EXIT
003300 END
======= ======================= BOTTOM OF DATA =======================
```

```
000100 PROC     0
000200 ISPEXEC  CONTROL  NOLIST  NOCONLIST  MSG  NOFLUSH
000300 ISPEXEC  CONTROL  ERRORS  RETURN
000400 /*-------------------------------------------------*/
000500 SET      TABLE = DDST000
000600 ISPEXEC  DISPLAY  PANEL(DDSP110A)
000700 IF       &LASTCC -= 0      THEN  EXIT
000800 IF       &APPL  = &STR(*)  THEN  ISPEXEC VPUT (APPL) PROFILE
000900 ELSE SET &APPL = &STR(*)
001000 ISPEXEC  TBOPEN   &TABLE WRITE
001100 IF       &LASTCC < 8       THEN  GOTO PROCESS
001200 CREATE:  ISPEXEC  TBCREATE &TABLE KEYS(APPL, VARNAME, PTYPE) +
001300                   NAMES    (DTYPE, LENTH, DESCRIPT)
001400 ISPEXEC  TBSORT   &TABLE +
001500                   FIELDS   (APPL,C,A, VARNAME,C,A, PTYPE,C,A)
001600 /*-------------------------------------------------*/
001700 PROCESS: SET      &TBLRC   = 0
001800 ISPEXEC  TBSARG   &TABLE
001900 ISPEXEC  TBSCAN   &TABLE
002000 IF       &LASTCC < 8       THEN  GOTO LOOP1
002100 SET      &VARNAME =
002200 SET      &PTYPE   =
002300 LOOP1:   ISPEXEC  TBADD    &TABLE ORDER
002400 DO       WHILE    &TBLRC   < 8
002500 ISPEXEC  TBDISPL  &TABLE PANEL(DDSP110B) AUTOSEL(NO)
002600 SET      &TBLRC = &LASTCC
002700 LOOP2:   DO       WHILE    &ZTDSELS > 0
002800 IF       &OPTION  = A  THEN  SET  &VARNAME =
002900 ISPEXEC  CONTROL  DISPLAY SAVE
003000 ISPEXEC  DISPLAY  PANEL(DDSP110C)
003100 SET      &PANCC = &LASTCC
003200 ISPEXEC  CONTROL  DISPLAY RESTORE
003300 IF       &PANCC   > 4  THEN  GOTO RESET
003400 IF       &OPTION  = A  THEN  ISPEXEC TBADD    &TABLE ORDER
003500 IF       &OPTION  = C  THEN  ISPEXEC TBMOD    &TABLE ORDER
003600 IF       &OPTION  = D  THEN  ISPEXEC TBDELETE &TABLE
003700 RESET:   SET      &DEL     =
003800 SET      &ZTDSELS > 1
003900 IF       &ZTDSELS > 1  THEN  ISPEXEC TBDISPL  &TABLE
004000 ELSE SET &ZTDSELS = 0
004100 ENDLP2:  END
004200 ENDLP1:  END
004300 /*-------------------------------------------------*/
004400 ISPEXEC  TBCLOSE  &TABLE
004500 EXIT
004600 END
======================== BOTTOM OF DATA ========================
```

Figure 9-17 Command Procedure DDSC110.

```
======================================= TOP OF DATA =======================================
000100 PROC    0
000200 CONTROL NOLIST  NOCONLIST NOMSG NOFLUSH
000300 ISPEXEC CONTROL ERRORS  RETURN
000400 /*--------------------------------------------------------------*/
000500 SET     TABLE = DDST000
000600 SET     SKEL  = DDSS120
000700 SET     DSN   = '&SYSUID..DDS.FTOUTPUT'
000800 ISPEXEC DISPLAY PANEL(DDSP120A)
000900 IF      &LASTCC ¬= 0 THEN EXIT
001000 FREE    FI(ISPFILE)
001100 ALLOCATE FI(ISPFILE) DA(&DSN.) OLD
001200 ISPEXEC FTOPEN
001300 IF      &LASTCC ¬= 0 THEN GOTO NOFTOPEN
001400 ISPEXEC FTINCL &SKEL
001500 IF      &LASTCC ¬= 0 THEN GOTO NOFTINCL
001600 ISPEXEC FTCLOSE
001700 IF      &LASTCC ¬= 0 THEN GOTO NOFTCLSE
001800 ISPEXEC SETMSG MSG(DDSM120A)
001900 GOTO    EXIT
002000 /*------------------------------------------------------*/
002100 NOFTOPEN: ISPEXEC SETMSG MSG(DDSM120B)
002200 GOTO    EXIT
002300 NOFTINCL: ISPEXEC SETMSG MSG(DDSM120C)
002400 ISPEXEC FTCLOSE NAME(DDSO120)
002500 GOTO    EXIT
002600 NOFTCLSE: ISPEXEC SETMSG MSG(DDSM120D)
002700 EXIT:   FREE FI(ISPFILE)
002800 EXIT
002900 END
======================================= BOTTOM OF DATA =======================================
```

Figure 9-18 Command Procedure DDSC120.

```
EDIT ---- userid.DDS.CLIST(DDSC130) - 01.07 ------------- COLUMNS 001 072
COMMAND ===>                                                SCROLL ===> CSR
======= ==================================== TOP OF DATA =======================
000100  PROC    0
000200  CONTROL NOLIST  NOCONLIST NOMSG NOFLUSH
000300  ISPEXEC CONTROL ERRORS    RETURN
000400  ISPEXEC BROWSE  DATASET(DDS.FTOUTPUT)
000500  EXIT
000600  END
======= ================================== BOTTOM OF DATA =====================
```

Figure 9-19 Command Procedure DDSC130.

```
EDIT ---- userid.DDS.CLIST(DDSC140) - 01.10 -------------- COLUMNS 001 072
COMMAND ===>                                               SCROLL ===> CSR
====== ============================= TOP OF DATA =============================
000100 PROC       0
000200 CONTROL    NOLIST   NOCONLIST NOMSG NOFLUSH
000300 ISPEXEC    CONTROL  ERRORS    RETURN
000400 /*                                                                    */
000500 SET        SKEL =   DDSS140
000600 ISPEXEC    DISPLAY  PANEL(DDSP140A)
000700 IF         &LASTCC  ¬= 0     THEN EXIT
000800 ISPEXEC    VPUT     (UNAME,ACCT,ROOM,CLASS) PROFILE
000900 ISPEXEC    FTOPEN   TEMP
001000 IF         &LASTCC  ¬= 0     THEN GOTO NOFTOPEN
001100 ISPEXEC    FTINCL   &SKEL
001200 IF         &LASTCC  ¬= 0     THEN GOTO NOFTINCL
001300 ISPEXEC    FTCLOSE
001400 IF         &LASTCC  ¬= 0     THEN GOTO NOFTCLSE
001500 ISPEXEC    VGET     ZTEMPF
001600 SUBMIT     '&ZTEMPF.'
001700 ISPEXEC    SETMSG   MSG(DDSM140A)
001800 EXIT
001900 /*                                                                    */
002000 NOFTOPEN:ISPEXEC   SETMSG   MSG(DDSM120B)
002100 EXIT
002200 NOFTINCL:ISPEXEC   SETMSG   MSG(DDSM120C)
002300 EXIT
002400 NOFTCLSE:ISPEXEC   SETMSG   MSG(DDSM120D)
002500 EXIT
002600 END
====== ========================== BOTTOM OF DATA ============================
```

Figure 9-20 Command Procedure DDSC140.

206

```
EDIT ---- userid.DDS.SKELS(DDSS120) - 01.24 ------------------- COLUMNS 001 072
COMMAND ===>                                                     SCROLL ===> CSR
====== ========================== TOP OF DATA ================================
000100 )DEFAULT )&?!<|>
000200 )TB   2  8 19 25 32 41
000300 )SET LINES = 255
000400 )CM ------------------------------------ start loop for all table rows
000500 )DOT &table
000600 )CM ------------------------------------- start row selection process
000700 )SEL     &appl = *        |      &sappl = &appl
000800 )SEL       &spool = *      |       &spool = &ptype
000900 )SEL         &sdata = *     |        &sdata = &dtype
001000 )CM            - row selected if all 3 true -
001100 )SEL            &LINES > 50
001200 )CM ------------------------------------- start heading routine
001300 1DDS TABLE ENTRIES FOR:  APPL=&sappl.,POOLTYPE=&spool.,DATATYPE=&sdata.
001400 0APPL  VARIABLE  POOL   DATA   FIELD   FIELD DESCRIPTION AND COMMENTS
001500  ID    NAME    TYPE   TYPE   LENGTH
001600 )BLANK
001700 )SET LINES = 5
001800 )CM ------------------------------------- end heading routine/resume row processing
001900 )ENDSEL
002000 &appl !&varname !&ptype !&dtype !&lenth !&descript
002100 )SET LINES = &LINES + 1
002200 )ENDSEL
002300 )ENDSEL
002400 )ENDSEL
002500 )CM ------------------------------------- end selection process
002600 )ENDDOT
002700 )CM ------------------------------------- end loop for table rows
====== ================= BOTTOM OF DATA ================================
```

Figure 9-21 Skeleton DDSS120.

```
EDIT ---- userid.DDS.SKELS(DDSS140) - 01.11 ------------------- COLUMNS 001 072
COMMAND ===>                                                        SCROLL ===> CSR
===== ========================== TOP OF DATA =================================
000100 //&ZUSER.A JOB (&acct.,&room.,TLIST),&uname.,MSGCLASS=&class.,
000200 //             USER=&ZUSER.,NOTIFY=&ZUSER.,PASSWORD=&pass.
000300 /*JOBPARM      COPIES=&cpy.
000400 //S1     EXEC  PGM=IEBGENER
000500 //SYSUT1   DD  DSN=&ZUSER..DDS.FTOUTPUT,DISP=SHR
000600 //SYSUT2   DD  SYSOUT=*,DCB=(&ZUSER..DDS.FTOUTPUT,RECFM=FBA)
000700 //SYSPRINT DD  SYSOUT=*
000800 //SYSIN    DD  DUMMY
000900 //
===== ======================= BOTTOM OF DATA =================================
```

Figure 9-22 Skeleton DDSS140.

```
EDIT ---- userid.DDS.PANELS(DDSH000) - 01.07 ---------------------------- COLUMNS 001 080
COMMAND ===>                                                              SCROLL ===> CSR
=====  ============================= TOP OF DATA ====================================
000001 )ATTR DEFAULT(%+_)
000002        /* % TYPE(TEXT) INTENS(HIGH)          defaults displayed for   */
000003        /* + TYPE(TEXT) INTENS(LOW)           information only         */
000004        /* _ TYPE(INPUT) INTENS(HIGH) CAPS(ON) JUST(LEFT)              */
000005 )BODY
000006 %TUTORIAL ---------------- DATA DICTIONARY SYSTEM ------------- TUTORIAL +
000007 %SELECTION ===>_ZCMD
000008 %
000009 %
000010 %                      |--------------------------------------|
000011                        |          TABLE OF CONTENTS           |
000012 +                      |--------------------------------------|
000013        You may "navigate" throughout this tutorial facility as if it were a
000014        normal book, i.e., you may proceed sequentially through each of the
000015        topics offered, or you may go directly to the desired one shown based
000016        on the one-character designators associated with each entry.
000017
000018        Once in a topic, you may go from one "page" to the next (if any) by
000019        pressing the%ENTER+key, you may back up with the%B(ack)+command, you
000020        may skip to the next topic with the%S(kip)+command, you may go up to
000021        the higher topic with the%U(p)+command, or you may go to the index
000022        (the%I(ndex)+command) or the table of contents (the%T(op)+command).
000023
000024        The following are the available topics:
000025
000026        %0+ GENERAL INFO       General system description
000027        %1+ UPDATE TABLE       Update/create master dictionary
000028        %2+ LIST  TABLE        List full dictionary or a subset
000029        %3+ VIEW  OUTPUT       View listing at the terminal
000030        %4+ PRINT OUTPUT       Send listing to the printer
000031
000032 )PROC
000033        &ZSEL = TRANS(&ZCMD
000034                     0, DDSH100
000035                     1,*DDSH110
000036                     2,*DDSH120
000037                     3,*DDSH130
000038                     4,*DDSH140
000039                     *,'?')
000040 )END
=====  ============================ BOTTOM OF DATA ===================================
```

Figure 9-23   Tutorial Panel DDSH000.

```
======= ================================= TOP OF DATA =================================
000001 )ATTR DEFAULT(%+_)
000002          /* % TYPE(TEXT) INTENS(HIGH)          defaults displayed for   */
000003          /* + TYPE(TEXT) INTENS(LOW)                 information only    */
000004          /* _ TYPE(INPUT) INTENS(HIGH) CAPS(ON) JUST(LEFT)               */
000005 )BODY
000006 %TUTORIAL ---------------------- DATA DICTIONARY SYSTEM -------------------- TUTORIAL +
000007 %SELECTION ===> _ZCMD
000008 %
000009 %                        |----------------------------------|
000010                          |           PRIMARY OPTIONS         |
000011                          |----------------------------------|
000012 +
000013        The%DATA DICTIONARY SYSTEM (DDS)+is designed to assist a dialog developer
000014        with the tracking and maintenance of all the VARIABLE NAMES required for
000015        a given application.  To further assist the developer, facilities have
000016        been incorporated to allow also the names of PANELS, MESSAGES, TABLES,
000017        SKELETONS, TUTORIALS, PROGRAMS, COMMANDS, etc.
000018
000019        The following topics may be viewed in sequence or selected directly:
000020
000021        %1+ UPDATE TABLE       Update/create master dictionary
000022        %2+ LIST   TABLE       List full dictionary or a subset
000023        %3+ VIEW   OUTPUT      View listing at the terminal
000024        %4+ PRINT  OUTPUT      Send listing to the printer
000025
000026 )PROC
000027        &ZUP  = DDSH000
000028        &ZSEL = TRANS (&ZCMD
000029                        1,DDSH110
000030                        2,DDSH120
000031                        3,DDSH130
000032                        4,DDSH140
000033                        *,'?')
000034 )END
======= ================================= BOTTOM OF DATA =================================
```

210

```
EDIT ---- userid.DDS.PANELS(DDSH110) - 01.04 --------------------- COLUMNS 001 080
COMMAND ===>                                                        SCROLL ===> CSR
======= ============================== TOP OF DATA ==============================
000001 )ATTR DEFAULT(%+_)
000002          /* % TYPE(TEXT) INTENS(HIGH)           defaults displayed for    */
000003          /* + TYPE(TEXT) INTENS(LOW)            information only           */
000004          /* _ TYPE(INPUT) INTENS(HIGH) CAPS(ON) JUST(LEFT)                 */
000005 )BODY
000006 %TUTORIAL ------------------ DATA DICTIONARY SYSTEM -------------- TUTORIAL_+
000007 %SELECTION ===>_ZCMD
000008 %
000009 %                     |-------------------------------|
000010                       |      UPDATE DICTIONARY         |
000011                       |-------------------------------|
000012 +
000013         This option allows a developer either to create a master dictionary (if
000014         none yet exists), or to update an existing one. Within this dictionary,
000015         entries are "partitioned" by application identifiers which logically
000016         should match the id given to ISPF. This "partitioning" allows one to
000017         subset the dictionary display so that scrolling for the needed data may
000018         be minimized.
000019
000020         This subsetting concept can also be used to reduce the display to names
000021         associated with a particular variable pool type and/or data type classes.
000022
000023         The following topics are presented in sequence, or may be selected by
000024         number:
000025
000026         %1+ SUBSET SELECTION     Dictionary subsetting parameters
000027         %2+ TABLE  DISPLAY       Dictionary entry selection
000028         %3+ DATA   ENTRY         Dictionary data entry
000029 )PROC
000030         &ZUP = DDSH100
000031         &ZSEL = TRANS (&ZCMD
000032                        1,DDSH110A
000033                        2,DDSH110B
000034                        3,DDSH110C
000035                        *,'?')
000036 )END
======= =========================== BOTTOM OF DATA ============================
```

Figure 9-25 Tutorial Panel DDSH110.

```
EDIT ---- userid.DDS.PANELS(DDSH110A) - 01.03 --------------------- COLUMNS 001 080
COMMAND ===>                                                         SCROLL ===> CSR
====== ================================ TOP OF DATA =================================
000001 )ATTR DEFAULT(%+_)
000002        /* % TYPE(TEXT) INTENS(HIGH)           defaults displayed for     */
000003        /* + TYPE(TEXT) INTENS(LOW)            information only            */
000004        /* _ TYPE(INPUT) INTENS(HIGH) CAPS(ON) JUST(LEFT)                  */
000005 )BODY
000006 %TUTORIAL ------------- DATA DICTIONARY SYSTEM ------------- TUTORIAL +
000007 %SELECTION ===> _ZCMD
000008 %
000009 %
000010                    |------------------------------------|
000011                    |          SUBSETTING OPTIONS         |
000012 +                  |------------------------------------|
000013         This option allows a developer to work with a subset of the complete
000014         dictionary. Normally, a developer is only concerned with a portion
000015         of the full dictionary either because it relates to the application
000016         being developed, or because he/she wishes to examine all of the names
000017         that fit a particular class.
000018
000019         By selecting specific classes, it should become easier to analyze the
000020         various names and to determine patterns and/or abnormalities.
000021         Selections may be performed based on%(1)+application id,%(2)+pool type
000022         and/or%(3)+data type.
000023
000024         For example, if one wanted to see all of the names that relate to
000025         the components of a dialog (PANELS, MESSAGES, TABLES, etc), one
000026         could give the dialog name and a pool of "N" (N/A). If a developer
000027         wanted to review all of the messages available for any application,
000028         the data type parameter of "MSGS", by itself, would accomplish this.
000029 )PROC
000030        &ZUP   = DDSH110
000031 )END
====== =============================== BOTTOM OF DATA ===============================
```

Figure 9-26 Tutorial Panel DDSH110A.

```
EDIT ---- userid.DDS.PANELS(DDSH110B) - 01.03 -------------------- COLUMNS 001 080
COMMAND ===>                                                       SCROLL ===> CSR
====== =============================== TOP OF DATA ===============================
000001 )ATTR DEFAULT(%+_)
000002       /* % TYPE(TEXT) INTENS(HIGH)            defaults displayed for    */
000003       /* + TYPE(TEXT) INTENS(LOW)             information only          */
000004       /* _ TYPE(INPUT) INTENS(HIGH) CAPS(ON) JUST(LEFT)                 */
000005 )BODY
000006 %TUTORIAL --------------- DATA DICTIONARY SYSTEM -------------- TUTORIAL_+
000007 %SELECTION ===> _ZCMD
000008 %
000009 %                        |----------------------------|
000010                          |    TABLE DISPLAY PANEL      |
000011                          |----------------------------|
000012 +
000013       This option display the dictionary contents based on the subsetting
000014       parameters (if any) given in the preceding panel.
000015
000016       Preceding each entry, provisions are made to accept a%command code+
000017       to allow additions (A), changes (C), or deletions (D). As many lines
000018       as necessary may be selected with one of these codes; for each line
000019       selected, an expanded panel display will be provided to allow the user
000020       to add/change/delete the selected entries.
000021 )PROC
000022     &ZUP  =  DDSH110
000023 )END
====== ============================= BOTTOM OF DATA =============================
```

Figure 9-27 Tutorial Panel DDSH110B.

```
====== =============================== TOP OF DATA ==============================
000001 )ATTR DEFAULT(%+_)
000002        /* % TYPE(TEXT) INTENS(HIGH)          defaults displayed for    */
000003        /* + TYPE(TEXT) INTENS(LOW)               information only       */
000004        /* _ TYPE(INPUT) INTENS(HIGH) CAPS(ON) JUST(LEFT)                */
000005 )BODY
000006 %TUTORIAL --------------- DATA DICTIONARY SYSTEM --------------- TUTORIAL +
000007 %SELECTION ===>_ZCMD
000008 %
000009 %                    |-----------------------------------|
000010 +                    |         DATA ENTRY PANEL          |
000011                      |-----------------------------------|
000012 +
000013        This panel is displayed whenever a valid command code is detected
000014        on any line, displayed by the table display panel. Depending on the
000015        command action (displayed at the top of the panel), the user may then
000016        add, change, or delete the entry.
000017
000018        For a%delete+action, one only needs to confirm it by entering a Yes or
000019        No on the last entry of the screen (the cursor will be placed there
000020        automatically.
000021
000022        For a%change+or%add+action, all fields (except the description) are
000023        required. For maximum flexibility, field checking has been limited
000024        to simple data type checks such as numeric, alphabetic, or name rules.
000025        The only entry which is checked for specific codes is the pool type
000026        which must contain a "P", "S", "F", or "N" (for N/A).
000027
000028        It should also be noted that the combination of APPLICATION ID, VARIABLE
000029        NAME, and POOL TYPE form a%composite key+which should yield a unique value
000030        when adding a new entry.
000031 )PROC
000032        &ZUP  =  DDSH110
000033 )END
====== ============================= BOTTOM OF DATA =============================
```

```
EDIT ---- userid.DDS.PANELS(DDSH120) - 01.04 ---------------------------- COLUMNS 001 080
COMMAND ===>                                                              SCROLL ===> CSR
======= =============================== TOP OF DATA ===============================
000001 )ATTR DEFAULT(%+_)
000002        /* % TYPE(TEXT) INTENS(HIGH)      defaults displayed for      */
000003        /* + TYPE(TEXT) INTENS(LOW)       information only            */
000004        /* _ TYPE(INPUT) INTENS(HIGH) CAPS(ON) JUST(LEFT)             */
000005 )BODY
000006 %TUTORIAL ------------ DATA DICTIONARY SYSTEM ------------ TUTORIAL +
000007 %SELECTION ===>_ZCMD
000008 %
000009 %                   |-------------------------------|
000010                     |        LIST DICTIONARY        |
000011                     |-------------------------------|
000012 +
000013      This option allows a developer to list the contents of the dictionary
000014      either for more extensive browsing capabilities or for hard-copy print,
000015      or both.
000016
000017      The dictionary can be processed in its entirety, or it may be selected
000018      by%(1)+application identifier,%(2)+by variable pool type, and/or%(3)+
000019      by data type class. These three entries may be used in any combination
000020      to provide a very selective listing of the desired items.
000021
000022      For a detailed explanation of each of the three entries, press the
000023      ENTER key.
000024 )PROC
000025      &ZUP   = DDSH100
000026      &ZCONT = DDSH120A
000027 )END
======= =============================== BOTTOM OF DATA ===============================
```

Figure 9-29 Tutorial Panel DDSH120.

215

```
===== ================================= TOP OF DATA =================================
000001 )ATTR DEFAULT(%+)
000002        /* % TYPE(TEXT) INTENS(HIGH)         defaults displayed for   */
000003        /* + TYPE(TEXT) INTENS(LOW)          information only          */
000004        /* _ TYPE(INPUT) INTENS(HIGH) CAPS(ON) JUST(LEFT)              */
000005 )BODY
000006 %TUTORIAL ---------------- DATA DICTIONARY SYSTEM --------------- TUTORIAL +
000007 %SELECTION ===>_ZCMD
000008 %
000009 %
000010               |---------------------------------------------|
000011               |          LIST SELECTION PARAMETERS          |
000012 +             |---------------------------------------------|
000013        This panel enables one to identify the selection parameters to control
000014        the contents of the dictionary listing about to be produced.
000015
000016        By selecting specific classes, it should become easier to analyze the
000017        various names and to determine patterns and/or abnormalities.
000018        Selections may be performed based on%(1)+application id,%(2)+pool type
000019        and/or%(3)+data type.
000020
000021        For example, if one wanted to see all of the names that relate to
000022        the components of a dialog (PANELS, MESSAGES, TABLES, etc), one
000023        could give the dialog name and a pool of "N" (N/A). If a developer
000024        wanted to review all of the messages available for any application,
000025        the data type parameter of "MSGS", by itself, would accomplish this.
000026
000027        An absence of a selection parameter indicates that no test is to be
000028        made; i.e., all variations of that entry are to be accepted.  As such,
000029        to list the entire dictionary, leave all entries blank.
000030 )PROC
000031        &ZUP  =  DDSH120
000032 )END
===== =============================== BOTTOM OF DATA ===============================
```

```
EDIT ---- userid.DDS.PANELS(DDSH130) - 01.03 ------------------------ COLUMNS 001 080
COMMAND ===>                                                          SCROLL ===> CSR
===== ================================= TOP OF DATA ==================================
000001 )ATTR DEFAULT(%+_)
000002        /* % TYPE(TEXT) INTENS(HIGH)          defaults displayed for     */
000003        /* + TYPE(TEXT) INTENS(LOW)           information only           */
000004        /* _ TYPE(INPUT) INTENS(HIGH) CAPS(ON) JUST(LEFT)                */
000005 )BODY
000006 %TUTORIAL ---------------- DATA DICTIONARY SYSTEM ---------------- TUTORIAL +
000007 %SELECTION ===>_ZCMD
000008 %
000009 %              |-------------------------------------------|
000010 +              |        REVIEW DICTIONARY LISTING          |
000011                |-------------------------------------------|
000012 +
000013        This option allows a developer to review the selected dictionary listing
000014        either for more extensive browsing capabilities or for a hard-copy print,
000015        or both.
000016
000017        The full capabilities of the BROWSE command will allow the developer
000018        to scan the contents of the listing for any field or word that one
000019        may need to locate. Any of the BROWSE commands may be used while in
000020        this option.
000021 )PROC
000022     &ZUP  =  DDSH100
000023 )END
===== ============================= BOTTOM OF DATA ==================================
```

Figure 9-31 Tutorial Panel DDSH130.

```
EDIT ---- userid.DDS.PANELS(DDSH140) - 01.04 ------------------ COLUMNS 001 080
COMMAND ===>                                                      SCROLL ===> CSR
======= ============================== TOP OF DATA ==============================
000001 )ATTR DEFAULT(%+ )
000002      /* % TYPE(TEXT) INTENS(HIGH)          defaults displayed for      */
000003      /* + TYPE(TEXT) INTENS(LOW)                 information only      */
000004      /* _ TYPE(INPUT) INTENS(HIGH) CAPS(ON) JUST(LEFT)                 */
000005 )BODY
000006 %TUTORIAL -------------- DATA DICTIONARY SYSTEM --------------- TUTORIAL +
000007 %SELECTION ===> _ZCMD
000008 %
000009 %                   |---------------------------------------|
000010                     |     PRINT DICTIONARY LISTING          |
000011                     |---------------------------------------|
000012 +
000013      This option allows a developer to print the selected dictionary listing
000014      on any printer available through the system using any of the output
000015      classes desired and for any number of copies allowed.
000016
000017      User profile data is maintained for each person so that the same data
000018      will not have to be repeated each time this service is requested. Of
000019      course, the first time that this is used, this profile will not exist.
000020
000021      For a detailed explanation of these user profile items, press the
000022      ENTER key.
000023 )PROC
000024      &ZUP   = DDSH100
000025      &ZCONT = DDSH140A
000026 )END
======= ============================= BOTTOM OF DATA =============================
```

Figure 9-32 Tutorial Panel DDSH140.

```
EDIT ---- userid.DDS.PANELS(DDSH140A) - 01.02 --------------------------------- COLUMNS 001 080
COMMAND ===>                                                                        SCROLL ===> CSR
====== ============================================ TOP OF DATA ===============================================
000001 )ATTR DEFAULT(%+_)
000002        /* % TYPE(TEXT) INTENS(HIGH)      defaults displayed for      */
000003        /* + TYPE(TEXT) INTENS(LOW)              information only      */
000004        /* _ TYPE(INPUT) INTENS(HIGH) CAPS(ON) JUST(LEFT)             */
000005 )BODY
000006 %TUTORIAL --------------- DATA DICTIONARY SYSTEM --------------- TUTORIAL_+
000007 %SELECTION ===>_ZCMD
000008 %
000009 %                  |---------------------------------------|
000010                    |         PRINT JOB PARAMETERS          |
000011                    |---------------------------------------|
000012 +
000013        This panel enables one to review/provide the necessary job control
000014        parameters in order to submit a job which will print the listing
000015        produced from a previous process.
000016
000017        All of the entries indicated are required except for the ACCESS
000018        PASSWORD which will depend on the security attached to the data
000019        set that holds the dictionary listing.
000020
000021        All parameters will be "remembered" across sessions except for
000022        the number of output copies which will always default to 1. The
000023        actual contents of each entry will depend on the installation
000024        requirements.
000025 )PROC
000026        &ZUP  =  DDSH140
000027 )END
====== =========================================== BOTTOM OF DATA ===============================================
```

Figure 9-33 Tutorial Panel DDSH140A.

219

```
======= ======================================= TOP OF DATA ====================
000001 )ATTR DEFAULT(%+_)
000002        /* % TYPE(TEXT) INTENS(HIGH)        defaults displayed for    */
000003        /* + TYPE(TEXT) INTENS(LOW)          information only          */
000004        /* _ TYPE(INPUT) INTENS(HIGH) CAPS(ON) JUST(LEFT)             */
000005 )BODY
000006 %TUTORIAL ------------------- DATA DICTIONARY SYSTEM ------------------- TUTORIAL +
000007 %COMMAND ===>_ZCMD
000008 %
000009 %
000010              |--------------------------|
000011              |          INDEX           |
000012              |--------------------------|
000013 +     Selected topics discussed in the tutorial can be found in this index.
000014
000015       To use the index, enter the first letter of the topic of interest. The
000016       index page containing subjects starting with that letter is displayed.
000017       On an index page, any subject can be selected by entering the two
000018       character option preceding that selection.
000019
000020       When you are on one index page, you can access any other index page by
000021       entering its letter identification. If you are in the tutorial but%not+
000022       on an index page, you can get to the index by entering%INDEX+or%I+in
000023       the command field.
000024
000025       The index pages are presented in sequence if you press the ENTER key.
000026
000027 )PROC
000028       &ZIND = YES                                    /* THIS IS AN INDEX PANEL */
000029       &ZCMD = TRUNC (&ZCMD,1)
000030       VER(&ZCMD, ALPHA)
000031       IF (&ZCMD -= ' ')  &ZSEL  = DDSH999&ZCMD
000032       IF (&ZCMD = ' ')  &ZCONT = DDSH999A
000033 )END
======= ============================ BOTTOM OF DATA =============================
```

```
                                                                     COLUMN 001 000
COMMAND ===>                                                         SCROLL ===> CSR
====== ===================================== TOP OF DATA ===============================
000001 )ATTR DEFAULT(%+_)
000002 )BODY
000003 %TUTORIAL ----------------- DATA DICTIONARY SYSTEM ----------------- TUTORIAL +
000004 %COMMAND ===>_ZCMD
000005 %
000006 %
000007                          |----------------|  |---|
000008                          |      INDEX:  'A'|  |   |
000009 +                        |----------------|  |---|
000010 +To select a topic, enter code (letter and number) in the option field:
000011 +
000012 %A1 +-                                               %A16+-
000013 %A2 +-ACCOUNTING                                     %A17+-
000014 %A3 +-                                               %A18+-
000015 %A4 +-ACTION                                         %A19+-
000016 %A5 +-                                               %A20+-
000017 %A6 +-ADD                                            %A21+-
000018 %A7 +-                                               %A22+-
000019 %A8 +-ANALYZE (Display)                              %A23+-
000020 %A9 +-ANALYZE (Listing)                              %A24+-
000021 %A10+-                                               %A25+-
000022 %A11+-APPLICATION                                    %A26+-
000023 %A12+-                                               %A27+-
000024 %A13+-                                               %A28+-
000025 %A14+-                                               %A29+-
000026 %A15+-                                               %A30+-
000027 )PROC
000028     &ZIND = YES                              /* THIS IS AN INDEX PANEL */
000029     &ZSEL = TRANS(&ZCMD
000030                  A2,*DDSH140
000031                  A4,*DDSH110C
000032                  A6,*DDSH110B
000033                  A8,*DDSH110A
000034                  A9,*DDSH120A
000035                  A11,*DDSH110A
000036                  )
000037     IF (&ZSEL = ' ')
000038     &ZCMD = TRUNC(&ZCMD,1)
000039     IF (&ZCMD ¬= ' ')           &ZSEL  = DDSH999&ZCMD
000040     IF (&ZCMD = ' ')            &ZCONT = DDSH999B
000041 )END
====== ===================================== BOTTOM OF DATA =============================
```

Figure 9-35 Tutorial Panel DDSH999A.

221

```
EDIT ---- userid.DDS.PANELS(DDSH999Z) - 01.01 ----------------------------- COLUMNS 001 080
COMMAND ===>                                                                  SCROLL ===> CSR
=====  ========================== TOP OF DATA ================================================
000001 )ATTR DEFAULT(%+_)
000002 )BODY
000003 %TUTORIAL --------------- DATA DICTIONARY SYSTEM --------------- TUTORIAL +
000004 %COMMAND ===>_ZCMD
000005 %
000006 %                      |------------------------------|
000007 %                      |          INDEX: 'Z'          |
000008 %                      |------------------------------|
000009 +
000010 +To select a topic, enter code (letter and number) in the option field:
000011 +
000012 %Z1 +-          %Z16+-
000013 %Z2 +-          %Z17+-
000014 %Z3 +-          %Z18+-
000015 %Z4 +-          %Z19+-
000016 %Z5 +-          %Z20+-
000017 %Z6 +-          %Z21+-
000018 %Z7 +-          %Z22+-
000019 %Z8 +-          %Z23+-
000020 %Z9 +-          %Z24+-
000021 %Z10+-          %Z25+-
000022 %Z11+-          %Z26+-
000023 %Z12+-          %Z27+-
000024 %Z13+-          %Z28+-
000025 %Z14+-          %Z29+-
000026 %Z15+-          %Z30+-
000027 )PROC
000028 &ZIND = YES                              /* THIS IS AN INDEX PANEL */
000029 &ZSEL = TRANS(&ZCMD
000030               Z1,*DDSH000
000031               )
000032 IF (&ZSEL =  ' ')        &ZSEL  = DDSH999&ZCMD
000033 IF (&ZCMD ¬= ' ')        &ZCONT = DDSH999A
000034 IF (&ZCMD =  ' ')
000035 )END
=====  ======================== BOTTOM OF DATA ===============================================
```

Figure 9-36   Tutorial Panel DDSH999Z.

10

Testing a New Application

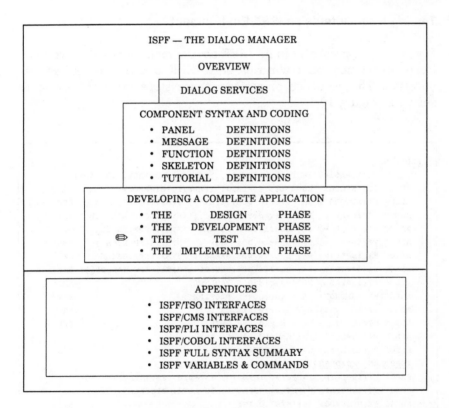

Now that the components are developed, the next phase is to test them. This is not to imply that you cannot test any component until all of them are in place; the panels, for example, can be tested as you develop each one. It is common for a developer to enter split-screen mode so that one screen can be used to edit the panel while the other screen is used to test the same panel. For ease of presentation, however, we will assume that all components are now ready to test as a group.

The method of testing depends on the environment in which you operate, i.e., whether you are already in an ISPF environment or not, and if so, whether you have access to PDF or not. We will start with the situation where you are not in an ISPF environment.

Testing from Outside an ISPF Environment

If you are not presently in an ISPF environment, you will have to allocate all the necessary libraries, start ISPF, and then enter your application. The sequence to perform these steps might be coded as shown in Figure 10-1.

```
PROC  0
    FREE  FI(ISPLLIB, ISPPLIB, ISPMLIB, ISPSLIB, ISPTABL, ISPPROF)
    FREE  FI(ISPCTL1, ISPCTL2, ISPLST1, ISPLST2, SYSPROC)
    ALLOC FI(SYSPROC) DA('userid.DDS.CLIST', 'SYS1.CLIST')          SHR
    ALLOC FI(ISPLLIB) DA('userid.DDS.LOAD',  'SYS1.ISPF.LINKLIB') SHR
    ALLOC FI(ISPPLIB) DA('userid.DDS.PANELS','SYS1.ISPF.PANELS') SHR
    ALLOC FI(ISPMLIB) DA('userid.DDS.MSGS',  'SYS1.ISPF.MSGS')   SHR
    ALLOC FI(ISPSLIB) DA('userid.DDS.SKELS', 'SYS1.ISPF.SKELS')  SHR
    ALLOC FI(ISPTLIB) DA('userid.DDS.TABLES','SYS1.ISPF.TABLES') SHR
    ALLOC FI(ISPTABL) DA('userid.DDS.TABLES')                     SHR
    ALLOC FI(ISPPROF) DA('userid.xxx.PROFILE')                    SHR
    ALLOC FI(ISPCTL1) DA('userid.xxx.CNTL')                       SHR
    ALLOC FI(ISPCTL2) DA('userid.yyy.CNTL')                       SHR
    ALLOC FI(ISPLST1) DA('userid.xxx.LIST')                       OLD
    ALLOC FI(ISPLST2) DA('userid.yyy.LIST')                       OLD
    ISPSTART CMD(DDSC000) NEWAPPL(DDS) TRACEX
    FREE  FI(ISPLLIB, ISPPLIB, ISPMLIB, ISPSLIB, ISPTABL, ISPPROF)
    FREE  FI(ISPCTL1, ISPCTL2, ISPLST1, ISPLST2, SYSPROC)
    ALLOC FI(SYSPROC) DA('SYS1.CLIST')                            SHR
    EXIT
    END
```

Figure 10-1   Sample ISPF Start-Up Procedure.

The names for each library would, of course, be installation dependent. Basically, all that we are doing with this procedure is allocating the various file names used by ISPF to the data sets that contain our application as well as those for ISPF proper. Once this is done, we then invoke the ISPSTART command which starts the Dialog Manager, which in turn SELECTs a panel, a command, or a program based on the parameters given. The full syntax of the ISPSTART command is very similar to that of the SELECT service already discussed:

```
 ISPSTART sel-options  [appl-options]  [test-options]


  where "sel-options" is one of the following:
  ♦      PANEL(name)  [OPT(option)]
  ♦      CMD(name     [parms])        [LANG(APL)]
  ♦      PGM(name)    [PARM(parms)]


  "appl-options" is:  NEWAPPL(appl-id)


  "test-options" is:  TEST | TESTX | TRACE | TRACEX
```

The "sel-options" and "appl-options" parameters are exactly the same as already explained under the SELECT service. What is new is the "test-options" which will be explained now.

The TEST parameter indicates that ISPF is to operate in *test mode* — a very useful facility for debugging any ISPF dialog application. In this mode, panels are refetched from the library each time, whereas in normal mode, definitions for the last six panels displayed are kept in core (to improve performance). It should be obvious, then, that if you are making adjustments to your panels as you test them and if you are not in test mode, the changes will not be visible until the copies in core are replaced.

In addition to this mechanism, some other features such as ABEND intercepts, tutorial chaining indications, etc., are also available only while in test mode.

The TESTX parameter is similar to TEST, but, in addition, all messages written to the log file are also written to the terminal.

The TRACE parameter provides the same features as TEST, but it also writes to the log file a trace of all the ISPEXEC service calls along with any errors detected.

The TRACEX parameter is similar to TRACE, but, in addition, all traces are also written to the terminal.

The ISPSTART command is to be used not only for testing a new application, but to execute as well any other application already in production that must be started from an environment where ISPF is not already running.

The example given in the previous procedure (Figure 10-1),

```
☞ ISPSTART CMD(DDSC000) NEWAPPL(DDS) TRACEX
```

indicates that the Dialog Manager is to be started, the command DDSC000 is to be selected with a profile pool named DDS, and TRACEX mode is to be activated.

Testing from Within an ISPF Environment

If you are already in an ISPF environment, which is the most common situation, then the basic ISPF libraries are already allocated. The problem here is how to "join" (concatenate) your new libraries with those already established for ISPF.

Using the LIBDEF Service

If you are using a recent ISPF release where the LIBDEF service is supported, this process can simplify your needs tremendously. We have already seen that any libraries allocated through the LIBDEF service are "concatenated" ahead of the ones already established for the existing environment. (It should be noted that this is not a concatenation process as generally understood. Although the general effect is the same for all ISPF services, it is accomplished by actually searching two different sets of definitions — one as established by the LIBDEF services, the other as established through the normal operating system functions.)

```
)BODY
%---------------- ISPF USER PRIMARY OPTION MENU ----------------
%OPTION  ===_ZCMD                                         +
%
%  1 +DEMO          - ISPF Demo/Test of Dialog Management
%  2 +DDS           - Data Dictionary System
%  3 +...           - ... ...
%  X +EXIT          - Terminate User Developed Dialogs
%
+Enter%END+command to terminate this application


)INIT
  &ZPRIM   = YES
  &ZHTOP   = USRH000
  .HELP    = USRH000
  &ZHINDEX = USRH999


)PROC
  &ZSEL = TRANS( TRUNC (&ZCMD,'.')
             1,'PANEL(DEMO000)  NEWAPPL(DEMO)'
             2,'CMD(DDSC000)    NEWAPPL(DDS)'
             3,... ...
             X,'EXIT'
             ' ',' '
             *,'?' )


)END
```

Figure 10-2   "Hooking" a New Application into an Existing Panel.

In any event, once the libraries are properly defined, ISPF is then able to find our application components. All that is left is to have some place — a selection panel or a function — where we can trigger the new application. The panel shown in Figure 10-2 illustrates this process.

This would start a command procedure like the one in Figure 10-3. This procedure would establish our needed environment which would be reset automatically when exited.

Please note that SYSPROC, which is a TSO — not ISPF — file, was handled in a special manner. While it is possible for the

```
   PROC    0
   CONTROL NOLIST NOCONLIST   MSG NOFLUSH
   ISPEXEC LIBDEF ISPPLIB DATASET ID(DDS.PANELS)
   ISPEXEC LIBDEF ISPMLIB DATASET ID(DDS.MSGS)
   ISPEXEC LIBDEF ISPTLIB DATASET ID(DDS.TABLES)
   ISPEXEC LIBDEF ISPTABL DATASET ID(DDS.TABLES)
   ISPEXEC LIBDEF ISPSLIB DATASET ID(DDS.SKELS)
 /*ISPEXEC LIBDEF ISPLLIB DATASET ID(DDS.LOAD)   if using pgms */
 /*needed:  LIBDEF SYSPROC DATASET ID(DDS.CLIST)                */
 /*since... LIBDEF SYSPROC not supported, need special handling: */
   FREE    FI(SYSPROC)
   ALLOC   FI(SYSPROC) DA(DDS.CLIST, 'SYS1.CLIST') SHR
   ISPEXEC SELECT PANEL(DDSP100)
   EXIT
   END
```

Figure 10-3   Starting Application with LIBDEFs.

ISPLLIB LIBDEF to access some commands, this process would only work if you always accessed them through SELECT services. If you attempted to have one command call another through the TSO EXEC command, for example, this would not work because it would be a TSO mechanism which does not know about the LIBDEF process.

Without LIBDEF Support

If your installation is using an older release of ISPF where this important service is not yet available, you will need a more complex procedure. Since this is heavily dependent on the specific environment under which you operate, we will be discussing that under Appendix A, "ISPF/TSO Interfaces" and Appendix B, ISPF/CMS Interfaces.

The ISPF/PDF TEST Option

Once the libraries are established, you may exercise your application from an existing selection panel or command procedure as previously

```
--------------- DIALOG TEST PRIMARY OPTION MENU ----------------
OPTION  ===>

  1  FUNCTIONS        - Invoke dialog functions/selection menus
  2  PANELS           - Display panels
  3  VARIABLES        - Display/set variable information
  4  TABLES           - Display/modify table information
  5  LOG              - Browse ISPF log
  6  DIALOG SERVICES - Invoke dialog services
  7  TRACES           - Specify trace definitions
  8  BREAKPOINTS      - Specify breakpoint definitions
  T  TUTORIAL         - Display information about Dialog Test
  X  EXIT             - Terminate dialog testing
```

Figure 10-4   Dialog Test Selection Panel.

shown. Another alternative is available if you have access to the PDF product (which is most likely).

Through the PDF TEST option (option 7) an array of tracing and debugging facilities are available that are not available through other means. Since this is a very important option, which relates totally to ISPF applications development, we will examine it in detail.

When you choose PDF Option 7 — the TEST Option — you are presented with a selection panel where you may establish the conditions for your test session (see Figure 10-4).

If you are testing panels, and the panel libraries have been properly allocated, you need only select option 2 to view the panels on the screen. If the libraries are not yet allocated, you can invoke option 6, DIALOG SERVICES, to define the panel library in a format such as:

```
⇨ ISPEXEC LIBDEF DATASET ID(DDS.PANELS)
```

After this service, any panel on that library could be displayed. If changes are necessary, enter SPLIT screen mode, EDIT the panel, SAVE it, SWAP screens, END the current panel display, and then request the same panel display. Once you have done this once or twice, it becomes second nature.

If you are testing functions, you have several options. If the functions are fairly simple, selecting option 1 may be all that is needed. If the functions are more complex, you may want to establish breakpoints, traces, examine variable pools, etc.

If you need these features, you should do the following:

1. Select option 7 to specify what to trace.
2. Select option 8 to specify breakpoints in the execution.
3. Select option 1 to execute your function.

When you reach a breakpoint, you will be given a similar selection panel where you may examine the results reached thus far. At this point, you may do any or all of the following:

• Select option 3 to examine the variables in the pools.
• Select option 4 to examine any tables being processed.
• Select option 5 if you would like to examine the log for the traces requested.
• etc.

As you examine the variables and/or the tables, you have the ability to modify them to further test your function. When you have completed the examination and want to resume processing from the point of interruption, simply type "GO" (or "G") and it will continue until it either reaches the next breakpoint or the application terminates.

To better illustrate this process, the following set of figures depict a possible scenario used in testing a small section of our DDS application. In order to keep the number of figures down to a manageable size, some of the intermediate panel displays have been omitted, either because of their simplicity or because they were redundant.

Please browse through these figures to gain a general idea of how the process works. If you should need a more detailed explanation on this process, you should refer to the ISPF/PDF manual published by IBM.

```
------------------  DIALOG TEST PRIMARY OPTION MENU  ------------------
OPTION  ===> 7

     1  FUNCTIONS         - Invoke dialog functions/selection menus
     2  PANELS            - Display panels
     3  VARIABLES         - Display/set variable information
     4  TABLES            - Display/modify table information
     5  LOG               - Browse ISPF log
     6  DIALOG SERVICES   - Invoke dialog services
     7  TRACES            - Specify trace definitions
     8  BREAKPOINTS       - Specify breakpoint definitions
     T  TUTORIAL          - Display information about Dialog Test
     X  EXIT              - Terminate dialog testing

Enter END command to terminate dialog testing.
```

--->

Figure 10-5 Selecting the TRACES Option.

```
------------------------------  TRACES  ------------------------------
OPTION  ===> 1

   1 FUNCTION TRACES - Monitor dialog service calls
   2 VARIABLE TRACES - Monitor dialog variable usage

--->
```

Figure 10-6   Selecting the FUNCTION TRACES.

```
-----------------  FUNCTION TRACES  -----------------  ROW 1 OF 16
COMMAND ===>                                           SCROLL ===> PAGE

ADD, DELETE, AND CHANGE TRACES.  UNDERSCORES NEED NOT BE BLANKED.
ENTER END COMMAND TO FINALIZE CHANGES.

      FUNCTION      ACTIVE      DIALOG SERVICES TO BE TRACED
      (Required)    (YES,NO)    (No entry=all)
                    (No entry=YES)  ("OR" is assumed between names)

--->  ALL_          yes         _____
      ¦¦¦¦          ¦¦¦         _____
      ¦¦¦¦          ¦¦¦         _____
      ¦¦¦¦          ¦¦¦         _____
      ¦¦¦¦          ¦¦¦         _____
      ¦¦¦¦          ¦¦¦         _____
      ¦¦¦¦          ¦¦¦         _____
      ¦¦¦¦          ¦¦¦         _____
      ¦¦¦¦          ¦¦¦         _____
      ¦¦¦¦          ¦¦¦         _____
======================================= BOTTOM OF DATA ========================
```

Figure 10-7 Defining Functions to Trace.

```
-------------   DIALOG TEST PRIMARY OPTION MENU   -------------
OPTION  ===> 8

    1  FUNCTIONS          -  Invoke dialog functions/selection menus
    2  PANELS             -  Display panels
    3  VARIABLES          -  Display/set variable information
    4  TABLES             -  Display/modify table information
    5  LOG                -  Browse ISPF log
    6  DIALOG SERVICES    -  Invoke dialog services
    7  TRACES             -  Specify trace definitions
    8  BREAKPOINTS        -  Specify breakpoint definitions
    T  TUTORIAL           -  Display information about Dialog Test
    X  EXIT               -  Terminate dialog testing

    Enter END command to terminate dialog testing.

--->
```

Figure 10-8   Selecting the BREAKPOINTS Option.

```
------------------------------- BREAKPOINTS -------------------------- ROW 1 OF 16
COMMAND ===>                                                        SCROLL ===> PAGE

ADD, DELETE, AND CHANGE BREAKPOINTS.  UNDERSCORES NEED NOT BE BLANKED.
ENTER END COMMAND TO FINALIZE CHANGES.

        SERVICE            WHEN              FUNCTION             ACTIVE
       (Required)    (BEFORE,AFTER,Rnn)   (No entry=all)        (YES,NO)
                       (No entry=all)                         (No entry=YES)

''''  display_       _____         _____          _____
''''  tbdispl_       _____         _____          _____
''''  _____       _____         _____          _____
''''  _____       _____         _____          _____
''''  _____       _____         _____          _____
''''  _____       _____         _____          _____
''''  _____       _____         _____          _____
''''  _____       _____         _____          _____
''''  _____       _____         _____          _____
''''  _____       _____         _____          _____
''''  _____       _____         _____          _____
''''  _____       _____         _____          _____
''''  _____       _____         _____          _____
''''  _____       _____         _____          _____
=============================== BOTTOM OF DATA ==================================
```

Figure 10-9 Defining Breakpoints.

235

```
------------------           DIALOG TEST PRIMARY OPTION MENU   -------------
OPTION  ===> 1

   1  FUNCTIONS          -  Invoke dialog functions/selection menus
   2  PANELS             -  Display panels
   3  VARIABLES          -  Display/set variable information
   4  TABLES             -  Display/modify table information
   5  LOG                -  Browse ISPF log
   6  DIALOG SERVICES    -  Invoke dialog services
   7  TRACES             -  Specify trace definitions
   8  BREAKPOINTS        -  Specify breakpoint definitions
   T  TUTORIAL           -  Display information about Dialog Test
   X  EXIT               -  Terminate dialog testing

Enter END command to terminate dialog testing.
```

Figure 10-10 Selecting FUNCTIONS.

```
------------------  INVOKE DIALOG FUNCTION/SELECTION MENU  ------------------
COMMAND ===>

INVOKE SELECTION MENU:
        PANEL   ===>                           OPT     ===>

INVOKE COMMAND:
        CMD     ===> ddsc000
        LANG    ===>                           (APL OR BLANK)

INVOKE PROGRAM:
        PGM     ===>                           PARM    ===>
NEWAPPL ===> yes                               ID      ===> dds
NEWPOOL ===> NO                                PASSLIB ===> NO
```

Figure 10-11   Defining Function to Test.

```
-------- BREAKPOINT PRIMARY OPTION MENU - BEFORE DISPLAY --------
OPTION ===> 5

    1  FUNCTIONS        - Invoke dialog functions/selection menus
    2  PANELS           - Display panels
    3  VARIABLES        - Display/set variable information
    4  TABLES           - Display/modify table information
    5  LOG              - Browse ISPF log
    6  DIALOG SERVICES  - Invoke dialog services
    7  TRACES           - Specify trace definitions
    8  BREAKPOINTS      - Specify breakpoint definitions
    T  TUTORIAL         - Display information about Dialog Test
    G  GO               - Continue execution from breakpoint
    C  CANCEL           - Cancel dialog testing


CURRENT STATUS:
   APPLICATION: DDS          FUNCTION: FDSC110
   BREAKPOINT : ISPEXEC   DISPLAY PANEL(DDSP110A)
```

--->

238

Figure 10-12 First Breakpoint — Selecting the LOG.

```
BROWSE LOG - userid.SPFLOG6.LIST ------------------------------------------------ LINE 000000 COL 001 120
COMMAND ===>                                                                      SCROLL ===> CSR
===================================================== TOP OF DATA =================================================*
TIME                  *** ISPF TRANSACTION LOG ***               USERID: userid   DATE: YY/08/04   PAGE: 1
---------------------------------------------------------------------------------------------------------------
16:08   START OF ISPF LOG - - -    SESSION # 1402
16:10   DIALOG TRACE -----------   APPLICATION(ISR)   FUNCTION(ISR@USER)   SCREEN(1)
16:10   SELECT.. BEGIN ... TEST    SELECT CMD(DDSC000) NEWAPPL(DDS)
16:10        TSO   - COMMAND -     DDSC000
16:10   DIALOG TRACE -----------   APPLICATION(DDS)   FUNCTION(DDSC000)   SCREEN(1)
16:10   LIBDEF.. BEGIN ........:   ISPEXEC LIBDEF ISPPLIB DATASET ID(DDS.PANELS)
16:10   LIBDEF.. END ..........:   ISPEXEC LIBDEF ISPPLIB DATASET ID(DDS.PANELS)
16:10       .RETURN CODE (0)   :   ISPEXEC
16:10   LIBDEF.. BEGIN ........:   ISPEXEC LIBDEF ISPMLIB DATASET ID(DDS.MSGS)
16:10   LIBDEF.. END ..........:   ISPEXEC LIBDEF ISPMLIB DATASET ID(DDS.MSGS)
16:10       .RETURN CODE (0)   :   ISPEXEC
16:10   LIBDEF.. BEGIN ........:   ISPEXEC LIBDEF ISPTLIB DATASET ID(DDS.TABLES)
16:10   LIBDEF.. END ..........:   ISPEXEC LIBDEF ISPTLIB DATASET ID(DDS.TABLES)
16:10       .RETURN CODE (0)   :   ISPEXEC
16:10   LIBDEF.. BEGIN ........:   ISPEXEC LIBDEF ISPTABL DATASET ID(DDS.TABLES)
16:10   LIBDEF.. END ..........:   ISPEXEC LIBDEF ISPTABL DATASET ID(DDS.TABLES)
16:10       .RETURN CODE (0)   :   ISPEXEC
16:10   LIBDEF.. BEGIN ........:   ISPEXEC LIBDEF ISPSLIB DATASET ID(DDS.SKELS)
16:10   LIBDEF.. END ..........:   ISPEXEC LIBDEF ISPSLIB DATASET ID(DDS.SKELS)
16:10       .RETURN CODE (0)   :   ISPEXEC
16:10   SELECT.. BEGIN ........:   ISPEXEC SELECT PANEL(DDSP100)
16:10        TSO   - COMMAND -     DDSC110
16:10   DIALOG TRACE -----------   APPLICATION(DDS)   FUNCTION(DDSC110)   SCREEN(1)
16:10   CONTROL. BEGIN ........:   ISPEXEC CONTROL ERRORS RETURN
16:10   CONTROL. END ..........:   ISPEXEC CONTROL ERRORS RETURN
16:10       .RETURN CODE (0)   :   ISPEXEC
16:10   DISPLAY. BEGIN ........:   ISPEXEC DISPLAY PANEL(DDSP110A)
                                 == BOTTOM OF DATA ==============================================================
```

Figure 10-13 Examining the Log.

239

```
 . . . . . . . . . . . . . . . . . . . . . . . . .

 BREAKPOINT PRIMARY OPTION MENU - BEFORE DISPLAY ------------
 OPTION  ===> go

    1  FUNCTIONS        - Invoke dialog functions/selection menus
    2  PANELS           - Display panels
    3  VARIABLES        - Display/set variable information
    4  TABLES           - Display/modify table information
    5  LOG              - Browse ISPF log
    6  DIALOG SERVICES  - Invoke dialog services
    7  TRACES           - Specify trace definitions
    8  BREAKPOINTS      - Specify breakpoint definitions
    T  TUTORIAL         - Display information about Dialog Test
    G  GO               - Continue execution from breakpoint
    C  CANCEL           - Cancel dialog testing

 CURRENT STATUS:
 APPLICATION: DDS        FUNCTION: DDSC110
 BREAKPOINT : ISPEXEC    DISPLAY  PANEL(DDSP110A)

 --->

 . . . . . . . . . . . . . . . . . . . . . . . . .
```

Figure 10-14 Resuming Test Process.

```
-------------  DDS APPLICATION SELECTION PANEL  -------------
COMMAND ===>

  TO ISOLATE AND PROCESS A GIVEN SUBSET, ENTER MATCHING PARAMETERS:

    APPLICATION ID . . . .  TEST
    POOL TYPE. . . . . .  _          (No entry processes all appl.)
    DATA TYPE. . . . . .  _____      (No entry processes all types)
                                     (No entry processes all types)
```

Figure 10-15 Application Displays Panel.

```
------------- BREAKPOINT PRIMARY OPTION MENU - AFTER DISPLAY -------------
      OPTION ===> 3

        1  FUNCTIONS        -  Invoke dialog functions/selection menus
        2  PANELS           -  Display panels
        3  VARIABLES        -  Display/set variable information
        4  TABLES           -  Display/modify table information
        5  LOG              -  Browse ISPF log
        6  DIALOG SERVICES  -  Invoke dialog services
        7  TRACES           -  Specify trace definitions
        8  BREAKPOINTS      -  Specify breakpoint definitions
        T  TUTORIAL         -  Display information about Dialog Test
        G  GO               -  Continue execution from breakpoint
        C  CANCEL           -  Cancel dialog testing

      CURRENT STATUS:
        APPLICATION: DDS              FUNCTION: DDSC110
        BREAKPOINT : ISPEXEC    DISPLAY  PANEL(DDSP110A)

        RETURN CODE ===> 0
```

--->

Figure 10-16   Next Breakpoint — Selecting VARIABLES.

```
           ------------ VARIABLE DISPLAY AND SET ------------ ROW 1 OF 89
COMMAND ===>                                             SCROLL ===> PAGE

ADD AND CHANGE VARIABLES.  UNDERSCORES NEED NOT BE BLANKED.
ENTER END COMMAND TO FINALIZE CHANGES.

          VARIABLE  P A VALUE
--->
''''      APPL      F   TEST
''''      DTYPE_    F
''''      LASTCC_   F   0
''''      MAXCC_    F   0
''''      PTYPE_    F
''''      TABLE_    F   DDST000
''''      ZCMD_     F
''''      SEL       S   CMD(DDSC110)
''''      ZAPPLID_  S N DDS
```

Figure 10-17 Examining Some Variables.

243

```
------------- BREAKPOINT PRIMARY OPTION MENU - BEFORE TBDISPL -------------
OPTION ===> 4

        1  FUNCTIONS        - Invoke dialog functions/selection menus
        2  PANELS           - Display panels
        3  VARIABLES        - Display/set variable information
        4  TABLES           - Display/modify table information
        5  LOG              - Browse ISPF log
        6  DIALOG SERVICES  - Invoke dialog services
        7  TRACES           - Specify trace definitions
        8  BREAKPOINTS      - Specify breakpoint definitions
        T  TUTORIAL         - Display information about Dialog Test
        G  GO               - Continue execution from breakpoint
        C  CANCEL           - Cancel dialog testing

CURRENT STATUS:
    APPLICATION: DDS           FUNCTION: DDSC110
    BREAKPOINT : ISPEXEC    TBDISPL  DDST000  PANEL(DDSP110B) AUTOSEL(NO)
```

--->

Figure 10-18   Another Breakpoint — Selecting TABLES Option.

```
--------------------------------- TABLES ---------------------------------
---> OPTION ===> 6

       1  Display row        4  Add row
       2  Delete row         5  Display structure
       3  Modify row         6  Display status

---> TABLE NAME    ===> DDST000        CURRENT ROW:  55

     ROW IDENTIFICATION:
       BY ROW NUMBER ===> *                (* = current row)

       BY VARIABLE      VALUE              (Search for row if row number blank)
       _____      _____
       _____      _____
       _____      _____

     DBCS COLUMN SPECIFICATION:
       _____      _____
       _____      _____
```

Figure 10-19 Selecting Table Status.

```
---------------------------------  STATUS  OF  TABLE  DDST000  --------------------------

COMMAND ===>

STATUS FOR THIS SCREEN   : OPEN          DATE CREATED        : YY/01/07
OPEN OPTION              : WRITE         TIME CREATED        : 10.50.56
TABLE ON DISK            : NO            LAST DATE MODIFIED  : YY/08/04
LAST TABLE SERVICE       : TBQUERY       LAST TIME MODIFIED  : 16.07.19
LAST SERVICE RETURN CODE : 00            LAST MODIFIED BY    : userid
CURRENT ROW POINTER      : 55            ORIGINAL ROW COUNT  : 7
                                         CURRENT ROW COUNT   : 56
                                         MODIFIED ROW COUNT  : 55
                                         UPDATE COUNT        : 31
```

Figure 10-20 Examining Table Status.

```
----------------- INVOKE DIALOG FUNCTION/SELECTION                FUNCTION RC =   0
COMMAND ===>

INVOKE SELECTION MENU:
     PANEL   ===>                    OPT    ===>

INVOKE COMMAND:
     CMD     ===> DDSC000
     LANG    ===>                    (APL OR BLANK)

INVOKE PROGRAM:
     PGM     ===>                    PARM   ===>

NEWAPPL    ===> YES                  ID     ===> DDS

NEWPOOL    ===> NO                   PASSLIB ===> NO
```

Figure 10-21 Function Terminated.

```
BROWSE LOG -  userid.SPFLOG6.LIST --------------------------------------------------- LINE 000025 COL 001 120
COMMAND ===>                                                                             SCROLL ===> CSR
  16:14   DISPLAY. END...... :   ISPEXEC   DISPLAY   PANEL(DDSP110A)
  16:14   ..RETURN CODE.(0) ... :   ISPEXEC   VPUT (APPL) PROFILE
  16:14   VPUT.... BEGIN ... :   ISPEXEC   VPUT (APPL) PROFILE
  16:14   VPUT.... END...... :
  16:14   ..RETURN CODE (0) ... :   ISPEXEC   TBOPEN    DDST000   WRITE
  16:14   TBOPEN.. BEGIN ... :   ISPEXEC   TBOPEN    DDST000   WRITE
  16:14   TBOPEN.. END...... :
  16:14   ..RETURN CODE (0) ... :   ISPEXEC   TBSARG    DDST000
  16:14   TBSARG.. BEGIN ... :   ISPEXEC   TBSARG    DDST000
  16:14   TBSARG.. END...... :
  16:14   ..RETURN CODE (0) ... :   ISPEXEC   TBSCAN    DDST000
  16:14   TBSCAN.. BEGIN ... :   ISPEXEC   TBSCAN    DDST000
  16:14   TBSCAN.. END...... :
  16:14   ..RETURN CODE (0) ... :   ISPEXEC   TBDISPL   DDST000   PANEL(DDSP110B) AUTOSEL(NO)
  16:14   TBDISPL. BEGIN ... :   ISPEXEC   TBDISPL   DDST000   PANEL(DDSP110B) AUTOSEL(NO)
  16:18   TBDISPL. END...... :
  16:18   ..RETURN CODE (8) ... :   ISPEXEC   TBCLOSE   DDST000
  16:18   TBCLOSE. BEGIN ... :   ISPEXEC   TBCLOSE   DDST000
  16:18   TBCLOSE. END...... :
  16:18   ..RETURN CODE (0) ... :   APPLICATION(DDS)   FUNCTION(DDSC000)
  16:18   DIALOG TRACE ------- :   ISPEXEC SELECT PANEL(DDSP100)     SCREEN(1)
  16:18   SELECT.. END...... :
  16:18   ..RETURN CODE (4) ... :   APPLICATION(ISR)   FUNCTION(ISR@USER)
  16:18   DIALOG TRACE ------- : TEST   SELECT CMD(DDSC000) NEWAPPL(DDS)    SCREEN(1)
  16:18   SELECT.. END...... :
  16:18   ..RETURN CODE (0) ... :   ============= BOTTOM OF DATA =====================================
```

Figure 10-22   End of Test — Reviewing Portion of Log.

11

Implementing a New Application

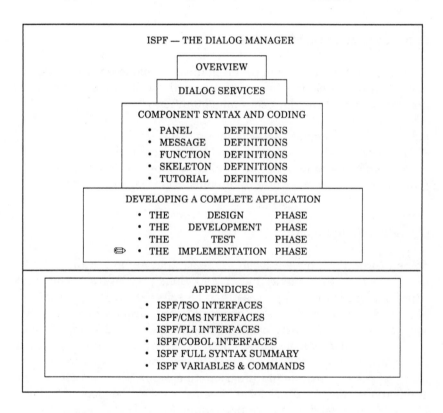

ISPF — THE DIALOG MANAGER

OVERVIEW

DIALOG SERVICES

COMPONENT SYNTAX AND CODING
- PANEL   DEFINITIONS
- MESSAGE   DEFINITIONS
- FUNCTION   DEFINITIONS
- SKELETON   DEFINITIONS
- TUTORIAL   DEFINITIONS

DEVELOPING A COMPLETE APPLICATION
- THE   DESIGN   PHASE
- THE   DEVELOPMENT   PHASE
- THE   TEST   PHASE
- THE   IMPLEMENTATION PHASE

APPENDICES
- ISPF/TSO INTERFACES
- ISPF/CMS INTERFACES
- ISPF/PLI INTERFACES
- ISPF/COBOL INTERFACES
- ISPF FULL SYNTAX SUMMARY
- ISPF VARIABLES & COMMANDS

General Considerations

We are now on the last phase of our new application. We have
designed it, coded it, tested it (successfully, I hope), and all that is

left is to promote it into production status by "elevating" the private libraries to public ones.

At this point, we really become dependent on whatever rules (if any) our installations impose on us. Generally, smaller installations have greater freedom in how this process is accomplished, while the larger ones may have very rigid standards that must be observed carefully.

We will be looking at various ways of accomplishing this process as we consider the possibilities.

Data Set Naming Considerations

Each installation may have its mechanism to name data sets. For illustration purposes, in this chapter we will use the following convention for the first-level data set name qualifiers:

- SYS1.*xxx*:   The data sets containing IBM products
- SYS2.*xxx*:   The installation production (protected) products
- SYS3.*xxx*:   The installation public (but unprotected) products
- userid.*xxx*:   The user private products

Operating Environment

Some installations have a logon sequence that automatically places a user into the ISPF environment and then presents a menu from which an application or process is to be selected. Other installations place the user into a general command mode from where, if necessary, a command can activate ISPF and then the needed application.

Often, the decision is based on the class of users involved, their needs, their skills, etc. If an installation develops applications for users who have little or no programming skills, then presenting an applications menu after logon seems to be the logical choice. However, if the end-users are programmers (as is the case in my installation), then either the menu or the native command mode may be chosen.

At my installation, for example, the logon sequence under MVS automatically concludes with the presentation of an ISPF/PDF selection panel. But the logon sequence under VM simply takes the users to CMS command mode; if an ISPF application should be needed under VM, a command would have to establish the proper ISPF environment before executing the application.

Many times, when there is a choice, as in the case just mentioned, the decision is based on the response time involved in performing the task. VM, which generally provides a very fast response time (usually because it does not carry the heavy burden of extensive batch processing that MVS does), makes it very easy to switch from one mode to another. In MVS, however, a considerable delay can occur each time that ISPF is initiated and terminated. Consequently, most MVS installations will normally place a user into the ISPF environment from where all other applications will run.

Non-ISPF Environment

If your users normally operate in a non-ISPF environment, you will need a command procedure similar to the one already described for the test process. The difference now is that the library names would probably be the public ones (production), and you would not invoke any trace options as before (please refer to Figure 11-1).

You will note that some of the data set names are now 'SYS2.DDS.---' while some others remain as 'userid.---.---'. The reason, of course, is that the SYS2 sets represent the public production libraries, whereas the userid sets represent private ones that apply to each user individually (the profile data set, the list, and the work files as well).

When you operate in this mode (where you initiate/terminate ISPF each time), it is very convenient to maintain separate sets of libraries for each application for ease of maintenance, portability, etc. In the other mode (next topic), this is not necessarily the most efficient way.

Assuming that we called this sample procedure DDS, and assuming that it resided in a public library already available to us (for example, 'SYS2.CLIST'), then to activate the process we would enter:

```
PROC  0
FREE  FI(ISPLLIB, ISPPLIB, ISPMLIB, ISPSLIB, ISPTABL, ISPPROF)
FREE  FI(ISPCTL1, ISPCTL2, ISPLST1, ISPLST2, SYSPROC)
ALLOC FI(SYSPROC) DA('SYS2.DDS.CLIST',   'SYS1.CLIST')           SHR
ALLOC FI(ISPLLIB) DA('SYS2.DDS.LOAD',    'SYS1.ISPF.LINKLIB')  SHR
ALLOC FI(ISPPLIB) DA('SYS2.DDS.PANELS',  'SYS1.ISPF.PANELS')   SHR
ALLOC FI(ISPMLIB) DA('SYS2.DDS.MSGS',    'SYS1.ISPF.MSGS')     SHR
ALLOC FI(ISPSLIB) DA('SYS2.DDS.SKELS',   'SYS1.ISPF.SKELS')    SHR
ALLOC FI(ISPTLIB) DA('SYS2.DDS.TABLES',  'SYS1.ISPF.TABLES')   SHR
ALLOC FI(ISPTABL) DA('SYS2.DDS.TABLES')                         SHR
ALLOC FI(ISPPROF) DA(xxx.PROFILE)                               SHR
ALLOC FI(ISPCTL1) DA(xxx.CNTL)                                  SHR
ALLOC FI(ISPCTL2) DA(yyy.CNTL)                                  SHR
ALLOC FI(ISPLST1) DA(xxx.LIST)                                  OLD
ALLOC FI(ISPLST2) DA(yyy.LIST)                                  OLD
ISPSTART CMD(DDSC000) NEWAPPL(DDS)
FREE  FI(ISPLLIB, ISPPLIB, ISPMLIB, ISPSLIB, ISPTABL, ISPPROF)
FREE  FI(ISPCTL1, ISPCTL2, ISPLST1, ISPLST2, SYSPROC)
ALLOC FI(SYSPROC) DA('SYS1.CLIST')                             SHR
EXIT
END
```

Figure 11-1   ISPF/DDS Start-Up Procedure.

```
☞ DDS
  or
☞ %DDS
  or
☞ EXEC 'SYS2.CLIST(DDS)'   /* if not in the cmd search seq */
```

ISPF Environment

When you operate within ISPF, data set allocation can either be performed at logon time or, if you have LIBDEF support (V2.2), as each
application is activated.

Without LIBDEF Support. If you do not yet have the LIBDEF service,
you have no choice but to allocate all data sets within the logon se-

quence. This can be either good or bad depending on how many libraries you will need.

On the positive side, allocating libraries through the JCL procedure triggered by the logon process is much faster than through the TSO dynamic allocation process. On the negative side, you will have to spend time allocating every possible library needed even if the user intends to access only one or two applications.

Some installations compromise this issue by combining all applications into one set of libraries. Although this resolves the problem just mentioned, it does create another one (although less critical) which is the library management, maintenance, portability, etc.

Another possibility is to have different logon procedures that allocate different sets of libraries. This would work well if the type of users could be easily divided by the type of applications that they will be exercising.

For a detailed examination of the logon process and the data set allocation, please refer to either Appendix A, "ISPF/TSO Interfaces," or Appendix B, "ISPF/CMS Interfaces."

With LIBDEF Support. If you have this service available with your release, you have even more choices. In addition to all that has been said, you can now allocate certain libraries only if certain paths are chosen.

This is without a doubt the most flexible method, but it does have its price. If each application performs the LIBDEF sequence necessary, and if the users are constantly entering and exiting applications, a very significant amount of time will be spent on this process.

There is considerable latitude in the two extremes: allocating all libraries at logon time, and allocating each set as each application is invoked. You may wish to compromise somewhere in between.

The bottom line of all this is that you will have to decide where your particular situation fits (within the ones described here) and then decide on one of these suggested methods (or a combination of methods).

Hooking Your Application into a Menu. Once you decide on the library allocation process, the next step is to determine where in the established hierarchy of applications you wish to place yours. Some installations, where the primary users are programmers, choose to start at the highest level with a PDF primary option menu. Other installations, where the primary users are mostly nonprogrammer types,

```
%----------------- ISPF MASTER APPLICATION MENU ----------------
%OPTION  ===>_ZCMD                                              +
%                                          +USERID   - &ZUSER
%   1 +DDS       - Data Dictionary System  +TIME     - &ZTIME
%   2 +...       - ...                      +TERMINAL - &ZTERM
%   3 +...       - ...                      +PF KEYS  - &ZKEYS
%   4 +PDF       - Program Development Facility
%   5 +...       - ...
%   X +EXIT      - Terminate ISPF using list/log defaults
%
+Enter%END+command to terminate ISPF.


)INIT
 .HELP    = ISP00005       /* Help for this master menu    */
 &ZPRIM   = YES            /* This is a primary option menu */


)PROC
 &ZSEL = TRANS( TRUNC (&ZCMD,'.')
                1,'CMD(DDSC0000)   NEWAPPL(DDS)'
                4,'PANEL(ISR@PRIM) NEWAPPL(ISR)'
                X,'EXIT'
                ' ',' '
                *,'?' )


)END
```

Figure 11-2   Hooking into ISP@MSTR Menu.

choose to begin with an application menu from which PDF may be one choice.

Hooking Applications to the ISPF master menu. If you choose to hook your application in this fashion, you may consider the ISP@MSTR panel provided by IBM as a model to use (see Figure 11-2).

One advantage of starting all selections from this level is that you do not have to perform any changes as new PDF releases are installed at your installation. The disadvantage is that if your users are heavily dependent on PDF, they will have to traverse one extra level of panels.

Hooking Applications to the PDF primary menu. If you choose to begin all selections with the PDF primary menu, you should hook your applications into the ISR@PRIM panel released with that product. For installations with "heavy" PDF users, this is normally the preferred method.

To prevent excessive maintenance of this panel, which would have to be repeated with each implementation of a new release, as well as to keep this menu from growing out of control, it is recommended that you make only one entry at this level for all applications that are added at your installation. Figure 11-3 illustrates how this could be done.

Thus, any applications beyond the PDF functions would branch from the next level of this tree structure, which would be the "A" option for the "ABC Corporation Functions." That panel, in turn, could then branch by general applications and group applications. The group applications could then branch into each individual's applications, etc.

Conclusion

This concludes the installation process. If you have followed all the steps carefully, you should have no problem implementing your first application. After that, you will find that this is a relatively simple procedure.

In the appendices provided, you will find additional points on specific environment considerations that go beyond the general needs. Some of you may find this additional information very useful. Good luck with your new projects!

```
%--------------- ISPF/PDF PRIMARY OPTION PANEL -----------------
%OPTION  ===>_ZCMD                                              +
%                                                               +...
%   0 +ISPF PARMS  - Specify terminal and user parameters   +...
%   1 +BROWSE      - Display source data or output listings +...
%   2 +EDIT        - Create or change source data           +...
%   3 +UTILITIES   - Perform utility functions
%   ... ... ...
%   A +ABC CORP.   - ABC Corporation Applications
%   ... ... ...
%   X +EXIT        - Terminate using console, log, list defaults
%
%
+Enter%END+command to terminate ISPF.
```

```
)INIT
  .HELP = ISR00003
  &ZPRIM = YES         /* ALWAYS A PRIMARY OPTION MENU */
  &ZHTOP = ISR00003    /* TUTORIAL TABLE OF CONTENTS   */
  &ZHINDEX = ISR91000  /* TUTORIAL INDEX - 1ST PAGE    */
  VPUT (ZHTOP,ZHINDEX) PROFILE
```

```
)PROC
  &Z1 = TRUNC(&ZCMD,1)
  IF (&Z1 = '.')
    &ZSEL = TRANS( TRUNC (&ZCMD,'.')
                   0,'PANEL(ISPOPTA)'
                   1,'PGM(ISRBRO)   PARM(ISRBRO01)'
                   2,'PGM(ISREDIT) PARM(P,ISREDM01)'
                   3,'PANEL(ISRUTIL)'
                   ... ... ...
                   A,'PANEL(ABCP000) NEWAPPL(ABC)'
                   ... ... ...
                   X,'EXIT'
                   ' ',' '
                   *,'?' )
```

```
)END
```

Figure 11-3   Hooking into ISR@PRIM Menu.

ISPF/TSO Interfaces

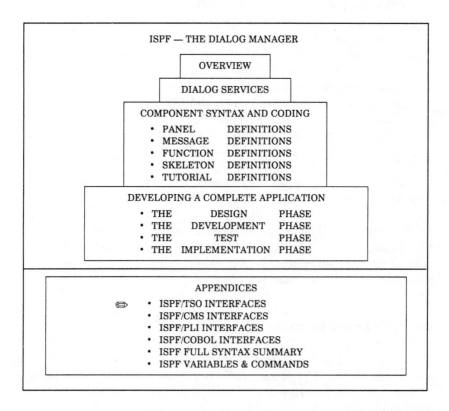

ISPF — THE DIALOG MANAGER

OVERVIEW

DIALOG SERVICES

COMPONENT SYNTAX AND CODING
- PANEL   DEFINITIONS
- MESSAGE   DEFINITIONS
- FUNCTION   DEFINITIONS
- SKELETON   DEFINITIONS
- TUTORIAL   DEFINITIONS

DEVELOPING A COMPLETE APPLICATION
- THE   DESIGN   PHASE
- THE   DEVELOPMENT   PHASE
- THE   TEST   PHASE
- THE   IMPLEMENTATION   PHASE

APPENDICES
- ISPF/TSO INTERFACES
- ISPF/CMS INTERFACES
- ISPF/PLI INTERFACES
- ISPF/COBOL INTERFACES
- ISPF FULL SYNTAX SUMMARY
- ISPF VARIABLES & COMMANDS

Some of you may have to establish logon procedures to allow some users the ability to develop and test new ISPF interactive applications. This is particularly critical for installations that do not yet have the LIBDEF service available.

Even if you are not usually responsible for providing these procedures, you may find this section very useful because it will give you the complete sequence of events — the Job Control Language (JCL) and the command procedures involved from the time that a person logs on to TSO until the first selection panel is presented. Once you understand this process, it will become easier for you to either develop these procedures for your installation or for you to understand how the various products locate the necessary libraries.

Three logon process sequences will be provided:

1. This first sequence will contain the basic logon process for the general TSO/ISPF users. It makes no special provisions for development of ISPF applications by any particular user.
2. The second sequence will extend the first one by providing customized logon procedures to some individuals. This logon process might be used either in smaller installations or in installations where there is a small number of dialog developers.
3. The third sequence is much more flexible, but it is also a little lengthier and more complex. It provides logic to automatically allocate the necessary ISPF user libraries if they are found.

In all cases, the data set names used will reflect the following conventions for the first-level qualifier:

- SYS1.*xxx*   — The data sets containing IBM products
- SYS2.*xxx*   — The installation production (protected) products
- SYS3.*xxx*   — The installation public (but unprotected) products
- userid.*xxx*   — The user private products

The Basic Logon Process

This sequence demonstrates the absolute minimum required in order for anyone to use ISPF under TSO. It makes no special provisions to allocate private libraries for individual users to develop their own ISPF applications.

To begin, let us examine the initial JCL system procedure used to define the major system libraries for all JCL procedures (see Figure A-1).

This procedure indicates that all future JCL procedure searches will be performed through SYS1.PROCLIB first, then, if necessary,

```
//JES2     PROC MEMBER=JES2PARM,ALTMEM=JES2PARM
//IEFPROC EXEC PGM=HASJES20,DPRTY=(15,15),TIME=1440,PERFORM=9
//PROC00   DD   DSN=SYS1.PROCLIB,DISP=SHR          <----------
//         DD   DSN=SYS2.PROCLIB,DISP=SHR          <----------
//         DD   DSN=SYS3.PROCLIB,DISP=SHR          <----------
//HASPPARM DD   DSN=SYS1.PROCLIB(&MEMBER),DISP=SHR
//ALTPARM  DD   DSN=SYS1.PARMLIB(&ALTMEM),DISP=SHR
//HASPLIST DD   DDNAME=IEFRDER
```

Figure A-1   System Procedure to Identify JCL Procedure Libraries.

through SYS2.PROCLIB, and finally, if still not found, through SYS3.PROCLIB.

Once this is given to the system, and as different users log on to TSO, the given (or implied) logon procedure name will be fetched from one of these three libraries and then executed.

Suppose, for example, that USRX logs on and specifies (or implies) that procedure ISPFUSE is to be used. This could be done as follows:

```
⇨ LOGON  usrx/password  [PROC(ispfuse)]
```

Following this command, MVS would search the libraries for ISPFUSE and execute it when found. This procedure might be similar to the one shown in Figure A-2.

This procedure causes the MVS Job Step Initiator/Terminator to allocate all the given file names to their respective data sets based on the Data Definition (DD) statements given.

You will note that for the ISPF files, two sets of libraries were used with each file. The first set (ISR) is for the PDF product libraries while the second set (ISP) is for the base product — ISPF. To avoid the extra processing time involved in always allocating (and searching) two sets of libraries, it is suggested that you merge the two into one, which you could simply call SYS1.xxx. We will do that for the remainder of this appendix.

You may also note that ISPTABL, ISPFILE, and ISPPROF were not defined. The first two are for table output and file tailoring output, which require specific applications to generate them; if needed,

```
//IKJACCNT PROC
//IKJACCNT EXEC PGM=IKJEFT01,DYNAMNBR=25,TIME=1440,PARM='LOGPROC'
//*---------------- TSO FILES ----------------------------------
//SYSUADS   DD  DSN=SYS1.UADS,DISP=SHR
//SYSLBC    DD  DSN=SYS1.BRODCAST,DISP=SHR
//SYSHELP   DD  DSN=SYS1.HELP,DISP=SHR
//SYSPROC   DD  DSN=SYS1.CLIST,DISP=SHR
//          DD  DSN=SYS2.CLIST,DISP=SHR
//          DD  DSN=SYS3.CLIST,DISP=SHR
//SYSPRINT  DD  TERM=TS,SYSOUT=A
//SYSTERM   DD  TERM=TS,SYSOUT=A
//SYSIN     DD  TERM=TS
//*---------------- ISPF FILES ----------------------------------
//ISPPLIB   DD  DSN=SYS1.ISR.PANELS,DISP=SHR
//          DD  DSN=SYS1.ISP.PANELS,DISP=SHR
//ISPMLIB   DD  DSN=SYS1.ISR.MSGS,DISP=SHR
//          DD  DSN=SYS1.ISP.MSGS,DISP=SHR
//ISPSLIB   DD  DSN=SYS1.ISR.SKELS,DISP=SHR
//          DD  DSN=SYS1.ISP.SKELS,DISP=SHR
//ISPTLIB   DD  DSN=SYS1.ISR.TABLES,DISP=SHR
//          DD  DSN=SYS1.ISP.TABLES,DISP=SHR
//ISPCTL1   DD  DISP=NEW,UNIT=DISK,SPACE=(CYL,(1,1)),
//              DCB=(RECFM=FB,LRECL=80,BLKSIZE=6160)
//ISPCTL2   DD  DISP=NEW,UNIT=DISK,SPACE=(CYL,(1,1)),
//              DCB=(RECFM=FB,LRECL=80,BLKSIZE=6160)
//ISPLST1   DD  DISP=NEW,UNIT=DISK,SPACE=(CYL,(1,1)),
//              DCB=(RECFM=FBA,LRECL=121,BLKSIZE=1210)
//ISPLST2   DD  DISP=NEW,UNIT=DISK,SPACE=(CYL,(1,1)),
//              DCB=(RECFM=FBA,LRECL=121,BLKSIZE=1210)
```

Figure A-2   ISPFUSE General Logon Procedure for ISPF Users.

they can be allocated at that time. The last one, ISPPROF, is unique to each user and will be allocated through a command procedure.

Once all the data sets are allocated, the program IKJEFT01 — the Terminal Monitor Program (TMP) — is executed. This is the program that will control the TSO session. This program receives a parameter of "LOGPROC," which is the name of a TSO command procedure to be executed just before the session begins.

This procedure, among other things, would allocate the data set for the ISPF profile tables where the various profile pools are maintained, and then finish with the invocation of ISPF (see Figure A-3.)

```
PROFILE  WTPMSG
ALLOCATE FI(ISPPROF)  DA('&SYSUID..PROFILE') OLD
ISPSTART PANEL(ISR@PRIM)  NEWAPPL(ISR)
```

Figure A-3   Possible LOGPROC Procedure.

The last command starts ISPF with the PDF panel. Thus, the logon sequence would terminate with the display of the ISR@PRIM panel (see Figure A-4).

Supporting a Few Developers

This sequence assumes that you have a small number of dialog developers and, as such, it is not a heavy burden to have separate special logon procedures for each one. Let us assume that we have one user (USR1) who needs a procedure to create, test, and execute a new ISPF application.

```
----------------- ISPF/PDF PRIMARY OPTION MENU -----------------
OPTION  ===>

    0  ISPF PARMS  - Specify terminal and user parameters
    1  BROWSE      - Display source data or output listings
    2  EDIT        - Create or change source data
    3  UTILITIES   - Perform utility functions
    4  FOREGROUND  - Invoke language processors in foreground
    5  BATCH       - Submit job for language processing
    6  COMMAND     - Enter TSO command or CLIST
    7  DIALOG TEST - Perform dialog testing
    T  TUTORIAL    - Display information about ISPF/PDF
    X  EXIT        - Terminate ISPF using log and list defaults

Enter END command to terminate ISPF.
```

Figure A-4   Display Following Logon Sequence.

In order not to disturb the existing processes, we will create a new version of the existing procedure (ISPFUSE) and we will call it ISPFDEV1. The only adjustment consists of concatenating the private libraries ahead of the ones for the other products (PDF and ISPF now combined into SYS1). The result would be as shown in Figure A-5.

```
//IKJACCNT PROC
//IKJACCNT EXEC PGM=IKJEFT01,DYNAMNBR=25,TIME=1440,PARM='LOGPROC'
//*---------------- TSO FILES ------------------------------
//SYSUADS   DD  DSN=SYS1.UADS,DISP=SHR
//SYSLBC    DD  DSN=SYS1.BRODCAST,DISP=SHR
//SYSHELP   DD  DSN=SYS1.HELP,DISP=SHR
//SYSPROC   DD  DSN=SYS1.CLIST,DISP=SHR
//          DD  DSN=SYS2.CLIST,DISP=SHR
//          DD  DSN=SYS3.CLIST,DISP=SHR
//          DD  DSN=USR1.CLIST,DISP=SHR       usr cmd procedures
//SYSPRINT  DD  TERM=TS
//SYSTERM   DD  TERM=TS
//SYSIN     DD  TERM=TS
//*---------------- ISPF FILES ------------------------------
//ISPLLIB   DD  DSN=USR1.LOAD,DISP=SHR        usr pgm modules
//ISPPLIB   DD  DSN=USR1.PANELS,DISP=SHR      usr panels
//          DD  DSN=SYS1.PANELS,DISP=SHR
//ISPMLIB   DD  DSN=USR1.MSGS,DISP=SHR        usr messages
//          DD  DSN=SYS1.MSGS,DISP=SHR
//ISPSLIB   DD  DSN=USR1.SKELS,DISP=SHR       usr skeletons
//          DD  DSN=SYS1.SKELS,DISP=SHR
//ISPTLIB   DD  DSN=USR1.TABLES,DISP=SHR      usr table input
//          DD  DSN=SYS1.TABLES,DISP=SHR
//ISPTABL   DD  DSN=USR1.TABLES,DISP=SHR      usr table output
//ISPFILE   DD  DSN=USR1.FTOUTPUT,DISP=SHR    usr file tail. output
//ISPCTL1   DD  DISP=NEW,UNIT=DISK,SPACE=(CYL,(1,1)),
//              DCB=(RECFM=FB,LRECL=80,BLKSIZE=6160)
//ISPCTL2   DD  DISP=NEW,UNIT=DISK,SPACE=(CYL,(1,1)),
//              DCB=(RECFM=FB,LRECL=80,BLKSIZE=6160)
//ISPLST1   DD  DISP=NEW,UNIT=DISK,SPACE=(CYL,(1,1)),
//              DCB=(RECFM=FBA,LRECL=121,BLKSIZE=1210)
//ISPLST2   DD  DISP=NEW,UNIT=DISK,SPACE=(CYL,(1,1)),
//              DCB=(RECFM=FBA,LRECL=121,BLKSIZE=1210)
```

Figure A-5   ISPFDEV1 Logon Procedure for ISPF Development.

Once established, user USR1 would log on to TSO in the following manner:

```
⇨ LOGON  usr1/password  [PROC(ispfdev1)]
```

The PROC parameter would only be required if the "User Attribute Data Set" (UADS) had not been changed to reflect this new procedure as a default for this user.

In order to exercise his or her new application, this user would have to get a copy of the ISR@PRIM selection panel (since this is the first panel that ISPF displays in this case), modify it to allow selection of the new application, and then file it in the USR1.PANELS library.

Thereafter, upon logon, when ISPF searches for the ISR@PRIM panel, it will find it in the user's library and will not use the one in the system's libraries. This is the reason for concatenating the user's data sets ahead of the system's. The logon sequence would then terminate with a panel similar to the one in Figure A-6.

```
----------------- ISPF/PDF PRIMARY OPTION MENU -----------------
OPTION ===>

   0   ISPF PARMS   - Specify terminal and user parameters
   1   BROWSE       - Display source data or output listings
   2   EDIT         - Create or change source data
   3   UTILITIES    - Perform utility functions
   4   FOREGROUND   - Invoke language processors in foreground
   5   BATCH        - Submit job for language processing
   6   COMMAND      - Enter TSO command or CLIST
   7   DIALOG TEST  - Perform dialog testing
   P   PRIVATE      - Private Applications
   T   TUTORIAL     - Display information about ISPF/PDF
   X   EXIT         - Terminate ISPF using log and list defaults

Enter END command to terminate ISPF.
```

Figure A-6   Display Following Special Logon Procedure.

Supporting Many Developers

If you are in a large installation where many developers may be producing ISPF applications, you probably do not want to have a different procedure for each one. In this case, you will have to consider a logon sequence with more elaborate logic.

Since the logic available through JCL is extremely limited, you will have to do most of the file allocation and control through TSO command procedures. The problem with this is that allocation of files through commands is considerably slower than through JCL, and this may have an impact on your system's performance and response time.

You must, therefore, weigh the alternatives between a faster but more cumbersome method as given before, or a more flexible but slower method as the one that follows.

Let us start with the basic logon process and transfer all the major ISPF file allocations from the JCL procedure to a command procedure. This would leave us with the procedure shown in Figure A-7.

```
//IKJACCNT PROC
//IKJACCNT EXEC PGM=IKJEFT01,DYNAMNBR=25,TIME=1440,PARM='LOGPROC'
//*---------------- TSO FILES ----------------------------
//SYSUADS   DD   DSN=SYS1.UADS,DISP=SHR
//SYSLBC    DD   DSN=SYS1.BRODCAST,DISP=SHR
//SYSHELP   DD   DSN=SYS1.HELP,DISP=SHR
//SYSPROC   DD   DSN=SYS1.CLIST,DISP=SHR
//          DD   DSN=SYS2.CLIST,DISP=SHR
//          DD   DSN=SYS3.CLIST,DISP=SHR
//SYSPRINT  DD   TERM=TS,SYSOUT=A
//SYSTERM   DD   TERM=TS,SYSOUT=A
//SYSIN     DD   TERM=TS
//*---------------- ISPF WORK FILES ----------------------
//ISPCTL1   DD   DISP=NEW,UNIT=DISK,SPACE=(CYL,(1,1)),
//               DCB=(RECFM=FB,LRECL=80,BLKSIZE=6160)
//ISPCTL2   DD   DISP=NEW,UNIT=DISK,SPACE=(CYL,(1,1)),
//               DCB=(RECFM=FB,LRECL=80,BLKSIZE=6160)
//ISPLST1   DD   DISP=NEW,UNIT=DISK,SPACE=(CYL,(1,1)),
//               DCB=(RECFM=FBA,LRECL=121,BLKSIZE=1210)
//ISPLST2   DD   DISP=NEW,UNIT=DISK,SPACE=(CYL,(1,1)),
//               DCB=(RECFM=FBA,LRECL=121,BLKSIZE=1210)
```

Figure A-7   Stripped Version of Logon Procedure for Developers.

This JCL procedure handles all the files that are not subject to change, regardless of whether the user is a developer or not. The one exception here is the allocation of SYSPROC. Although this will be redefined in the next section, it is included here so that the LOGPROC command procedure passed as a parameter can be located in one of the libraries given under SYSPROC.

The remaining file allocations will be done in the LOGPROC command procedure that follows (please refer to Figure A-8). In this complementary procedure, a series of allocations is performed for each major file needed for ISPF. These allocations are given in sets, where each set will perform the following:

1. Assign the name of the data set to the variable &DS1.
2. Allocate the data set represented by &DS1.
3. Test the outcome of the allocation to see if &DS1 exists.
4. If it does not exist, clear &DS1 to a null value.
5. Free this last allocation.
6. Now allocate all the necessary data sets including &DS1 which may be null.

Of course, in order for this procedure to work for everyone, each user would have to name the data sets as the procedure expects them.

You may also note that at the end of the procedure, two other command procedures are executed: USEREXIT and ISPFKICK. The USEREXIT allows for any special user processes to take place before ISPF is invoked (see Figure A-9).

The ISPFKICK procedure provides one last place where any special installation processes may be performed before ISPF takes control. Its basic format could be as shown in Figure A-10.

Again, the ISR@PRIM panel should be customized by the user to reflect any personal preferences and paths into the private applications being developed.

```
PROC   0
PROFILE     WTPMSG
CONTROL     NOMSG NOLIST NOFLUSH
ALLOCATE    FI(ISPPROF) DA('&SYSUID..PROFILE')   SHR
/*-----------------------------------------------------------*/
SET         DS1 = '&SYSUID.CLIST'
ALLOCATE    FI(DD1)       DA(&DS1)                 SHR
IF          &LASTCC NE 0 THEN SET DS1 =
FREE        FI(DD1)
ALLOCATE    FI(SYSPROC) DA('SYS1.CLIST',    +
            'SYS2.CLIST','SYS3.CLIST'  &DS1)      SHR
/*-----------------------------------------------------------*/
SET         DS1 = '&SYSUID..PANELS'
ALLOCATE    FI(DD1)       DA(&DS1)                 SHR
IF          &LASTCC NE 0 THEN SET DS1 =
FREE        FI(DD1)
ALLOCATE    FI(ISPPLIB) DA(&DS1  'SYS1.PANELS') SHR
/*-----------------------------------------------------------*/
SET         DS1 = '&SYSUID..MSGS'
ALLOCATE    FI(DD1)       DA(&DS1)                 SHR
IF          &LASTCC NE 0 THEN SET DS1 =
FREE        FI(DD1)
ALLOCATE    FI(ISPMLIB) DA(&DS1  'SYS1.MSGS')   SHR
/*-----------------------------------------------------------*/
SET         DS1 = '&SYSUID..SKELS'
ALLOCATE    FI(DD1)       DA(&DS1)                 SHR
IF          &LASTCC NE 0 THEN SET DS1 =
FREE        FI(DD1)
ALLOCATE    FI(ISPSLIB) DA(&DS1  'SYS1.SKELS')  SHR
/*-----------------------------------------------------------*/
SET         DS1 = '&SYSUID..TABLES'
ALLOCATE    FI(DD1)       DA(&DS1)                 SHR
IF          &LASTCC NE 0 THEN SET DS1 =
FREE        FI(DD1)
ALLOCATE    FI(ISPTLIB) DA(&DS1  'SYS1.TABLES') SHR
/*-----------------------------------------------------------*/
%USEREXIT
CONTROL     MSG NOLIST    NOPROMPT NOCONLIST NOSYMLIST FLUSH
%ISPFKICK
END
```

Figure A-8   Command Procedure to Complement JCL Procedure.

```
PROC 0
ALLOCATE   FI(ISPTABL)   DA(DDS.TABLES)     SHR
ALLOCATE   FI(ISPFILE)   DA(DDS.FTOUTPUT)   OLD
/* any other special user needs */
END
```

Figure A-9   Sample USEREXIT Procedure.

```
PROC 0
/* any other final adjustments */
ISPSTART   PANEL(ISR@PRIM)   NEWAPPL(ISR)
END
```

Figure A-10   Sample ISPF Final Procedure.

B

ISPF/CMS Interfaces

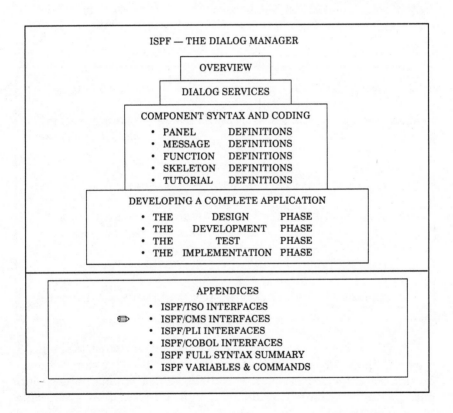

ISPF — THE DIALOG MANAGER

OVERVIEW

DIALOG SERVICES

COMPONENT SYNTAX AND CODING
- PANEL DEFINITIONS
- MESSAGE DEFINITIONS
- FUNCTION DEFINITIONS
- SKELETON DEFINITIONS
- TUTORIAL DEFINITIONS

DEVELOPING A COMPLETE APPLICATION
- THE DESIGN PHASE
- THE DEVELOPMENT PHASE
- THE TEST PHASE
- THE IMPLEMENTATION PHASE

APPENDICES
- ISPF/TSO INTERFACES
- ISPF/CMS INTERFACES
- ISPF/PLI INTERFACES
- ISPF/COBOL INTERFACES
- ISPF FULL SYNTAX SUMMARY
- ISPF VARIABLES & COMMANDS

The Basic Differences

Everything stated for ISPF under MVS (services, syntax, processes, etc.) applies equally to CMS with the exception of the file-handling definitions. And even these differences are not that significant or difficult to comprehend. Basically, *MVS data sets* become *CMS files*, and *MVS libraries* become *CMS MACLIBs*. Understandably, the syntax for the file definitions and for the LIBDEF service will be slightly different.

The FILEDEF Command

In CMS, we identify the files needed for ISPF through the FILEDEF command. The syntax for this command — as it relates to ISPF — is:

```
⊜ FILEDEF ddname DISK filename filetype filemode [(options)]

where "ddname" would be:   ISPPLIB, ISPMLIB, ISPSLIB, ISPTLIB,
                           ISPTABL, ISPFILE, ISPLLIB, ISPXLIB,
                           ISPPROF

    "filename" would be:   ISPNULL  or the actual name

    "filetype" would be:   PANEL,    MESSAGE, SKELETON,TABLE,
                           LOADLIB, TXTLIB,  MACLIB,  etc.

    "filemode" would be:   *        or the actual disk

    "options"  would be:   [PERM] [CONCAT] [RECFM x] [LRECL nn]
```

The *ddname* entry, as in MVS, is the name that connects the ISPF symbolic file references to the actual CMS files. The names shown are for the panels, messages, skeletons, tables (input), tables (output), file tailoring output, load module libraries, text files, and profile tables respectively.

The *filename filetype filemode* sequence is, of course, the manner in which we identify all CMS files.

Filename is the actual name assigned to our file. A special case here (available with ISPF Version 2.2) is the ISPNULL entry. This is a dummy entry (called a place holder) which is used when we wish to reference a variable file name (more on this later).

Filetype generally reflects the type of data that the file contains. The names shown are the defaults used by ISPF when trying to locate a file that has not been defined. In the case of "libraries," the file type should be MACLIB.

Filemode is the "minidisk" where this file can be located. Whenever possible, the actual letter for the disk should be used since it is more efficient than the generic *.

The PERM option simply indicates that this file definition is to remain even if a general file definition clear (FILEDEF * CLEAR) is issued.

The CONCAT option allows you to concatenate several file definitions. RECFM indicates the record format for the file, while LRECL indicates the desired logical record length.

To illustrate the usage of this statement, assume that you wish to indicate that the user's profile is to be assigned to a "library" called TABLES MACLIB which will be in your A-Disk. You would define this as follows:

```
⇨ FILEDEF ISPPROF DISK TABLES MACLIB A (PERM
```

Suppose, now, that you need to define the panel libraries for both the PDF and the ISPF products to the Dialog Manager. You could code the following:

```
⇨ FILEDEF ISPPLIB DISK ISRPLIB MACLIB * (PERM CONCAT
⇨ FILEDEF ISPPLIB DISK ISPPLIB MACLIB * (PERM CONCAT
```

NOTE: The fact that the ddname (ISPPLIB) and the file name (ISPPLIB) are the same in the second example is only a coincidence, not a requirement.

Now suppose that you had a series of panel files with various names, but with a common file type of PANEL in your A-Disk. Assuming that you wanted to concatenate these to the other ISPPLIBs, you could define this as follows:

```
☞ FILEDEF ISPPLIB DISK ISPNULL PANEL A (PERM CONCAT
```

In this case, ISPNULL, which acts only as a place holder, indicates that the actual file name will be extracted from the ISPF service request. For example:

```
☞ ISPEXEC DISPLAY PANEL(DDSP110A)
```

This would cause a search for a file named "DDSP110A PANEL A".

Please note that if you have two such definitions for the same FILEDEF where the file type is the same in both cases, then you have to use ISPNULL1, ISPNULL2, etc. For example:

```
☞ FILEDEF ISPPLIB DISK ISPNULL1 PANEL A (PERM CONCAT
☞ FILEDEF ISPPLIB DISK ISPNULL2 PANEL D (PERM CONCAT
```

When the needed panels are stored in a "library," you do not use the ISPNULL option. You simply give the name of the MACLIB, and the panel name becomes the member to be found in such a library. For example, if you wanted the DDSP110A panel in the preceding DISPLAY service from a MACLIB called DDSPANLS, you would code the file definition as follows:

```
☞ FILEDEF ISPPLIB DISK DDSPANLS MACLIB A (PERM CONCAT
```

Figure B-1 shows a possible sequence of file definitions to allocate all the necessary ISPF files for an application, followed by the PDF libraries, followed by the ISPF libraries, and then to start the Dialog Manager.

```
&TRACE  OFF
*------ profile ----------------------------------
FILEDEF  ISPPROF  DISK   TABLES   MACLIB   A   (PERM
*------- panels  ----------------------------------
FILEDEF  ISPPLIB  DISK   ISPNULL PANEL    A   (PERM CONCAT
FILEDEF  ISPPLIB  DISK   ISRPLIB MACLIB   P   (PERM CONCAT
FILEDEF  ISPPLIB  DISK   ISPPLIB MACLIB   P   (PERM CONCAT
*------- messages ----------------------------------
FILEDEF  ISPMLIB  DISK   ISPNULL MESSAGE  A   (PERM CONCAT
FILEDEF  ISPMLIB  DISK   ISRMLIB MACLIB   P   (PERM CONCAT
FILEDEF  ISPMLIB  DISK   ISPMLIB MACLIB   P   (PERM CONCAT
*------- skeletons ---------------------------------
FILEDEF  ISPSLIB  DISK   ISPNULL SKELETON A   (PERM CONCAT
FILEDEF  ISPSLIB  DISK   ISRSLIB MACLIB   P   (PERM CONCAT
*------- table input -------------------------------
FILEDEF  ISPTLIB  DISK   ISPNULL TABLE    A   (PERM CONCAT
FILEDEF  ISPTLIB  DISK   ISRTLIB MACLIB   P   (PERM CONCAT
FILEDEF  ISPTLIB  DISK   ISPTLIB MACLIB   P   (PERM CONCAT
*------- table output ------------------------------
FILEDEF  ISPTABL  DISK   ISPNULL TABLE    A   (PERM
*------- begin ISPF with PDF -----------------------
ISPSTART PANEL(ISR@PRIM) NEWAPPL(ISR)
*------- clear all filedefs ------------------------
FILEDEF  ISPPROF  CLEAR
FILEDEF  ISPPLIB  CLEAR
FILEDEF  ISPMLIB  CLEAR
FILEDEF  ISPSLIB  CLEAR
FILEDEF  ISPTLIB  CLEAR
FILEDEF  ISPTABL  CLEAR
*------- done --------------------------------------
&EXIT
```

Figure B-1   Possible CMS Sequence to Start ISPF.

The LIBDEF Service

This service performs the same function in CMS as it does in the
MVS environment. The syntax, which is only slightly different, is as
follows:

```
⊜ ISPEXEC LIBDEF libtype ┌ FILE      ID(fileid) ┐   [COND|UNCOND]
                         │                      │
                         └ LIBRARY ID(ddname)  ┘
```

You will note that instead of DATASET, we now use FILE, and the options EXCLDATA and EXCLLIBR do not apply here. As in MVS, when FILE is used, we provide the complete file ID (file name, file type, file mode); when LIBRARY is used, we provide a ddname which refers to a FILEDEF previously executed.

Suppose, for example, that we wanted to invoke a LIBDEF service so that we could access a new set of panel files. We could do it one of two ways:

```
⊜ ISPEXEC LIBDEF ISPPLIB FILE ID(ISPNULL PANEL A)


   or


⊜ FILEDEF PANELS DISK ISPNULL PANEL A (PERM
       L _ _ _ _ _ _
   ...                        ⌐
⊜ ISPEXEC LIBDEF ISPPLIB LIBRARY ID(PANELS)
```

In either case, if we requested a display of panel DDSP110A, ISPF would search for a file named "DDSP110A PANEL A".

Addressing the Command Environment

EXEC2 Procedures

In a CMS EXEC2 procedure, any statement that is not recognized as an EXEC2 control statement (it begins with an "&") is generally passed through to the operating system (CMS) for handling. If CMS recognizes it as one of its commands, it executes; if not, it passes it through to CP — the Control Program. Of course, if CP does not recognize it as one of its own, it will reject it.

In order to identify ISPEXEC as the proper handler for our ISPF service requests, we must use the following technique:

```
   *  to identify the command receiver:
 &PRESUME &SUBCOMMAND ISPEXEC
 ISPEXEC  service parameter(s)
 ... ...
 ISPEXEC  service parameter(s)
 ... ...


   *  to reset the receiver back to CMS:
 &PRESUME [&COMMAND]
```

To illustrate a small example, please consider the file tailoring example given in Figure 5-7. Translated to CMS EXEC2 language, the coding would be similar to that shown in Figure B-2.

REXX Procedures

The same principles mentioned previously apply to REXX procedures as well. The only difference is in the syntax, which is:

```
 /*  variables must not be in 'quotes' */
 /*  to identify the command receiver: */
 ADDRESS ISPEXEC
 'service parameter(s)'
 ... ...
 'service parameter(s)'
 ... ...
 /*  to reset the receiver back to CMS: */
 ADDRESS CMS
```

```
          &TRACE     OFF
          &PRESUME   &SUBCOMMAND  ISPEXEC
          ISPEXEC    CONTROL  ERRORS   RETURN
*----------------------------------------------------------------
          &TABLE =   DDST000
          &SKEL  =   DDSS120
          &DSN   =   &STRING  OF DDSO120 FTOUTPUT A
          ISPEXEC    DISPLAY  PANEL(DDSP120A)
          &IF &RC    ¬= 0     &THEN &GOTO -EXIT
          &COMMAND   FILEDEF  ISPFILE      CLEAR
          &COMMAND   FILEDEF  ISPFILE DISK &DSN (PERM
          ISPEXEC    FTOPEN
          &IF &RC    ¬= 0     &THEN &GOTO -NOFTOPN
          ISPEXEC    FTINCL   &SKEL
          &IF &RC    ¬= 0     &THEN &GOTO -NOFTINC
          ISPEXEC    FTCLOSE
          &IF &RC    ¬= 0     &THEN &GOTO -NOFTCLS
          ISPEXEC    SETMSG   MSG(DDSM120A)
          &GOTO      -EXIT
*----------------------------------------------------------------
-NOFTOPN  ISPEXEC    SETMSG   MSG(DDSM120B)
          &GOTO      -EXIT
-NOFTINC  ISPEXEC    SETMSG   MSG(DDSM120C)
          ISPEXEC    FTCLOSE
          &GOTO      -EXIT
-NOFTCLS  ISPEXEC    SETMSG   MSG(DDSM120D)
-EXIT     &PRESUME   &COMMAND
```

Figure B-2   CMS EXEC2 Coding Example.

C

ISPF/PLI Interfaces

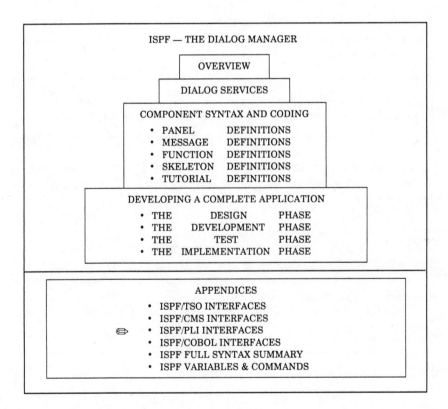

ISPF — THE DIALOG MANAGER

OVERVIEW

DIALOG SERVICES

COMPONENT SYNTAX AND CODING
- PANEL DEFINITIONS
- MESSAGE DEFINITIONS
- FUNCTION DEFINITIONS
- SKELETON DEFINITIONS
- TUTORIAL DEFINITIONS

DEVELOPING A COMPLETE APPLICATION
- THE DESIGN PHASE
- THE DEVELOPMENT PHASE
- THE TEST PHASE
- THE IMPLEMENTATION PHASE

APPENDICES
- ISPF/TSO INTERFACES
- ISPF/CMS INTERFACES
- ISPF/PLI INTERFACES
- ISPF/COBOL INTERFACES
- ISPF FULL SYNTAX SUMMARY
- ISPF VARIABLES & COMMANDS

General Concepts

Starting with Version 2 of ISPF, the mechanism to invoke the ISPF services from a program is such that we can code the requests with basically the same format as we do for command procedures. Prior to that (and still available), all service requests were coded with a call to a different subroutine and with a syntax slightly different from what we learned.

The two subroutine calls available are:

1. ISPEXEC — all parameters are based on *keyword notation*.
2. ISPLINK — all parameters are based on *positional notation*. (The only exception to this rule is in the SELECT service call which will be explained later.)

Whether we use ISPEXEC or ISPLINK, we should inform the PL/I compiler of the attributes of these external entry points. This is accomplished through statements such as:

```
⇨ DECLARE ISPEXEC ENTRY EXTERNAL OPTIONS(ASM,INTER,RETCODE);
⇨ DECLARE ISPLINK ENTRY EXTERNAL OPTIONS(ASM,INTER,RETCODE);
```

ASM informs PL/I that the entry point is an assembler subroutine. As such, arguments will be passed directly rather than through control blocks.

INTER indicates that, in case of exceptional conditions in this entry point, PL/I is to handle the interrupts.

RETCODE indicates that you expect a return code to be given by this entry point and PL/I is to extract the lower half of register 15 for subsequent interrogation. This value can then be made available through the PL/I built-in function PLIRETV.

To declare that you wish to use PLIRETV as the built-in function, you could code:

```
⇨ DECLARE PLIRETV BUILTIN;
```

If you do not make this declaration, you need to imply that PLIRETV is a function by coding each reference as "PLIRETV()".

For a general overview of the programming sequence, please refer to Figure C-1.

```
SAMPLE: PROCEDURE OPTIONS (MAIN);
        DECLARE(ISPEXEC,ISPLINK) ENTRY EXTERNAL
                                OPTIONS(ASM,INTER,RETCODE);
        DECLARE PLIRETV BUILTIN;
        ...
        CALL ISPEXEC (... ... ...);
        IF PLIRETV ¬= 0 THEN GO TO ERROR1;
        ...
        CALL ISPLINK (... ... ...);
        IF PLIRETV ¬= 0 THEN GO TO ERROR2;
        ...
        END SAMPLE;
```

Figure C-1 General Overview of a PL/I Program.

And now, let us examine the details of the two call formats: ISPEXEC and ISPLINK.

The ISPEXEC Format

The general syntax for this call is as follows:

```
☞ CALL ISPEXEC (buffer-length, buffer);
```

This format simply requires a *BINARY FIXED (31)* value as the first parameter which indicates the length of the buffer area that follows. The buffer area itself contains the service request coded exactly as already specified for command procedures.

For example, assume that we want to invoke a service request to display panel DDSP110A. The coding could be as simple as:

```
☞ CALL ISPEXEC (BINARY(23,31),'DISPLAY PANEL(DDSP110A)');
```

In this example, we are passing a buffer length of 23, which will be given with a base, scale, and precision of BINARY FIXED (31). The buffer is made up of 23 characters which contain the service and the parameters needed.

There are many other ways of coding these services. To give just one other one, you could code two general fields for all calls, assign values to these fields, and then perform the call. This could even be turned into a generalized subroutine which could then perform other functions such as examining the return code, taking special actions, etc.

For example:

```
DECLARE BUFLEN BIN FIXED (31),
        BUFFER CHARACTER(100);
...
BUFFER = 'DISPLAY PANEL(DDSP110A)';
BUFLEN = 23;
CALL ISPEXEC (BUFLEN, BUFFER);
IF PLIRETV ¬= 0 THEN GO TO DONE;
...
```

The ISPLINK Format

With this format, each parameter is positional, i.e., it must be coded in a specific sequence. If you wish to skip an optional intervening parameter, you will have to code the skipped item as a dummy one by coding a blank (' '). If the parameters that you are skipping follow the last significant parameter, you can ignore this scheme and simply close the parameter list.

The general syntax for this format is as follows:

```
CALL ISPLINK (service, parameter [,parameter [...]] );
```

The actual parameters for each ISPLINK service request are the same as for the ISPEXEC calls with the following restrictions:

- Any keyword in the format "KEYWORD(parameter)" is simply coded as "parameter". The only exception applies to the coding of the SELECT service.
- For SELECT service calls, we really have a mixture of the two call formats: The "service" is coded as 'SELECT', but the remainder of the parameters are coded as if this were an ISPEXEC call (i.e., we pass a buffer length, then the buffer is coded with the same rules as we did for &ZSEL under panels). Example:

```
⇨ CALL ISPLINK ('SELECT ', BIN(13,31), 'CMD(DDSC140A)');
```

- The order of each parameter must be the same as that given in Appendix E, "ISPF Syntax Summary." (Please note that the sequence of parameters as shown in Chapter 5, "Function Definitions," is slightly different from the one in the appendix: In the chapter, a logical sequencing and grouping was chosen for ease of understanding; in the appendix, the exact positional sequencing was observed.)
- And finally, the following services are only available through the ISPLINK format:

    - VCOPY   — Copy a pool variable into a program variable
    - VREPLACE   — Copy a program variable into a pool variable
    - VDEFINE   — Correlate a program variable to a pool variable
    - VDELETE   — Cancel a VDEFINE correlation
    - VRESET   — Cancel correlation of all variables
    - GRINIT   — Graphics initialization
    - GRERROR   — Graphics error block service
    - GRTERM   — Graphics termination

Each of these services will be explained in detail in the following sections and in the order shown.

To gain a general idea of how these calls are coded, please consider the following two examples (which give the exact same results):

```
☞ CALL ISPLINK ('DISPLAY ', 'DDSP110A', ' ', 'ZCMD ');


   or ...


☞ panelid  =  'DDSP110A';     fldx = 'ZCMD ';
☞ CALL ISPLINK ('DISPLAY ',  panelid,    ' ',   fldx);
```

You may notice that in some parameters an extra blank is placed at the end of the entry. This is used as a separation item whenever the entry is less than 8 characters.

And now, let us cover the few services that are only available through the ISPLINK formats.

Variable Correlation Services

As previously mentioned, although command procedure (CLIST, EXEC, REXX, etc.) variables are automatically known in the function pool, program variables are not — even when they have the same names. The reason, of course, is that, whereas command procedures are interpreted on demand and thus their names are known at that time, programs are compiled into object code and the names are converted into internal address values.

It is possible, however, to manipulate or associate variables in the program areas with those of the dialog pools through the use of specific ISPF service calls. Two basic processes are available:

1. *Transfer* the data values from one area to another through the VCOPY and VREPLACE services.
2. *Associate* a program variable with that of a function pool variable so that their usage becomes common to both the program and the ISPF services.

We will examine first the VCOPY and the VREPLACE services and then we will proceed to the others.

VCOPY — Copy a Pool Variable into a Program Variable.   For infrequent access to pool data, the VCOPY service is quite adequate. Its mechanism consists of searching the function pool first, then the shared pool, then the profile for the requested variable(s) and copying them into our program area(s) or simply giving us the needed address(es). The syntax is:

```
⊜ CALL ISPLINK ('VCOPY ',namelist,len-array,val-array
                          [,'LOCATE' | 'MOVE']);
```

The *namelist* parameter should be a character string containing one or more pool variable names to be copied. If it is more than one name, it must be in parentheses and separated with blanks and/or commas.

The *len-array* should be one or more fullword binary values containing the lengths of the program areas that will receive the pool variables. On return from the service, these areas will contain the actual lengths of the variables copied.

The *val-array* must contain either the pointers to the program areas receiving the values (if in LOCATE mode), or the name of the structure mapped by the *len-array* (if in MOVE mode).

The LOCATE parameter indicates that you wish to receive the addresses of the desired variables (to be stored into the pointer array named by *val-array*). The MOVE parameter indicates that you wish to receive the actual data (to be stored in the structure named by *val-array* and mapped by *len-array*).

The return code of greatest concern would be 8, which would indicate that one or more variables were not found.

To illustrate, assume that we wish to retrieve the ISPF system variable called &ZUSER (userid). This could be coded as follows:

```
⊜ DECLARE USERID CHARACTER ( 8),
            LENTH  BIN FIXED (31)   INITIAL (LENGTH(USERID));
⊜ CALL ISPLINK ('VCOPY ', 'ZUSER ', LENTH, USERID, 'MOVE');
```

For a second illustration, suppose that we had two values in one of the dialog pools containing the user name (&UNAME) and the user's room number (&ROOM). If we wanted to copy these values, we would code the following:

```
⮞ DCL 1 UINFO, 2 NAME CHAR (10), 2 ROOM CHAR ( 4);
⮞ DCL  LENTHS(2) BIN FIXED (31)  INITIAL (10, 4);
⮞ CALL ISPLINK('VCOPY ','(UNAME,ROOM)',LENTHS,UINFO,'MOVE');
```

VREPLACE — Copy a Program Variable into a Pool Variable. This service performs the reverse of the VCOPY except that it always
operates in MOVE mode and it always writes to the function pool.
The syntax is:

```
⮞ CALL ISPLINK ('VREPLACE',namelist,lengths,values);
```

The meaning of each parameter is the same as for the VCOPY service. Suppose, for example, that we wanted to alter (or create) a pool
variable called &ACCT to reflect the current value in our program.
The coding could be as follows:

```
⮞ DECLARE ACTDATA CHARACTER (10) INIT ('ABC-XYZ-87');
        LENTH    BIN FIXED (31) INIT (10);
⮞ CALL ISPLINK ('VREPLACE', 'ACCT ', LENTH, ACTDATA);
```

VDEFINE — Correlate a Program Variable to a Pool Variable. For   fre-
quent accesses to pool variables, the VDEFINE service will allow you
to correlate program variables with function pool variables and then
continue as if they were one class only. An update in one will be
reflected in the other automatically.
The syntax for this service is:

```
⮞ CALL ISPLINK ('VDEFINE ',namelist,variable,format,length,
                    [,COPY][,NOBSCAN] [,userdata]);

   where "format" is: CHAR | FIXED | BIT | HEX | USER
```

The *namelist* parameter follows the same rules as already explained for VCOPY. The *variable* parameter indicates the program area where the *namelist* variables are to be found. If more than one was specified, *variable* would have to be an array.

The *format* parameter indicates the type of data in the *variable* (as shown in the syntax box). The *length* parameter is a fullword binary value giving the length of each *variable* to be defined.

The COPY parameter indicates that, for initialization, this *variable* is to receive the value currently in one of the three types of pools. The NOBSCAN parameter indicates that "no blank scanning" is to be performed (to remove trailing blanks).

The *userdata* is the address of a program subroutine to perform special data type conversions. Because of its extremely limited application, we will not go into that here.

After this service request, you may wish to check for a return code of 8, which would indicate that one or more variables were not found.

A typical application of this service would be:

```
⇨ DCL APPL CHAR(4), VNAME CHAR(8), PTYPE CHAR(1);
⇨ CALL ISPLINK('VDEFINE ','APPL ', APPL, 'CHAR', BIN(4,31));
⇨ CALL ISPLINK('VDEFINE ','VNAME ',VNAME,'CHAR', BIN(8,31));
⇨ CALL ISPLINK('VDEFINE ','PTYPE ',PTYPE,'CHAR', BIN(1,31));
```

NOTE: You must be aware that successive VDEFINEs on the same variable are possible. This is equivalent to creating a stack for a given variable where the current reference applies to the one presently at the top of the stack.

You should also be careful with the usage of BASED storage variables. If the value of the base pointer should change *after* the VDEFINE service, the program and ISPF will be working with different addresses.

VDELETE — Cancel a VDEFINE Correlation. This service cancels the effect of previous VDEFINEs. The syntax is:

```
⇨ CALL ISPLINK ('VDELETE ', namelist | *);
```

The parameter is fairly simple: either you give a name list, or you code an "*" which indicates "all variables." A return code value of 8 would, again, indicate that one or more variables were not found.

To illustrate, if we wanted to cancel the three correlations given in the VDEFINE example, we could code:

```
☞ CALL ISPLINK('VDELETE ','(APPL,VNAME,PTYPE)');
```

VRESET — Cancel Correlation of All Variables.   This service is a super-set of the VDELETE service. It operates as if a VDELETE had been performed on each variable in a VDEFINE. The syntax is:

```
☞ CALL ISPLINK ('VRESET');
```

Graphics Interface Services

If the dialog uses a GRAPHIC area in a panel, an ISPF to GDDM in-terface must be established and, once completed, the interface must be removed. This connection and disconnection is performed through the GRINIT and the GRTERM services.

It is not the intent here to discuss the details about GDDM — it is assumed that, if you need these services, you must be familiar with GDDM. Consequently, only the syntax of the three calls that will allow you to interface with GDDM will be discussed.

GRINIT — Graphics Initialization.

```
☞ CALL ISPLINK('GRINIT ', apl-block [,panelid]);
```

All communications with GDDM involve the usage of an Applica-tions Anchor Block (AAB) which is an 8-byte area on a word boundary. The *apl-block* parameter is the name of the AAB area provided by the calling program. The *panelid* is the name of a panel where the GRAPHIC area is defined.

The possible return codes to check would be: 8 — the panel does not have a GRAPHIC area; 12 — the panel could not be found.

A simple example would be:

```
⇨ CALL ISPLINK ('GRINIT ', 'AAB1 ', 'DDSP500X');
```

GRERROR — Graphics Error Block Service. This service enables a function to process the error feedback information given by GDDM through its own service calls. The syntax is:

```
⇨ CALL ISPLINK('GRERROR ', err-pointer, pdt-pointer);
```

The *err-pointer* is a pointer field in the program to receive the address of the GDDM error feedback block. The *pdt-pointer* is another pointer field to receive the GDDM parameter descriptor table.

GRTERM — Graphics Termination. This service informs ISPF that GDDM is no longer needed and may be terminated. The syntax is extremely simple:

```
⇨ CALL ISPLINK('GRTERM ');
```

Comprehensive Example

To conclude this appendix, let us look at a complete program that uses a variety of services. For comparison purposes, the function DDSC140 previously shown has been translated into PL/I syntax.

The purpose of the function is to display an options panel (DDSP140A), then to create a job stream output through the use of a skeleton named DDSS140, and then to submit the created job stream (&ZTEMPF). This function was chosen because of its simplicity as well as to show how we can now invoke TSO services (such as the SUBMIT command) from a PL/I program by calling a command procedure as if it were a subroutine.

```
PROC        0
CONTROL     NOLIST     NOCONLIST NOMSG NOFLUSH
ISPEXEC     CONTROL    ERRORS    RETURN
ISPEXEC     VGET       ZTEMPF
SUBMIT      '&ZTEMPF.'
EXIT
END
```

Figure C-2   Supplementary Procedure to Submit FT Output.

Please note that ISPEXEC and ISPLINK call formats are used in this program. The purpose of this is primarily to show different ways of coding various services.

The DDSC140A "subroutine" shown in Figure C-2 (called by the DDSG140 program, see Figure C-3) submits the job stream created by the program as a temporary file whose name is stored in &ZTEMPF.

```
 DDSG140:PROCEDURE OPTIONS (MAIN);
          /*------------------------------------ declarations */
          DCL  ISPEXEC ENTRY EXTERNAL OPTIONS (ASM,INTER,RETCODE),
               ISPLINK ENTRY EXTERNAL OPTIONS (ASM,INTER,RETCODE),
               BINARY  BUILTIN,
               LENGTH  BUILTIN,
               PLIRETV BUILTIN;
          DCL  SKEL    CHARACTER ( 8) INITIAL ('DDSS140 '),
               LENSKEL BIN FIXED (31) INITIAL (LENGTH(SKEL));
          /*--------------------------------- initialization */
          CALL ISPEXEC (BINARY(21,31),  'CONTROL ERRORS RETURN');
          CALL ISPLINK ('VDEFINE','SKEL ',SKEL, 'CHAR ',LENSKEL);
          /*-------------------------- process options panel */
          CALL ISPLINK ('DISPLAY ', 'DDSP140A');
          IF   PLIRETV   ¬= 0      THEN  GO TO EXIT;
          CALL ISPEXEC (BINARY(36,31),
                        'VPUT (UNAME,ACCT,ROOM,CLASS) PROFILE');
          /*-------------------------- perform file tailoring */
          CALL ISPLINK ('FTOPEN ','TEMP ');
          IF   PLIRETV   ¬= 0      THEN  GOTO  NOFTOPN;
          CALL ISPLINK ('FTINCL ', SKEL);
          IF   PLIRETV   ¬= 0      THEN  GOTO  NOFTINC;
          CALL ISPLINK ('FTCLOSE ');
          IF   PLIRETV   ¬= 0      THEN  GOTO  NOFTCLS;
          /*-------------------- call procedure to submit job */
          CALL ISPEXEC (BINARY(20,31), 'SELECT CMD(DDSC140A)');
          CALL ISPLINK ('SETMSG ', 'DDSM140A');
          GOTO EXIT;
          /*-------------------------- error messages and exit */
 NOFTOPN:CALL ISPLINK ('SETMSG ', 'DDSM120B'); GO TO EXIT;
 NOFTINC:CALL ISPLINK ('SETMSG ', 'DDSM120C'); GO TO EXIT;
 NOFTCLS:CALL ISPLINK ('SETMSG ', 'DDSM120D');
 EXIT:   CALL ISPLINK ('VDELETE ', SKEL);
          /*----------------------------------------------------*/
 END  DDSG140;
```

Figure C-3   Program DDSG140 Translated from Procedure DDSC140.

D

ISPF/COBOL Interfaces

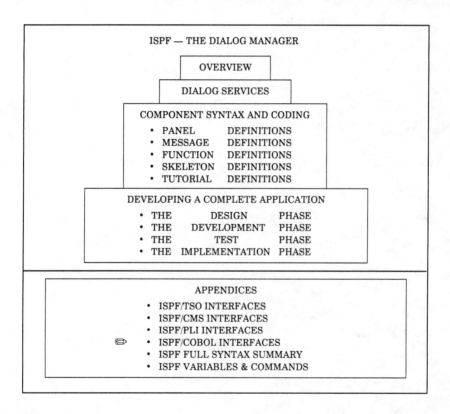

```
ISPF — THE DIALOG MANAGER

        OVERVIEW

      DIALOG SERVICES

  COMPONENT SYNTAX AND CODING
    • PANEL      DEFINITIONS
    • MESSAGE    DEFINITIONS
    • FUNCTION   DEFINITIONS
    • SKELETON   DEFINITIONS
    • TUTORIAL   DEFINITIONS

  DEVELOPING A COMPLETE APPLICATION
    • THE        DESIGN        PHASE
    • THE        DEVELOPMENT   PHASE
    • THE        TEST          PHASE
    • THE    IMPLEMENTATION    PHASE

          APPENDICES
    • ISPF/TSO INTERFACES
    • ISPF/CMS INTERFACES
    • ISPF/PLI INTERFACES
    • ISPF/COBOL INTERFACES
    • ISPF FULL SYNTAX SUMMARY
    • ISPF VARIABLES & COMMANDS
```

Every concept described under Appendix C, "ISPF/PLI Interfaces," applies to COBOL interfaces as well. The only obvious differences are those concerning the language syntax rules. Since all else is the same, we only need to see the same program (DDSG140) coded in

COBOL to understand how to code in this language. If you have skipped the previous appendix on PL/I, it is recommended that you read it now.

For best understanding of the similarities of the coding processes across the various languages, we will again translate the logic previously presented as a PL/I equivalent of the command procedure DDSC140.

This program could be coded in COBOL, as shown in Figure D-1.

```
      IDENTIFICATION DIVISION.
      PROGRAM-ID.  DDSG140.
      ENVIRONMENT DIVISION.
      DATA DIVISION.
      WORKING-STORAGE SECTION.


      01  SKEL            PIC    X(8)     VALUE   "DDSS140 ".
      01  LENSKEL         PIC    9(4)     VALUE   8     COMP.


      01  BUFLEN          PIC    9(4)     VALUE   0     COMP.
      01  BUFR            PIC    X(80)    VALUE   SPACES.
      01  PARMA           PIC    X(8)     VALUE   SPACES.
      01  PARMB           PIC    X(8)     VALUE   SPACES.


      01  SCONTROL        PIC    X(8)     VALUE   "CONTROL ".
      01  SVDEFINE        PIC    X(8)     VALUE   "VDEFINE ".
      01  SDISPLAY        PIC    X(8)     VALUE   "DISPLAY ".
      01  SVPUT           PIC    X(8)     VALUE   "VPUT    ".
      01  SFTOPEN         PIC    X(8)     VALUE   "FTOPEN  ".
      01  SFTINCL         PIC    X(8)     VALUE   "FTINCL  ".
      01  SFTCLOSE        PIC    X(8)     VALUE   "FTCLOSE ".
      01  SFTSELEC        PIC    X(8)     VALUE   "SELECT  ".
      01  SSETMSG         PIC    X(8)     VALUE   "SETMSG  ".
      01  SVDELETE        PIC    X(8)     VALUE   "VDELETE ".


      PROCEDURE DIVISION.
      *--- INITIALIZATION -----------------------------------------
      *     CALL ISPEXEC (21,  "CONTROL ERRORS RETURN");
            MOVE 21 TO BUFLEN.
            MOVE "CONTROL ERRORS RETURN" TO BUFR.
            CALL "ISPEXEC" USING BUFLEN BUFR.

      *     CALL ISPLINK ("VDEFINE","SKEL ",SKEL, "CHAR ",LENSKEL);
            MOVE "SKEL " TO PARMA.
            MOVE "CHAR " TO PARMB.
            CALL "ISPLINK" USING SVDEFINE PARMA SKEL PARMB LENSKEL.

      *--- PROCESS OPTIONS PANEL ----------------------------------
      *     CALL ISPLINK ("DISPLAY ", "DDSP140A");
            MOVE "DDSP140A" TO PARMA.
            CALL "ISPLINK" USING SDISPLAY PARMA.
            IF RETURN-CODE NOT = 0 THEN GO TO DONE.
```

Figure D-1   COBOL Translation of DDSC140.

```
      *     CALL ISPEXEC (36, "VPUT (UNAME,ACCT,ROOM,CLASS) PROFILE");
            MOVE 36 TO BUFLEN.
            MOVE "VPUT (UNAME,ACCT,ROOM,CLASS) PROFILE" TO BUFR.
            CALL "ISPEXEC" USING BUFLEN BUFR.

      *--- PERFORM FILE TAILORING -------------------------------
      *     CALL ISPLINK ("FTOPEN ","TEMP ");
            MOVE "TEMP" TO PARMA.
            CALL "ISPLINK" USING SFTOPEN PARMA.
            IF RETURN-CODE NOT = 0 THEN GO TO NOFTOPN;

      *     CALL ISPLINK ("FTINCL ", SKEL);
            CALL "ISPLINK" USING SFTINCL SKEL.
            IF RETURN-CODE NOT = 0 THEN GO TO NOFTINC.

      *     CALL ISPLINK ("FTCLOSE ");
            CALL "ISPLINK" USING SFTCLOSE.
            IF RETURN-CODE NOT = 0 THEN GO TO NOFTCLS.

      *--- CALL PROCEDURE TO SUBMIT JOB -------------------------
      *     CALL ISPEXEC (20, "SELECT CMD(DDSC140A)");
            MOVE 20 TO BUFLEN.
            MOVE "SELECT CMD(DDSC140A)" TO BUFR.
            CALL "ISPEXEC" USING BUFLEN BUFR.

      *   CALL ISPLINK ("SETMSG ", "DDSM140A");
            MOVE "DDSM140A" TO PARMA.
            CALL "ISPLINK" USING SSETMSG PARMA.
            GO TO DONE.

      *--- ERROR MESSAGES AND EXIT ------------------------------
      NOFTOPN.
      *     CALL ISPLINK ("SETMSG ", "DDSM120B");
            MOVE "DDSM120B" TO PARMA.
            CALL "ISPLINK" USING SSETMSG PARMA.
            GO TO DONE.
      NOFTINC.
      *     CALL ISPLINK ("SETMSG ", "DDSM120C");
            MOVE "DDSM120C" TO PARMA.
            CALL "ISPLINK" USING SSETMSG PARMA.
            GO TO DONE.
```

Figure D-1   (continued from previous page)

```
     NOFTCLS.
*       CALL ISPLINK ("SETMSG ", "DDSM120D");
        MOVE "DDSM120D" TO PARMA.
        CALL "ISPLINK" USING SSETMSG PARMA.
     DONE.
*       CALL ISPLINK ("VDELETE ", SKEL);
        CALL "ISPLINK" USING SVDELETE SKEL.
*--- DONE ----------------------------------------------------
        GOBACK.
```

Figure D-1   (continued from previous page)

E

ISPF Syntax Summary

```
ISPF — THE DIALOG MANAGER

        OVERVIEW

     DIALOG SERVICES

   COMPONENT SYNTAX AND CODING
     • PANEL      DEFINITIONS
     • MESSAGE    DEFINITIONS
     • FUNCTION   DEFINITIONS
     • SKELETON   DEFINITIONS
     • TUTORIAL   DEFINITIONS

   DEVELOPING A COMPLETE APPLICATION
     • THE      DESIGN         PHASE
     • THE      DEVELOPMENT    PHASE
     • THE      TEST           PHASE
     • THE  IMPLEMENTATION  PHASE

           APPENDICES
     • ISPF/TSO INTERFACES
     • ISPF/CMS INTERFACES
     • ISPF/PLI INTERFACES
     • ISPF/COBOL INTERFACES
  ☞  • ISPF FULL SYNTAX SUMMARY
     • ISPF VARIABLES & COMMANDS
```

PANEL Definitions

)ATTR Section

```
☞ )ATTR  [DEFAULT(abc  |  %+_)]
```

```
☞ char [TYPE   (TEXT  | INPUT  | OUTPUT  | DATAIN  | DATAOUT)]
       [COLOR (WHITE | RED    | BLUE    | GREEN
                     | PINK   | YELLOW  | TURQ)]
       [INTENS (HIGH | LOW    | NONE)]
       [HILITE(BLINK | USCORE | REVERSE)]
       [CAPS   (ON   | OFF    | IN      | OUT)]
       [JUST   (LEFT | RIGHT  | ASIS)]
       [PAD    (NULLS | USER  | char)]
       [PADC   (NULLS | USER  | char)]
       [SKIP   (ON   | OFF)]
       [ATTN   (ON   | OFF)]
       [AREA(DYNAMIC | GRAPHIC)]
       [EXTEND  (ON  | OFF)]
       [SCROLL  (ON  | OFF)]
       [USERMOD(code)]
       [DATAMOD(code)]
```

)BODY Section

```
☞ BODY [DEFAULT(abc)] [WIDTH(width)]  [EXPAND(xy)]    [KANA]
       [CMD(fldname)] [SMSG(fldname)] [LMSG(fldname)] [ASIS]
```

)MODEL Section

```
☞ )MODEL  [ROWS (ALL  | SCAN)]  [CLEAR(vname1 [vname2 ...])]
```

)INIT +)REINIT +)PROC Sections

```
⊜ )INIT
⊜ )REINIT
⊜ )PROC
```

Assignment Statements

```
⊜ &varname = value
```

The TRUNC Function

```
⊜ &varname = TRUNC (&variable, {nn | 'char'})
```

The TRANS Function

```
⊜ &varname = TRANS (&variable, value,value [...] [MSG=id])

   where: "value,value"  may be:  string,string
                            or:         *,string
                            or:         *,*
```

The PFK Function

```
⊜ &varname = PFK (nn | string)
```

The LVLINE Function

```
⊜ &varname = LVLINE (areaname)
```

VERify Statements

```
⊕ VER (&vname [NONBLANK | NB] keyword [value(s)] [MSG=msgid])


   where: "keyword" can be:
          ALPHA              (A-Z, a-z, @, >, $)
          NUM                (0-9)
          HEX                (0-9, A-F, a-f)
          BIT                (0, 1)
          PICT 'string'      (C=char, A=alpha, N | 9=numeric,
                              X=hex,  any other character
                              will represent itself)
          NAME               (OS name rules...1-8)
          DSNAME             (OS name rules...1-44)
          FILEID             (CMS rules for LISTFILE names)
          RANGE lower,upper  (Numeric ranges max 16 digits each)
          LIST  val1, val2, ...
```

IF Statements

```
⊕ IF (operand operator operand [,operand ...]) statement


   where: "operand"   can be a variable or a constant,
          "operator"  can be the conditions "=" or "¬="
          "statement" can be any of the statements given
                      in this section (including other IFs)
```

VPUT Statements

```
⊕ VPUT   vname-list  [SHARED | PROFILE | ASIS]


   where "vname-list" may be: (vname [vname ...])
```

REFRESH Statements

```
⊜ REFRESH (*  |  vname-list)
```

Selection Panel Considerations — &ZSEL

```
⊜ 'PANEL(name)  [OPT(option)]                        [appl-options]'
⊜ 'CMD(name    [parms])   [LANG(APL)] [NOCHECK] [appl-options]'
⊜ 'PGM(name)   [PARM(parms)]          [NOCHECK] [appl-options]'
⊜ EXIT


  where "appl-options" is:  NEWAPPL[[(appl-id)] [PASSLIB]]
                      or:  NEWPOOL
```

Tutorial Panel Considerations — &ZSEL

```
⊜ &ZSEL = [*]panelid

  where:  "*" indicates explicit selection
```

MESSAGE Definitions

```
⊜ msg-id ['short msg'] [.HELP={panel | *}] [.ALARM={YES | NO}]
⊜ 'long message'
```

FUNCTION Definitions

BROWSE — Invoke the BROWSE Program from a Dialog

```
⊜ ISPEXEC BROWSE DATASET(dsname)    [VOLUME(vol)]
                  [PASSWORD(pass)]  [PANEL(name)]
```

CONTROL — Specify Screen and Error-Handling Options

```
⊜ ISPEXEC CONTROL {DISPLAY  {LOCK               } }
                  {         {LINE               } }
                  {         {REFRESH            } }
                  {         {SAVE   | RESTORE}   }
                  {                             }
                  {NONDISPL [ENTER  | END]      }
                  {                             }
                  {ERRORS   [CANCEL | RETURN]   }
                  {                             }
                  {SPLIT    {ENABLE | DISABLE}  }
                  {                             }
                  {NOCMD                        }
```

DISPLAY — Display Data Panel

```
⊜ ISPEXEC DISPLAY [PANEL(name)]      [MSG(msgid)]
                  [CURSOR(field)]    [CSRPOS(position)]
```

EDIT — Invoke the EDIT Program from a Dialog

```
⊜ ISPEXEC EDIT DATASET(dsname)    [VOLUME(vol)]
               [PASSWORD(pass)]   [PANEL(name)]
               [MACRO(mname)]     [PROFILE(pname)]
```

EDREC — Edit Recovery Table Processing

```
⊜ ISPEXEC EDREC {INIT      [CMD(cmdname)]                     }
                {QUERY                                        }
                {PROCESS [DATAID(id)]   [PASSWORD(word)]}
                {CANCEL                                       }
                {DEFER                                        }
```

FTCLOSE — Close Out the File Tailoring Process

```
⊜ ISPEXEC FTCLOSE [NAME(member)] [LIBRARY(ddname)] [NOREPL]
```

FTERASE — Erase the Created Output File

```
⊜ ISPEXEC FTERASE member [LIBRARY(ddname)]
```

FTINCL — Include a Skeleton to Control Output

```
⊜ ISPEXEC FTINCL skelname [NOFT]
```

FTOPEN — Create an Output File for File Tailoring

```
⊜ ISPEXEC FTOPEN [TEMP]
```

GETMSG — Obtain Information on a Particular Message

```
⊜ ISPEXEC GETMSG MSG(id) [SHORTMSG(vname1)] [LONGMSG(vname2)]
                         [ALARM(vname3)]    [HELP(vname4)]
```

GRERROR — Graphics Error Block Service

```
☞ CALL ISPLINK('GRERROR ', err-pointer, pdt-pointer);
```

GRINIT — Graphics Initialization

```
☞ CALL ISPLINK('GRINIT ', apl-block [,panelid]);
```

GRTERM — Graphics Termination

```
☞ CALL ISPLINK('GRTERM ');
```

ISREDIT — Invoke EDIT Macros from a Dialog

```
☞ ISPEXEC ISREDIT macro [parm ...]
```

LIBDEF — Define ISPF Libraries for a Dialog

```
☞ ISPEXEC LIBDEF libtype  DATASET   ID(dslist)    [COND|UNCOND]
                          EXCLDATA  ID(dslist)
                          LIBRARY   ID(ddname)
                          EXCLLIBR  ID(ddname)
```

LMxxxxxx — Use PDF Library Access Services

```
☞ ISPEXEC LMxxxxx DATAID(id) [MEMBER(name)] [parm ...]
```

LOG — Write Dialog Messages to a Log File

```
☞ ISPEXEC LOG MSG(messageid)
```

PQUERY — Obtain Information on a Particular Panel

```
☞ ISPEXEC PQUERY  PANEL(panelname)    AREANAME(name)
                  [AREATYPE(vname1)]
                  [WIDTH(vname2)]    [DEPTH(vname3)]
                  [ROW(vname4)]      [COLUMN(vname5)]
```

SELECT — Display Selection Panel

```
☞ ISPEXEC SELECT sel-options  [appl-options]

   where "sel-options" is one of the following:
   ◆    PANEL(name) [OPT(option)]
   ◆    CMD(name    [parms])      [LANG(APL)]
   ◆    PGM(name)   [PARM(parms)]

   and "appl-options" is:  NEWAPPL[[(appl-id)] [PASSLIB]]
                      or:  NEWPOOL
```

SETMSG — Set Message for Display

```
☞ ISPEXEC SETMSG MSG(msgid)
```

TBADD — Add a Row to a Table

```
☞ ISPEXEC TBADD tblname [SAVE(namelist)] [ORDER]
```

TBBOTTOM — Point to Bottom of Table (Last Row)

```
☞ ISPEXEC TBBOTTOM tblname [SAVENAME(vname1)] [ROWID(vname2)]
                           [NOREAD]          [POSITION(vname3)]
```

TBCLOSE — File a Table and Disconnect It from Use

```
☞ ISPEXEC TBCLOSE tblname [NEWCOPY | REPLCOPY] [NAME(name)]
                          [PAD(percent)]  [LIBRARY(ddname)]
```

TBCREATE — Create a Table

```
☞ ISPEXEC TBCREATE tblname [KEYS(list)]       [NAMES(list)]
                           [WRITE | NOWRITE]  [REPLACE]
                           [LIBRARY(ddname)]  [SHARE]
```

TBDELETE — Delete a Row from a Table

```
☞ ISPEXEC TBDELETE tblname
```

TBDISPL — Display Table Panel

```
☞ ISPEXEC TBDISPL tblname [PANEL(name)]        [MSG(msgid)]
                          [CURSOR(field)]      [CSRROW(row)]
                          [CSRPOS(position)] [AUTOSEL(YES | NO)]
                          [POSITION(vname1)] [ROWID(vname2)]
```

TBEND — End Table Processing without Saving

```
⊜ ISPEXEC TBEND tblname
```

TBERASE — Erase a Table from a Library

```
⊜ ISPEXEC TBERASE tblname [LIBRARY(ddname)]
```

TBEXIST — Check Existence of a Given Key

```
⊜ ISPEXEC TBEXIST tblname
```

TBGET — Get a Row from a Table

```
⊜ ISPEXEC TBGET tblname [SAVENAME(vname1)] [ROWID(vname2)]
                        [NOREAD]            [POSITION(vname3)]
```

TBMOD — Modify/Add a Row to a Table

```
⊜ ISPEXEC TBMOD tblname [SAVE(namelist)] [ORDER]
```

TBOPEN — Open a Table for Processing

```
☞ ISPEXEC TBOPEN tblname [WRITE | NOWRITE]
                         [LIBRARY(ddname)] [SHARE]
```

TBPUT — Put a Row into a Table

```
☞ ISPEXEC TBPUT tblname [SAVE(namelist)] [ORDER]
```

TBQUERY — Query Information about a Table

```
☞ ISPEXEC TBQUERY tblname [KEYS(vname1)]      [NAMES(vname2)]
                          [ROWNUM(vname3)]   [KEYNUM(vname4)]
                          [NAMENUM(vname5)]  [POSITION(vname6)]
```

TBSARG — Set Search Arguments for a Scan

```
☞ ISPEXEC TBSARG tblname [ARGLIST(list)] [NEXT | PREVIOUS]
                         [NAMECOND(conditions)]

  where "conditions" represents: name,condition, ...
     and "condition"        may be: LT | LE | EQ | NE | GE | GT
```

TBSAVE — File a Table and Continue

```
⊜ ISPEXEC TBSAVE tblname [NEWCOPY | REPLCOPY] [NAME(name)]
                         [PAD(percent)]   [LIBRARY(ddname)]
```

TBSCAN — Search Table Based on TBSARG

```
⊜ ISPEXEC TBSCAN tblname [ARGLIST(list)] [SAVENAME(vname1)]
                         [ROWID(vname2)] [NEXT | PREVIOUS]
                         [NOREAD]        [POSITION(vname3)]
                         [CONDLIST(conditions)]

  where "conditions" represents: name,condition, ...
    and "condition"  may     be: LT | LE | EQ | NE | GE | GT
```

TBSKIP — Skip to the Next Row

```
⊜ ISPEXEC TBSKIP tblname [NUMBER(nbr)]   [SAVENAME(vname1)]
                         [ROWID(vname2)] [ROW(rowid)]
                         [NOREAD]        [POSITION(vname3)]
```

TBSORT — Sort a Table

```
⊜ ISPEXEC TBSORT tblname FIELDS(sortlist)

  where "sortlist" is: field, C | N, A | D, ...
```

TBSTATS — Obtain Statistical Data on a Table

```
⊜ ISPEXEC TBSTATS tblname [CDATE(vname1)]      [CTIME(vname2)]
                          [UDATE(vname3)]      [UTIME(vname4)]
                          [USER(vname5)]       [ROWCREAT(vname6)]
                          [ROWCURR(vname7)]    [ROWUPD(vname8)]
                          [TABLEUPD(vname9)]   [SERVICE(vname10)]
                          [RETCODE(vname11)]   [STATUS1(vname12)]
                          [STATUS2(vname13)]   [STATUS3(vname14)]
                          [LIBRARY(ddname)]
```

TBTOP — Point to TOP of Table (Row 0)

```
⊜ ISPEXEC TBTOP tblname
```

TBVCLEAR — Clear Table Variables to Null

```
⊜ ISPEXEC TBVCLEAR tblname
```

VCOPY — Copy a Pool Variable into a Program Variable

```
⊜ CALL ISPLINK ('VCOPY ',namelist,len-array,val-array
                         [,'LOCATE' | 'MOVE']);
```

VDEFINE — Correlate a Program Variable to a Pool Variable

```
⊜ CALL ISPLINK ('VDEFINE ',namelist,variable,format,length,
                         [,COPY][,NOBSCAN] [,userdata]);

  where "format" is: CHAR | FIXED | BIT | HEX | USER
```

VDELETE — Cancel a Variable Correlation between Program and Pool

```
☞ CALL ISPLINK ('VDELETE ', namelist | *);
```

VGET — Get Variable from Shared or Profile Pool

```
☞ ISPEXEC VGET (list) [SHARED | PROFILE | ASIS]
```

VPUT — Put Variable in Shared or Profile Pool

```
☞ ISPEXEC VPUT (list) [SHARED | PROFILE | ASIS]
```

VREPLACE — Copy a Program Variable into a Pool Variable

```
☞ CALL ISPLINK ('VREPLACE',namelist,lengths,values);
```

VRESET — Cancel Correlation of All Variables

```
☞ CALL ISPLINK ('VRESET');
```

SKELETON Definitions

)DEFAULT — Establish Control Characters

```
☞ )DEFAULT abcdefg

    where "abcdefg" are the characters to substitute
    for ")&?!<|>"
```

)TB — Establish Tab Positions

```
)TB position1 [ ... [ position16 ] ]
```

)CM — Comment Line

```
)CM any comment desired
```

)BLANK — Generate Blank Line(s)

```
)BLANK [nn]
```

)SET — Set Values in Variables

```
)SET vname = op1 [ ± op2 [ ± ... [ ± op15 ] ] ]

   where "op1" ... "op15" may be variables or constants
     and ± may be "+" or "-"
```

)SEL +)ENDSEL — Conditional Selection of Data

```
⊜ )SEL expl [ op exp2 [ ... [ op exp8 ] ] ]
⊜ ... ...
⊜ )ENDSEL

  where "exp" may be a logical expression
    and "op"  may be a logical condition: "|" (OR), "&&" (AND)

 further, "logical expression" may be: operand operator operand
 where  "operator" may be: NL | LT | LE | EQ | NE | GE | GT | NG
                   or: ¬< |  <  | <= | =  | ¬= | >= |  >  | ¬>
```

)DOT +)ENDDOT — Do-loop for a Table

```
⊜ )DOT &tablename
⊜ ...
⊜ )ENDDOT
```

)IM — Imbed Another Skeleton

```
⊜ )IM skeleton [NT] [OPT]
```

TUTORIAL Definitons

COMMAND	ABV	FUNCTION	VARIABLE	LOCATION
HELP	n/a	Enter tutorial	.HELP	)INIT, etc.
TOP INDEX	T I	Table of contents Index	&ZHTOP &ZHINDEX	)INIT)INIT
UP SKIP	U S	Parent topic Next topic	&ZUP n/a	)PROC (automatic)
enter BACK	n/a B	Next page Previous page	&ZCONT n/a	)PROC (automatic)

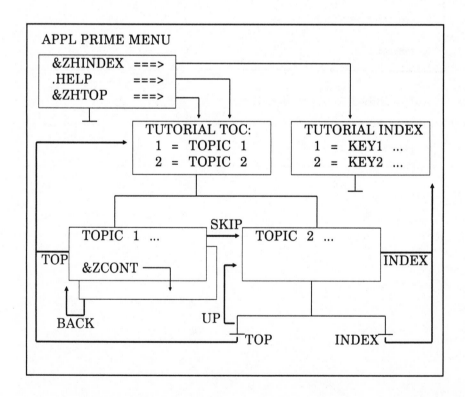

ISPF START Command

```
⌨ ISPSTART sel-options  [appl-options]  [test-options]

  where "sel-options" is one of the following:
  ♦    PANEL(name) [OPT(option)]
  ♦    CMD(name    [parms])      [LANG(APL)]
  ♦    PGM(name)   [PARM(parms)]


   and "appl-options" is:  NEWAPPL(appl-id)


   and "test-options" is:  TEST | TESTX | TRACE | TRACEX
```

CMS LIBDEF Service

```
⌨ ISPEXEC LIBDEF libtype ┌ FILE     ID(fileid) ┐  [COND|UNCOND]
                         │ LIBRARY  ID(ddname)  │
                         └                      ┘
```

ISPF System Variables

ISPF — THE DIALOG MANAGER

OVERVIEW

DIALOG SERVICES

COMPONENT SYNTAX AND CODING
- PANEL   DEFINITIONS
- MESSAGE   DEFINITIONS
- FUNCTION   DEFINITIONS
- SKELETON   DEFINITIONS
- TUTORIAL   DEFINITIONS

DEVELOPING A COMPLETE APPLICATION
- THE   DESIGN   PHASE
- THE   DEVELOPMENT   PHASE
- THE   TEST   PHASE
- THE   IMPLEMENTATION   PHASE

APPENDICES
- ISPF/TSO INTERFACES
- ISPF/CMS INTERFACES
- ISPF/PLI INTERFACES
- ISPF/COBOL INTERFACES
- ISPF FULL SYNTAX SUMMARY
- ISPF VARIABLES & COMMANDS

Panel Control Variables

.ALARM — Control sounding of terminal alarm

```
☞ .ALARM = [YES | NO]
```

.ATTR — Change attributes of a panel field

```
☞ .ATTR(&varname | .CURSOR) = 'attr-name(value) ...'
```

.ATTRCHAR — Change attributes for a character

```
☞ .ATTRCHAR(character)  = 'attr-name(value) ...'
```

.AUTOSEL — Control automatic row selection

```
☞ .AUTOSEL = [YES | NO]
```

.CURSOR — Control cursor on display

```
☞ .CURSOR = varname
```

.CSRPOS — Control cursor position in field

```
☞ .CSRPOS = [nn | &varname] or &varname = .CSRPOS
```

.CSRROW — Place cursor in table row

```
☞ .CSRROW = [nn | &varname]
```

.HELP — Identify tutorial panel

```
☞ .HELP = panelid
```

.MSG — Message ID to display

```
☞ .MSG = messageid
```

.PFKEY — Get PF key data

```
☞ IF (.PFKEY = PF01) ...
```

.RESP — Query response type

```
☞ IF (.RESP = END) ...
```

.TRAIL — Get remainder of TRUNCate operation

```
☞ &varname = .TRAIL
```

.ZVARS — Correlate z variables to actual names

```
☞  .ZVARS = '(vname1, vname2, ...)'
```

System Variables

These variables are of a more general and global nature and contain values such as current date, time, user identification, terminal type, etc. A complete list will be presented in alphabetical order within the following classes:

- General Variables
- Date and Time Variables
- Terminal and PF Keys
- Selection Panel Variables
- Table Display Variables
- Scrolling Variables
- Dialog Error Variables
- Tutorial Variables

For each class, the list will show:

- The variable's name
- The pool where it resides or is defined
- Whether or not it is updated by ISPF or the application
- The length of each variable area
- A brief description of the variable

General Variables

VAR NAME	LOCAT	UPDT	LEN	DESCRIPTION
Z	Shrd	ISPF	0	Null variable (gives null string)
ZAPLCNT	Shrd	ISPF	4	Nbr logical screen calls for appl
ZAPPLID	Shrd	ISPF	8	Application identifier
ZENVIR	Shrd	ISPF	32	Environment description:
				1 -8: Product name,version,release
				9-16: Operating system name
				17-24: Operating system environment
				25-32: Future use
ZPLACE	Prof	Appl	7	Command line location (ASIS, BOTTOM)
ZPROFAPP	Prof	ISPF	8	Appl profile pool extension table
ZTEMPF	Shrd	ISPF	44	Name temporary file for file tailor.
ZTEMPN	Shrd	ISPF	8	DDNAME for ZTEMPF
ZUSER	Shrd	ISPF	8	Userid
ZVERB	Shrd	ISPF	8	Value from SETVERB command

Date and Time Variables

VAR NAME	LOCAT	UPDT	LEN	DESCRIPTION
ZDATE	Shrd	ISPF	8	Current date in YY/MM/DD format
ZDAY	Shrd	ISPF	2	Current day of month in DD format
ZJDATE	Shrd	ISPF	6	Current Julian date in YY.DDD format
ZMONTH	Shrd	ISPF	2	Current month in MM format
ZTIME	Shrd	ISPF	5	Current time in HH:MM format
ZYEAR	Shrd	ISPF	2	Current year in YY format

Terminal and PF Keys

VAR NAME	LOCAT	UPDT	LEN	DESCRIPTION
ZCOLORS	Shrd	ISPF	4	Number of colors supported (1 or 7)
ZHILITE	Shrd	ISPF	3	Highlighting available? (YES, NO)
ZKEYS	Prof	ISPF	4	Number of PF keys
ZPFCTL	Prof	Appl	5	User authorization to use PFSHOW
ZPFFMT	Prof	Appl	4	Nbr PF key definitions per line
ZPFnn	Prof	Appl	255	PF key settings (ZPF01-ZPF24)
ZPFSET	Prof	Appl	4	PF key definition set displayed
ZPFSHOW	Prof	Appl	4	PFSHOW command status
ZSCREEN	Shrd	ISPF	1	Logical screen number (1 - 4)
ZSCREEND	Shrd	ISPF	4	Screen depth available for use
ZSCREENW	Shrd	ISPF	4	Screen width available for use
ZSPLIT	Shrd	ISPF	3	Split screen in effect (YES, NO)
ZTERM	Prof	ISPF	8	Terminal type (from option 0.1)

Selection Panel Variables

VAR NAME	LOCAT	UPDT	LEN	DESCRIPTION
ZCMD	Panel	Appl	var	Command field
ZPARENT	Panel	Appl	8	Parent menu name
ZPRIM	Panel	Appl	8	Primary menu indicator (YES, NO)
ZSEL	Panel	Appl	var	Command input field truncated at "."

Table Display Variables

VAR NAME	LOCAT	UPDT	LEN	DESCRIPTION
ZTDMARK	Any	ISPF	var	Bottom-of-data marker
ZTDMSG	Any	ISPF	8	Top-row-displayed msg id
ZTDROWS	Funct	ISPF	6	Nbr table rows from display
ZTDSELS	Funct	ISPF	4	Nbr selected rows in display
ZTDTOP	Funct	ISPF	6	Top row nbr displayed

Scrolling Variables

VAR NAME	LOCAT	UPDT	LEN	DESCRIPTION
ZSCBR	Prof	Appl	4	Scroll amount for BROWSE
ZSCED	Prof	Appl	4	Scroll amount for EDIT
ZSCML	Prof	Appl	4	Scroll amount for member lists
ZSCROLLA	Shrd	ISPF	4	Scroll amount field
ZSCROLLN	Shrd	ISPF	4	Scroll number (lines)
ZSCROLLD	Any	ISPF	4	Default for dynamic and tbl display

Dialog Error Variables

VAR NAME	LOCAT	UPDT	LEN	DESCRIPTION
ZERRALRM	Funct	ISPF	3	Error alarm indicator (YES, NO)
ZERRHM	Funct	ISPF	8	Error help panel ID
ZERRLM	Funct	ISPF	78	Long message text
ZERRMSG	Funct	ISPF	8	Error message ID
ZERRSM	Funct	ISPF	24	Short message text

Tutorial Variables

VAR NAME	LOCAT	UPDT	LEN	DESCRIPTION
ZCONT	Panel	Appl	8	Continuation panel name
ZHINDEX	Panel	Appl	8	First index panel name
ZHTOP	Panel	Appl	8	Table of Contents panel name
ZIND	Panel	Appl	8	Index page indicator (YES, NO)
ZUP	Panel	Appl	8	Parent topic panel name

System Commands

These are the standard ISPF commands that can generally be used within any application dialog. The full list, in alphabetical order, is:

- CMS — Invoke a CMS command
- CP — Invoke a CP command
- CURSOR — Move the cursor to the first input field
- DOWN — Scroll downward (toward bottom of data)
- END — Terminate the current display process
- HELP — Provide assistance with a given panel and/or message
- KEYS — Review and/or update the PF key settings
- LEFT — Scroll left
- PANELID — ON: display the current panelid; OFF: do not display
- PFSHOW — ON: show current PF key values; OFF: do not show; TAILOR: enter a panel to customize PF key display
- PRINT — Take a "snapshot" of the physical screen into the ISPF list file
- PRINT-HI — Same as PRINT but show high-intensity displays
- PRINTL — Take a "snapshot" of the logical screen (as if split screen were not in effect) into the ISPF list file
- PRINTL-HI — Same as PRINTL but show high-intensity displays
- RCHANGE — Repeat the change operation last given
- RETURN — Return to the most current primary option menu
- RFIND — Repeat the find operation last given
- RIGHT — Scroll right

- SPLIT — Split the screen horizontally (or change the current split) at the current cursor position
- SPLITV — For 3290 terminals, split the screen vertically along the middle
- STOPAT — When SELECTing a program in CMS, display a message and enter CMS SUBSET mode
- SWAP — Swap the cursor position to the other logical screen
- TSO — Invoke a TSO command
- UP — Scroll upward (toward top of data)

Standard PF Keys

PF01 HELP	PF02 SPLIT	PF03 END
PF04 RETURN	PF05 RFIND	PF06 RCHANGE
PF07 UP	PF08 DOWN	PF09 SWAP
PF10 LEFT	PF11 RIGHT	PF12 CURSOR

PF13 HELP	PF14 SPLIT	PF15 END
PF16 RETURN	PF17 RFIND	PF18 RCHANGE
PF19 UP	PF20 DOWN	PF21 SWAP
PF22 LEFT	PF23 RIGHT	PF24 CURSOR

Bibliography

The following is a list of the IBM manuals that relate to ISPF, PDF, TSO, and GDDM for both VM and MVS as mentioned in this book:

- GC34-2136 MVS *ISPF General Information*
- SC34-4019 MVS *ISPF Installation and Customization*
- SC34-4021 MVS *ISPF Dialog Management Services*
- SC34-4024 MVS *ISPF/PDF Program Reference*
- SC34-4018 MVS *ISPF/PDF Edit Macros*
- SC34-4023 MVS *ISPF/PDF Services*
- SC34-2135 MVS *ISPF/PDF Library Management*
- GC28-0646 OS/VS2 *TSO Command Language Reference*
- GC28-0647 OS/VS2 *TSO Terminal User's Guide*
- GC34-4036 VM/SP *ISPF General Information*
- SC34-4015 VM/SP *ISPF Installation and Customization*
- SC34-4009 VM/SP *ISPF Dialog Management Guide*
- SC34-2090 VM/SP *ISPF/PDF Program Reference*
- SC34-4011 VM/SP *ISPF/PDF Guide*
- SC34-4014 VM/SP *ISPF/PDF Edit Macros*
- SC34-4012 VM/SP *ISPF/PDF Services*
- SC34-4013 VM/SP *ISPF/PDF Library Management*
- ST00-1583 VM/SP *CMS Command and Macro Reference*
- SQ24-5239 VM/SP *SP Interpreter Reference*
- ST00-1593 VM/SP *SP Interpreter User's Guide*
- SC33-0332 GDDM *Base Application Programming Reference*

Index